Matter and Memory

Authorized Translation by Nancy Margaret Paul

and W. Scott Palmer

Matter and Memory

Henri Bergson

ZONE BOOKS · NEW YORK

1991

Published exclusively in the United States
© 1988 Urzone, Inc.

ZONE BOOKS
611 Broadway, Suite 608
New York, NY 10012

Originally published in France as *Matière et Mémoire* by
Presses Universitaires de France.

Printed in the United States of America.

Distributed by The MIT Press,
Cambridge, Massachusetts, and London, England

Library of Congress Cataloging in Publication Data

Bergson, Henri, 1859–1941.
    [Matière et mémoire. English]
    Matter and memory / Henri Bergson; authorized
translation by Nancy Margaret Paul and W. Scott Palmer.
    p.   cm.
    Bibliography: p.
    ISBN 0-942299-05-1 (pbk.)
    1. Mind and body. 2. Matter. I. Title.
B2430.B4M313   1988   87-37124
128'.3—DC19   CIP

Translators' Note

This translation of Monsieur Bergson's *Matière et mémoire* has been made from the fifth edition of 1908, and has had the great advantage of being revised in proof by the author. Monsieur Bergson has also written a new Introduction for it, which supersedes that which accompanied the original work.

The translators offer their sincere thanks to the author for his invaluable help in these matters and for many suggestions made by him while the book was in manuscript.

N.M.P.

W.S.P.

Contents

Introduction

This book affirms the reality of spirit and the reality of matter, and tries to determine the relation of the one to the other by the study of a definite example, that of memory. It is, then, frankly dualistic. But, on the other hand, it deals with body and mind in such a way as, we hope, to lessen greatly, if not to overcome, the theoretical difficulties which have always beset dualism, and which cause it, though suggested by the immediate verdict of consciousness and adopted by common sense, to be held in small honor among philosophers.

These difficulties are due, for the most part, to the conception, now realistic, now idealistic, which philosophers have of matter. The aim of our first chapter is to show that realism and idealism both go too far, that it is a mistake to reduce matter to the perception which we have of it, a mistake also to make of it a thing able to produce in us perceptions, but in itself of another nature than they. Matter, in our view, is an aggregate of "images." And by "image" we mean a certain existence which is more than that which the idealist calls a *representation*, but less than that which the realist calls a *thing* — an existence placed halfway between the "thing" and the "representation." This conception of matter is simply that of common sense. It would greatly astonish a man unaware of the speculations of philosophy if we told him that the object before him, which he sees and touches, exists only in his mind and for his mind or even, more generally, exists only for mind, as Berkeley held. Such a man would always maintain that the object exists independently of the consciousness which perceives it. But, on the other hand, we should astonish him quite as much by telling him that the object is entirely different from that which is perceived in it, that it has neither the color ascribed to it by the eye nor the resistance found in it by the hand. The color, the resistance, are, for him, in the object: they are not states of our mind; they are part and parcel of an existence really independent of our own. For common sense, then, the object exists in itself, and, on the other hand, the object is, in itself, pictorial, as we perceive it: image it is, but a self-existing image.

This is just the sense in which we use the word image in our first chapter. We place ourselves at the point of view of a mind unaware of the disputes between philosophers. Such a mind would naturally believe that matter exists just as it is perceived; and, since it is perceived as an image, the mind would make of it, in itself, an image. In a word, we consider matter before the dissociation which idealism and realism have brought about between its existence and its appearance. No doubt it has become difficult to avoid this dissociation now that philosophers have made it. To forget it, however, is what we ask of the reader. If, in the course of this first chapter, objections arise in his mind against any of the views that we put forward, let him ask himself whether these objections do not imply his return to one or the other of the two points of view above which we urge him to rise.

Philosophy made a great step forward on the day when Berkeley proved, as against the "mechanical philosophers," that the secondary qualities of matter have at least as much reality as the primary qualities. His mistake lay in believing that, for this, it was necessary to place matter within the mind and make it into a pure idea. Descartes, no doubt, had put matter too far from us when he made it one with geometrical extensity. But, in order to bring it nearer to us, there was no need to go to the point of making it one with our own mind. Because he did go as far as this, Berkeley was unable to account for the success of physics, and, whereas Descartes had set up the mathematical relations between phenomena as their very essence, he was obliged to regard the mathematical order of the universe as a mere accident. So the Kantian criticism became necessary, to show the reason of this mathematical order and to give back to our physics a solid foundation — a task in which, however, it succeeded only by limiting the range and value of our senses and of our understanding. The criticism of Kant, on this point at least, would have been unnecessary; the human mind, in this direction at least, would not have been led to limit its own range; metaphysics would not have been sacrificed to physics, if philosophy had been content to leave matter half way between the place to which Descartes had driven it and that to which Berkeley drew it back — to leave it, in fact, where it is seen by common sense.

There we shall try to see it ourselves. Our first chapter defines this way of looking at matter; the last sets forth the consequences of such a view. But, as we said before, we treat of matter only in so far as it concerns the problem dealt with in our second and third chapters, that which is the subject of this essay: the problem of the relation between soul and body.

This relation, though it has been a favorite theme throughout the history of philosophy, has really been very little studied. If we leave on one side the theories which are content to state the "union of soul and body" as an irreducible and inexplicable fact, and those which speak vaguely of the body as an instrument of the soul, there remains hardly any other conception of the psychophysiological relation than the hypothesis of "epiphenomenalism" or that of "parallelism," which in practice — I mean in the interpretation of particular facts — both end in the same conclusions. For whether, indeed, thought is regarded as a mere function of the brain and the state of consciousness as an epiphenomenon of the state of the brain, or whether mental states and brain states are held to be two versions, in two different languages, of one and the same original, in either case it is laid down that, could we penetrate into the inside of a brain at work and behold the dance of the atoms which make up the cortex, and if, on the other hand, we possessed the key to psychophysiology, we should know every detail of what is going on in the corresponding consciousness.

This, indeed, is what is most commonly maintained by philosophers as well as by men of science. Yet it would be well to ask whether the facts, when examined without any preconceived idea, really suggest an hypothesis of this kind. That there is a close connection between a state of consciousness and the brain we do not dispute. But there is also a close connection between a coat and the nail on which it hangs, for, if the nail is pulled out, the coat falls to the ground. Shall we say, then, that the shape of the nail gives us the shape of the coat, or in any way corresponds to it? No more are we entitled to conclude, because the physical fact is hung onto a cerebral state, that there is any parallelism between the two series psychical and physiological. When philosophy pleads that the theory of parallelism is borne out by the results of positive science, it enters upon an unmistakably vicious circle; for, if science interprets connection, which is a fact, as signifying parallelism, which is an hypothesis (and an hypothesis to which it is difficult to attach an intelligible meaning[1]), it does so, consciously or unconsciously, for reasons of a philosophic order: it is because science has been accustomed by a certain type of philosophy to believe that there is no hypothesis more probable, more in accordance with the interests of scientific inquiry.

Now, as soon as we do, indeed, apply to positive facts for such information as may help us to solve the problem, we find it is with memory that we have to deal. This was to be expected, because memory — we shall try to prove it in the course of this work — is just the intersection of mind and matter. But we may leave out the reason here: no one, at any rate, will deny that, among all the facts capable of throwing light on the psychophysiological relation, those which concern memory, whether in the normal or in the pathological state, hold a privileged position. Not only is the evidence here extremely abundant (consider the enormous mass of observations collected in regard to the various kinds of aphasia), but nowhere else have anatomy, physiology and psychology been able to lend each other such valuable aid. Anyone who approaches, without preconceived ideas and on the firm ground of facts, the classical problem of the relations of soul and body, will soon see this problem as centering upon the subject of memory, and, even more particularly, upon the memory of words: it is from this quarter, undoubtedly, that will come the light which will illumine the obscurer parts of the problem.

The reader will see how we try to solve it. Speaking generally, the physical state seems to us to be, in most cases, immensely wider than the cerebral state. I mean that the brain state indicates only a very small part of the mental state, that part which is capable of translating itself into movements of locomotion. Take a complex thought which unrolls itself in a chain of abstract reasoning. This thought is accompanied by images, that are at least nascent. And these images themselves are not pictured in consciousness without some foreshadowing, in the form of a sketch or a tendency, of the movements by which these images would be acted or played in space — would, that is to say, impress particular attitudes upon the body, and set free all that they implicitly contain of spatial movement. Now, of all the thought which is unrolling, this, in our view, is what the cerebral state indicates at every moment. He who could penetrate into the interior of a brain and see what happens there, would probably obtain full details of these sketched-out, or prepared, movements; there is no proof that he would learn anything else. Were he endowed with a superhuman intellect, did he possess the key to psychophysiology, he would know no more of what is going on in the corresponding conscious-ness than we should know of a play from the comings and goings of the actors upon the stage.

That is to say, the relation of the mental to the cerebral is not a constant, any more than it is a simple, relation. According to the nature of the play that is being acted, the movements of the players tell us more or less about it: nearly everything, if it is a pantomime; next to nothing, if it is a delicate comedy. Thus our cerebral state contains more or less of our mental state in the measure that we reel off our psychic life into action or wind it up into pure knowledge.

There are then, in short, divers *tones* of mental life, or, in other words, our psychic life may be lived at different heights, now nearer to action, now further removed from it, according to the degree of our *attention to life*. Here we have one of the ruling ideas of this book – the idea, indeed, which served as the starting point of our inquiry. That which is usually held to be a greater complexity of the psychical state appears to us, from our point of view, to be a greater dilatation of the whole personality, which, normally nar-rowed down by action, expands with the unscrewing of the vice in which it has allowed itself to be squeezed, and, always whole and undivided, spreads itself over a wider and wider surface. That which is commonly held to be a disturbance of the psychic life itself, an inward disorder, a disease of the personality, appears to us, from our point of view, to be an unloosing or a breaking of the tie which binds this psychic life to its motor accompaniment, a weakening or an impairing of our attention to outward life. This opinion, as also that which denies the localization of the memory-images of words and explains aphasia quite otherwise than by such localization, was considered paradoxical at the date of the first publication of the present work (1896). It will appear much less so now. The conception of aphasia then classical, universally admitted, believed to be unshakable, has been considerably shaken in the last few years, chiefly by reasons of an anatomical order, but partly also by reasons of the same kind as those which we then advanced.[2] And the profound and original study of neuroses made by Professor Pierre Janet has led him, of late years, to explain all *psychasthenic* forms of disease by these same considerations of psychic "tension" and of attention to reality which were then presumed to be metaphysical.[3]

In truth, it was not altogether a mistake to call them by that name. Without denying to psychology, any more than to metaphysics, the right to make itself into an independent science, we believe that each of these two sciences should set problems to the other and can, in a measure, help it to solve them. How should it be otherwise, if psychology has for its object the study of the human mind working for practical utility, and if metaphysics is but this same mind striving to transcend the conditions of useful action and to come back to itself as to a pure creative energy? Many problems, which appear foreign to each other as long as we are bound by the letter of the terms in which these two sciences state them, are seen to be very near akin, and to be able to solve each other when we thus penetrate into their inner meaning. We little thought, at the beginning of our inquiry, that there could be any connection between the analytical study of memory and the question, which is debated between realists and idealists or between mechanists and dynamists, with regard to the existence or the essence of matter. Yet this connection is real, it is even intimate; and, if we take it into account, a cardinal metaphysical problem is carried into the open field of observation, where it may be solved progressively, instead of forever giving rise to fresh disputes of the schools within the closed lists of pure dialectic. The complexity of some parts of the present work is due to the inevitable dovetailing of problems which results from approaching philosophy in such a way. But through this complexity, which is due to the complexity of reality itself, we believe that the reader will find his way if he keeps a fast hold on the two principles which we have used as a clue throughout our own researches. The first is that in psychological analysis we must never forget the utilitarian character of our mental functions, which are essentially turned toward action. The second is that the habits formed in action find their way up to the sphere of speculation, where they create fictitious problems, and that metaphysics must begin by dispersing this artificial obscurity.

H. BERGSON

PARIS,
October 1910

Chapter I

Of The Selection of Images for Conscious Presentation.

What Our Body Means and Does.

We will assume for the moment that we know nothing of theories of matter and theories of spirit, nothing of the discussions as to the reality or ideality of the external world. Here I am in the presence of images, in the vaguest sense of the word, images perceived when my senses are opened to them, unperceived when they are closed. All these images act and react upon one another in all their elementary parts according to constant laws which I call laws of nature, and, as a perfect knowledge of these laws would probably allow us to calculate and to foresee what will happen in each of these images, the future of the images must be contained in their present and will add to them nothing new.

Yet there is *one* of them which is distinct from all the others, in that I do not know it only from without by perceptions, but from within by affections: it is my body. I examine the conditions in which these affections are produced: I find that they always interpose themselves between the excitations that I receive from without and the movements which I am about to execute, as though they had some undefined influence on the final issue. I pass in review my different affections: it seems to me that each of them contains, after its kind, an invitation to act, with at the same time leave to wait and even to do nothing. I look closer: I find movements begun, but not executed, the indication of a more or less useful decision, but not that constraint which precludes choice. I call up, I compare my recollections: I remember that everywhere, in the organic world, I have thought I saw this same sensibility appear at the very moment when nature, having conferred upon the living being the power of mobility in space, gives warning to the species, by means of sensation, of the general dangers which threaten it, leaving to the individual the precautions necessary for escaping from them. Lastly, I interrogate my consciousness as to the part which it plays in affection: consciousness replies that it is present indeed, in the form of feeling or of sensation, at all the steps in which I believe that I take the initiative, and that it fades and disappears as soon as my activity, by becoming automatic, shows that consciousness is no longer needed. Therefore, either all these appearances are deceptive, or the act in which the affective state issues is not one of those which might be rigorously deduced from antecedent phenomena, as a movement from a movement; and, hence, it really adds something new to the universe and to its history. Let us hold to the appearances; I will formulate purely and simply what I feel and what I see: *All seems to take place as if, in this aggregate of images which I call the universe, nothing really new could happen except through the medium of certain particular images, the type of which is furnished me by my body.*

I pass now to the study, in bodies similar to my own, of the structure of that particular image which I call my body. I perceive afferent nerves which transmit a disturbance to the nerve centers; then efferent nerves which start from the center, conduct the disturbance to the periphery, and set in motion parts of the body or the body as a whole. I question the physiologist and the psychologist as to the purpose of both kinds. They answer that, as the centrifugal movements of the nervous system can call forth a movement of the body or of parts of the body, so the centripetal movements, or at least some of them, give birth to the representation[1] of the external world. What are we to think of this?

The afferent nerves are images, the brain is an image, the disturbance traveling through the sensory nerves and propagated in the brain is an image too. If the image which I term cerebral disturbance really begot external images, it would contain them in one way or another, and the representation of the whole material universe would be implied in that of this molecular movement. Now to state this proposition is enough to show its absurdity. The brain is part of the material world; the material world is not part of the brain. Eliminate the image which bears the name material world, and you destroy at the same time the brain and the cerebral disturbance which are parts of it. Suppose, on the contrary, that these two images, the brain and the cerebral disturbance, vanish: *ex hypothesi* you efface only these, that is to say very little, an insignificant detail from an immense picture. The picture in its totality, that is to say the whole universe, remains. To make of the brain the condition on which the whole image depends is, in truth, a contradiction in terms, since the brain is by hypothesis a part of this image. Neither nerves nor nerve centers can, then, condition the image of the universe.

Let us consider this last point. Here are external images, then my body, and, lastly, the changes brought about by my body in the surrounding images. I see plainly how external images influence the image that I call my body: they transmit movement to it. And I also see how this body influences external images: it gives back movement to them. My body is, then, in the aggregate of the material world, an image which acts like other images, receiving and giving back movement, with, perhaps, this difference only, that my body appears to choose, within certain limits, the manner in which it shall restore what it receives. But how could my body in

19

general, and my nervous system in particular, beget the whole or a part of my representation of the universe? You may say that my body is matter, or that it is an image: the word is of no importance. If it is matter, it is a part of the material world; and the material world, consequently, exists around it and without it. If it is an image, that image can give but what has been put into it, and since it is, by hypothesis, the image of my body only, it would be absurd to expect to get from it that of the whole universe. *My body, an object destined to move other objects, is, then, a center of action; it cannot give birth to a representation.*

But if my body is an object capable of exercising a genuine and therefore a *new* action upon the surrounding objects, it must occupy a privileged position in regard to them. As a rule, any image influences other images in a manner which is determined, and even calculable, through what are called the laws of nature. As it has not to choose, so neither has it any need to explore the region round about it, nor to try its hand at several merely *eventual* actions. The *necessary* action will take place automatically, when its hour strikes. But I have supposed that the office of the image which I call my body was to exercise on other images a real influence, and, consequently, to decide which step to take among several which are all materially possible. And since these steps are probably suggested to it by the greater or lesser advantage which it can derive from the surrounding images, these images must display in some way, upon the aspect which they present to my body, the profit which my body can gain from them. In fact, I note that the size, shape, even the color, of external objects is modified as my body approaches or recedes from them; that the strength of an odor, the intensity of a sound, increases or diminishes with distance; finally, that this very distance represents, above all, the measure in which surrounding bodies are insured, in some way, against the immediate action of my body. To the degree that my horizon widens, the images which surround me seem to be painted upon a more uniform background and become to me more indifferent. The more I narrow this horizon, the more the objects which it circumscribes space themselves out distinctly according to the greater or lesser ease with which my body can touch and move them. They send back, then, to my body, as would a mirror, its eventual influence; they take rank in an order corresponding to the growing or decreasing powers of my body. *The objects which surround my body reflect its possible action upon them.*

I will now, without touching the other images, modify slightly that image which I call my body. In this image I cut asunder, in thought, all the afferent nerves of the cerebro-spinal system. What will happen? A few cuts with the scalpel have severed a few bundles of fibres: the rest of the universe, and even the rest of my body, remain what they were before. The change effected is therefore insignificant. As a matter of fact, my perception has entirely vanished. Let us consider more closely what has just occurred. Here are the images which compose the universe in general, then those which are near to my body, and finally my body itself. In this last image the habitual office of the centripetal nerves is to transmit movements to the brain and to the cord; the centrifugal nerves send back this movement to the periphery. Sectioning of the centripetal nerves can, therefore, produce only one intelligible effect: that is, to interrupt the current which goes from the periphery to the periphery by way of the center, and, consequently, to make it impossible for my body to extract, from among all the things which surround it, the quantity and quality of movement necessary in order to act upon them. Here is something which concerns action, and action alone. Yet it is my perception which has vanished. What does this mean, if not that my perception displays, in the midst of the image world, as would their outward reflection or shadow, the eventual or possible actions of my body? Now the system of images in which the scalpel has effected only an insignificant change is what is generally called the material world; and, on the other hand, that which has just vanished is "my perception" of matter. Whence, provisionally, these two definitions: *I call* matter *the aggregate of images, and* perception of matter *these same images referred to the eventual action of one particular image, my body*.

Let us go more deeply into this reference. I consider my body, with its centripetal and centrifugal nerves, with its nerve centers. I know that external objects make in the afferent nerves a disturbance which passes onward to the centers, that the centers are the theater of very varied molecular movements, and that these movements depend on the nature and position of the objects. Change the objects, or modify their relation to my body, and everything is changed in the interior movements of my perceptive centers. But everything is also changed in "my perception." My perception is, then, a function of these molecular movements; it depends upon them. But how does it depend upon them? It will perhaps be said that it translates them, and that, in the main, I represent to myself nothing but the molecular movements of cerebral substance. But how should this have any meaning, since the image of the nervous system and of its internal movements is only, by hypothesis, that of a certain material object, whereas I represent to myself the whole material universe? It is true that many philosophers attempt to evade the difficulty. They show us a brain, analogous in its essence to the rest of the material universe, an image, consequently, if the universe is an image. Then, since they want the internal movements of this brain to create or determine the representation of the whole material world — an image infinitely greater than that of the cerebral vibrations — they maintain that these molecular movements, and movement in general, are not images like others, but something which is either more or less than an image — in any case is of another nature than an image — and from which representation will issue as by a miracle. Thus matter is made into something radically different from representation, something of which, consequently, we have no image; over against it they place a consciousness empty of images, of which we are unable to form any idea; lastly, to fill consciousness, they invent an incomprehensible action of this formless matter upon this matterless thought. But the truth is that the movements of matter are very clear, regarded as images, and that there is no need to look in movement for anything more than what we see in it. The sole difficulty would consist in bringing forth from these very particular images the infinite variety of representations; but why seek to do so, since we all agree that the cerebral vibrations *are contained in* the material world, and that these images, consequently, are only a part of the representation? What then are these movements, and what part do these particular images play in the representation of the whole? The answer is obvious: they are, within my body, the movements intended to prepare, while beginning it, the reaction of my body to the action of external objects. Images themselves cannot create images; but they indicate at each moment, like a compass that is being moved about, the position of a certain given image, my body, in relation to the surrounding images. In the totality of representation they are very little; but they are of capital importance for that part of representation which I call my body, since they foreshadow at each successive moment its virtual acts. There is, then, only a difference of degree — there can be no difference in kind — between what is called the perceptive faculty of the brain and the reflex functions of the spinal cord. The cord transforms into movements the stimulation received; the brain prolongs them into reactions which are merely nascent; but, in the one case as in the other, the function of the nerve substance is to conduct, to coordinate, or to inhibit movements. How then does it come about that "my perception of the universe" appears to depend upon the internal movements of the cerebral substance, to change when they vary, and to vanish when they cease?

The difficulty of this problem is mainly due to the fact that the grey matter and its modifications are regarded as things which are sufficient to themselves and might be isolated from the rest of the universe. Materialists and dualists are fundamentally agreed on this point. They consider certain molecular movements of the cerebral matter apart: then, some see in our conscious perception a phosphorescence which follows these movements and illuminates their track; for others, our perceptions succeed each other like an unwinding scroll in a consciousness which expresses continuously, in its own way, the molecular vibrations of the cortical substance: in the one case, as in the other, our perception is supposed to *translate* or to *picture* the states of our nervous system. But is it possible to conceive the nervous system as living apart from the organism which nourishes it, from the atmosphere in which the organism breathes, from the earth which that atmosphere envelopes, from the sun round which the earth revolves? More generally, does not the fiction of an isolated material object imply a kind of absurdity, since this object borrows its physical properties from the relations which it maintains with all others, and owes each of its determinations, and, consequently, its very existence, to the place which it occupies in the universe as a whole? Let us no longer say, then, that our perceptions depend simply upon the molecular movements of the cerebral mass. We must say rather that they *vary with* them, but that these movements themselves remain inseparably bound up with the rest of the material world. The question, then, is not only how our perceptions are connected with the modifications of the grey matter. The problem widens, and can also be put in much clearer terms.

It might be stated as follows: Here is a system of images which I term my perception of the universe, and which may be entirely altered by a very slight change in a certain privileged image — *my body*. This image occupies the center; by it all the others are conditioned; at each of its movements everything changes, as though by a turn of a kaleidoscope. Here, on the other hand, are the same images, but referred each one to itself, influencing each other no doubt, but in such a manner that the effect is always in proportion to the cause: this is what I term *the universe*. The question is: how can these two systems coexist, and why are the same images relatively invariable in the universe and infinitely variable in perception? The problem at issue between realism and idealism, perhaps even between materialism and spiritualism, should be stated, then, it seems to us, in the following terms: *How is it that the same images can belong at the same time to two different systems: one in which each image varies for itself and in the well-defined measure that it is patient of the real action of surrounding images; and another in which all images change for a single image and in the varying measure that they reflect the eventual action of this privileged image?*

Every image is within certain images and without others; but of the aggregate of images we cannot say that it is within us or without us, since interiority and exteriority are only relations among images. To ask whether the universe exists only in our thought, or outside of our thought, is to put the problem in terms that are insoluble, even if we suppose them to be intelligible; it is to condemn ourselves to a barren discussion, in which the terms *thought, being, universe*, will always be taken on either hand in entirely different senses. To settle the matter, we must first find a common ground where combatants may meet; and since on both sides it is agreed that we can only grasp things in the form of images, we must state the problem in terms of images, and of images alone. Now no philosophical doctrine denies that the same images can enter at the same time into two distinct systems, one belonging to *science*, wherein each image, related only to itself, possesses an absolute value; and the other, the world of *consciousness*, wherein all the images depend on a central image, our body, the variations of which they follow. The question raised between realism and idealism then becomes quite clear: what are the relations which these two systems of images maintain with each other? And it is easy to see that subjective idealism consists in deriving the first system from the second, materialistic realism in deriving the second from the first.

The realist starts, in fact, from the universe, that is to say from an aggregate of images governed, as to their mutual relations, by fixed laws, in which effects are in strict proportion to their causes, and of which the character is an absence of center, all the images unfolding on one and the same plane indefinitely prolonged. But he is at once bound to recognize that, besides this system, there are *perceptions*, that is to say, systems in which these same images seem to depend on a single one among them, around which they range themselves on different planes, so as to be wholly transformed by the slightest modification of this central image. Now this perception is just what the idealist starts from: in the system of images which he adopts there is a privileged image, his body, by which the other images are conditioned. But as soon as he attempts to connect the present with the past and to foretell the future, he is obliged to abandon this central position, to replace all the images on the same plane, to suppose that they no longer vary for him, but for themselves; and to treat them as though they made part of a system in which every change gives the exact measure of its cause. On this condition alone a science of the universe becomes possible; and, since this science exists, since it succeeds in foreseeing the future, its fundamental hypothesis cannot be arbitrary. The first system alone is *given* to present experience; but we *believe* in the second, if only because we affirm the continuity of the past, present and future. Thus in idealism, as in realism, we posit one of the two systems and seek to deduce the other from it.

But in this deduction neither realism nor idealism can succeed, because neither of the two systems of images is implied in the other, and each of them is sufficient to itself. If you posit the system of images which has no center, and in which each element possesses its absolute dimensions and value, I see no reason why to this system should accrue a second, in which each image has an undetermined value, subject to all the vicissitudes of a central image. You must, then, to engender perception, conjure up some deus ex machina, such as the materialistic hypothesis of the epiphenomenal consciousness, whereby you choose, among all the images that vary absolutely and that you posited to begin with, the one which we term our brain — conferring on the internal states of this image the singular and inexplicable privilege of adding to itself a reproduction, this time relative and variable, of all the others. It is true that you afterwards pretend to attach no importance to this representation, to see in it a mere phosphorescence which the cerebral vibrations leave behind them: as if the cerebral matter and cerebral vibrations, set in the images which compose this representation, could be of another nature than they are! All realism is thus bound to make perception an accident, and, consequently, a mystery. But, inversely, if you posit a system of unstable images disposed about a privileged center, and profoundly modified by trifling displacements of this center, you begin by excluding the order of nature, that order which is indifferent to the point at which we take our stand and to the particular end from which we begin. You will have to bring back this order by conjuring up in your turn a deus ex machina; I mean that you will have to assume, by an arbitrary hypothesis, some sort of pre-established harmony between things and mind, or, at least (to use Kant's terms), between sense and understanding. It is science now that will become an accident, and its success a mystery. You cannot, then, deduce the first system of images from the second, nor the second from the first; and these two antagonistic doctrines, realism and idealism, as soon as they decide to enter the same lists, hurl themselves from opposite directions against the same obstacle.

If we now look closely at the two doctrines, we shall discover in them a common postulate, which we may formulate thus: *perception has a wholly speculative interest; it is pure knowledge.* The whole discussion turns upon the importance to be attributed to this knowledge as compared with *scientific* knowledge. The one doctrine starts from the order required by science, and sees in perception only a confused and provisional science. The other puts perception in the first place, erects it into an absolute, and then holds science to be a symbolic expression of the real. But, for both parties, to perceive means above all to know.

Now it is just this postulate that we dispute. Even the most superficial examination of the structure of the nervous system in the animal series gives it the lie. And it is not possible to accept it without profoundly obscuring the threefold problem of matter, consciousness and their relation.

For if we follow, step by step, the progress of external perception from the monera to the higher vertebrates, we find that living matter, even as a simple mass of protoplasm, is already irritable and contractile, that it is open to the influence of external stimulation, and answers to it by mechanical, physical and chemical reactions. As we rise in the organic series, we find a division of

28

physiological labor. Nerve cells appear, are diversified, tend to group themselves into a system; at the same time, the animal reacts by more varied movements to external stimulation. But even when the stimulation received is not at once prolonged into movement, it appears merely to await its occasion; and the same impression, which makes the organism aware of changes in the environment, determines it or prepares it to adapt itself to them. No doubt there is in the higher vertebrates a radical distinction between pure automatism, of which the seat is mainly in the spinal cord, and voluntary activity, which requires the intervention of the brain. It might be imagined that the impression received, instead of expanding into more movements, spiritualizes itself into consciousness. But as soon as we compare the structure of the spinal cord with that of the brain, we are bound to infer that there is merely a difference of complication, and not a difference in kind, between the functions of the brain and the reflex activity of the medullary system. For what takes place in reflex action? The centripetal movement communicated by the stimulus is reflected at once, by the intermediary of the nerve centers of the spinal cord, in a centrifugal movement determining a muscular contraction. In what, on the other hand, does the function of the cerebral system consist? The peripheral excitation, instead of proceeding directly to the motorcells of the spinal cord and impressing on the muscle a necessary contraction, mounts first to the brain, and then descends again to the very same motor cells of the spinal cord which intervened in the reflex action. Now what has it gained by this roundabout course, and what did it seek in the so-called sensory cells of the cerebral cortex? I do not understand, I shall never understand, that it draws thence a miraculous power of changing itself into a representation of things; and, moreover, I hold this hypothesis to be useless, as will shortly appear. But what I do see clearly is that the cells of the various regions of the cortex which are termed

29

sensory — cells interposed between the terminal branches of the centripetal fibers and the motor cells of the Rolandic area — allow the stimulation received to reach *at will* this or that motor mechanism of the spinal cord, and so to *choose* its effect. The more these intercalated cells are multiplied and the more they project amoeboid prolongations which are probably capable of approaching each other in various ways, the more numerous and more varied will be the paths capable of opening to one and the same disturbance from the periphery, and, consequently, the more systems of movements will there be among which one and the same stimulation will allow of choice. In our opinion, then, the brain is no more than a kind of central telephonic exchange: its office is to allow communication or to delay it. It adds nothing to what it receives; but, as all the organs of perception send it to their ultimate prolongations, and, as all the motor mechanisms of the spinal cord and of the medulla oblongata have in it their accredited representatives, it really constitutes a center, where the peripheral excitation gets into relation with this or that motor mechanism, chosen and no longer prescribed. Yet, as a great multitude of motor tracks can open simultaneously in this substance to one and the same excitation from the periphery, this disturbance may subdivide to any extent, and consequently dissipate itself in innumerable motor reactions which are merely nascent. Hence the office of the brain is sometimes to conduct the movement received to a *chosen* organ of reaction, and sometimes to open to this movement the *totality* of the motor tracts, so that it may manifest there all the potential reactions with which it is charged, and may divide and so disperse. In other words, the brain appears to us to be an instrument of analysis in regard to the movement received and an instrument of selection in regard to the movement executed. But, in the one case as in the other, its office is limited to the transmission and division of movement. And no more in the higher centers of the

spondence with reality. But we hope to show that the individual accidents are merely grafted on to this impersonal perception, which is at the very root of our knowledge of things; and that just because philosophers have overlooked it, because they have not distinguished it from that which memory adds to or subtracts from it, they have taken perception as a whole for a kind of *interior* and *subjective* vision, which would then differ from memory only by its greater intensity. This will be our first hypothesis. But it leads naturally to another. However brief we suppose any perception to be, it always occupies a certain duration, and involves, consequently, an effort of memory which prolongs, one into another, a plurality of moments. As we shall endeavor to show, even the "subjectivity" of sensible qualities consists above all else in a kind of contraction of the real, effected by our memory. In short, memory in these two forms, covering as it does with a cloak of recollections a core of immediate perception, and also contracting a number of external moments into a single internal moment, constitutes the principal share of individual consciousness in perception, the subjective side of the knowledge of things; and, since we must neglect this share in order to make our idea clearer, we shall go too far along the path we have chosen. But we shall only have to retrace our steps and to correct, especially by bringing memory back again, whatever may be excessive in our conclusions. What follows, therefore, must be regarded as only a schematic rendering, and we ask that perception should be provisionally understood to mean not my concrete and complex perception — that which is enlarged by memories and offers always a certain breadth of duration — but a *pure* perception. By this I mean a perception which exists in theory rather than in fact and would be possessed by a being placed where I am, living as I live, but absorbed in the present and capable, by giving up every form of memory, of obtaining a vision of matter both immediate and instantaneous. Adopting this hypoth-

cortex than in the spinal cord do the nervous elements work with a view to knowledge: they do but indicate a number of possible actions at once, or organize one of them.

That is to say that the nervous system is in no sense an apparatus which may serve to fabricate, or even to prepare, representations. Its function is to receive stimulation, to provide motor apparatus, and to present the largest possible number of these apparatuses to a given stimulus. The more it develops, the more numerous and the more distant are the points of space which it brings into relation with ever more complex motor mechanisms. In this way the scope which it allows to our action enlarges: its growing perfection consists in nothing else. But, if the nervous system is thus constructed, from one end of the animal series to the other, in view of an action which is less and less necessary, must we not think that perception, of which the progress is regulated by that of the nervous system, is also entirely directed toward action, and not toward pure knowledge? And, if this be so, is not the growing richness of this perception likely to symbolize the wider range of indetermination left to the choice of the living being in its conduct with regard to things? Let us start, then, from this indetermination as from the true principle, and try whether we cannot deduce from it the possibility, and even the necessity, of conscious perception. In other words, let us posit that system of closely-linked images which we call the material world, and imagine here and there, within the system, *centers of real action*, represented by living matter: what we mean to prove is that *there must* be, ranged round each one of these centers, images that are subordinated to its position and variable with it; that conscious perception is *bound* to occur, and that, moreover, it is possible to understand how it arises.

We note, in the first place, that a strict law connects the amount of conscious perception with the intensity of action at the disposal of the living being. If our hypothesis is well founded, this perception appears at the precise moment when a stimulation received by matter is not prolonged into a necessary action. In the case of a rudimentary organism, it is true that immediate contact with the object which interests it is necessary to produce the stimulation and that reaction can then hardly be delayed. Thus, in the lower organisms, touch is active and passive at one and the same time, enabling them to recognize their prey and seize it, to feel a danger and make the effort to avoid it. The various prolongations of the protozoa, the ambulacra of the echinodermata, are organs of movement as well as of tactile perception; the stinging apparatus of the coelenterata is an instrument of perception as well as a means of defence. In a word, the more immediate the reaction is compelled to be, the more must perception resemble a mere contact; and the complete process of perception and of reaction can then hardly be distinguished from a mechanical impulsion followed by a necessary movement. But in the measure that the reaction becomes more uncertain, and allows more room for suspense, does the distance increase at which the animal is sensible of the action of that which interests it. By sight, by hearing, it enters into relation with an ever greater number of things, and is subject to more and more distant influences; and, whether these objects promise an advantage or threaten a danger, both promises and threats defer the date of their fulfillment. The degree of independence of which a living being is master, or, as we shall say, the zone of indetermination which surrounds its activity, allows, then, of an a priori estimate of the number and the distance of the things with which it is in relation. Whatever this relation may be, whatever be the inner nature of perception, we can affirm that its amplitude gives the exact measure of the indetermination of the act which is to follow. So that we can formulate this law: *perception is master of space in the exact measure in which action is master of time.* But why does this relation of the organism to more or less dis-

tant objects take the particular form of conscious perception? We have examined what takes place in the organized body, we have seen movements transmitted or inhibited, metamorphosed into accomplished actions or broken up into nascent actions. These movements appear to us to concern action, and action alone; they remain absolutely foreign to the process of representation. We then considered action itself, and the indetermination which surrounds it and is implied in the structure of the nervous system — an indetermination to which this system seems to point much more than to representation. From this indetermination, accepted as a fact, we have been able to infer the necessity of a perception, that is to say, a *variable* relation between the living being and the more-or-less distant influence of the objects which interest it. How is it that this perception is consciousness, and why does everything happen *as if* this consciousness were born of the internal movements of the cerebral substance?

To answer this question, we will first simplify considerably the conditions under which conscious perception takes place. In fact, there is no perception which is not full of memories. With the immediate and present data of our senses, we mingle a thousand details out of our past experience. In most cases these memories supplant our actual perceptions, of which we then retain only a few hints, thus using them merely as "signs" that recall to us former images. The convenience and the rapidity of perception are bought at this price; but hence also springs every kind of illusion. Let us, for the purposes of study, substitute for this perception, impregnated with our past, a perception that a consciousness would have if it were supposed to be ripe and full-grown, yet confined to the present and absorbed, to the exclusion of all else, in the task of molding itself upon the external object. It may be urged that this is an arbitrary hypothesis, and that such an ideal perception, obtained by the elimination of individual accidents, has no corre-

esis, let us consider how conscious perception may be explained.

To deduce consciousness would be, indeed, a bold undertaking; but it is really not necessary here, because by positing the material world we assume an aggregate of images, and, moreover, because it is impossible to assume anything else. No theory of matter escapes this necessity. Reduce matter to atoms in motion: these atoms, though denuded of physical qualities, are determined only in relation to an eventual vision and an eventual contact, the one without light and the other without materiality. Condense atoms into centers of force, dissolve them into vortices revolving in a continuous fluid: this fluid, these movements, these centers, can themselves be determined only in relation to an impotent touch, an ineffectual impulsion, a colorless light; they are still images. It is true that an image may *be* without *being perceived* — it may be present without being represented — and the distance between these two terms, presence and representation, seems just to measure the interval between matter itself and our conscious perception of matter. But let us examine the point more closely and see in what this difference consists. If there were *more* in the second term than in the first, if, in order to pass from presence to representation, it were necessary to add something, the barrier would indeed be insuperable, and the passage from matter to perception would remain wrapped in impenetrable mystery. It would not be the same if it were possible to pass from the first term to the second by way of diminution, and if the representation of an image were *less* than its presence; for it would then suffice that the images present should be compelled to abandon something of themselves in order that their mere presence should convert them into representations. Now, here is the image which I call a material object; I have the representation of it. How then does it not appear to be in itself that which it is for me? It is because, being bound up with all other images, it is continued in those which follow it,

35

just as it prolonged those which preceded it. To transform its existence into representation, it would be enough to suppress what follows it, what precedes it, and also all that fills it, and to retain only its external crust, its superficial skin. That which distinguishes it as a *present* image, as an objective reality, from a *represented* image is the necessity which obliges it to act through every one of its points upon all the points of all other images, to transmit the whole of what it receives, to oppose to every action an equal and contrary reaction, to be, in short, merely a road by which pass, in every direction, the modifications propagated throughout the immensity of the universe. I should convert it into representation if I could isolate it, especially if I could isolate its shell. Representation is there, but always virtual — being neutralized, at the very moment when it might become actual, by the obligation to continue itself and to lose itself in something else. To obtain this conversion from the virtual to the actual, it would be necessary, not to throw more light on the object, but, on the contrary, to obscure some of its aspects, to diminish it by the greater part of itself, so that the remainder, instead of being encased in its surroundings as a *thing*, should detach itself from them as a *picture*. Now, if living beings are, within the universe, just "centers of indetermination," and if the degree of this indetermination is measured by the number and rank of their functions, we can conceive that their mere presence is equivalent to the suppression of all those parts of objects in which their functions find no interest. They allow to pass through them, so to speak, those external influences which are indifferent to them; the others isolated, become "perceptions" by their very isolation. Everything thus happens for us as though we reflected back to surfaces the light which emanates from them, the light which, had it passed on unopposed, would never have been revealed. The images which surround us will appear to turn toward our body the side, emphasized by the light upon it, which interests our body.

They will detach from themselves that which we have arrested on its way, that which we are capable of influencing. Indifferent to each other because of the radical mechanism which binds them together, they present each to the others all their sides at once: which means that they act and react mutually by all their elements, and that none of them perceives or is perceived consciously. Suppose, on the contrary, that they encounter somewhere a certain spontaneity of reaction: their action is so far diminished, and this diminution of their action is just the representation which we have of them. Our representation of things would thus arise from the fact that they are thrown back and reflected by our freedom.

When a ray of light passes from one medium into another, it usually traverses it with a change of direction. But the respective densities of the two media may be such that, for a given angle of incidence, refraction is no longer possible. Then we have total reflection. The luminous point gives rise to a *virtual* image which symbolizes, so to speak, the fact that the luminous rays cannot pursue their way. Perception is just a phenomenon of the same kind. That which is given is the totality of the images of the material world, with the totality of their internal elements. But, if we suppose centers of real, that is to say of spontaneous, activity, the rays which reach it, and which interest that activity, instead of passing through those centers, will appear to be reflected and thus to indicate the outlines of the object which emits them. There is nothing positive here, nothing added to the image, nothing new. The objects merely abandon something of their real action in order to manifest their virtual influence of the living being upon them. Perception therefore resembles those phenomena of reflexion which result from an impeded refraction; it is like an effect of mirage.

This is as much as to say that there is for images merely a difference of degree, and not of kind, between *being* and *being consciously perceived*. The reality of matter consists in the totality of its elements and of their actions of every kind. Our representation of matter is the measure of our possible action upon bodies: it results from the discarding of what has no interest for our needs, or more generally, for our functions. In one sense we might say that the perception of any unconscious material point whatever, in its instantaneousness, is infinitely greater and more complete than ours, since this point gathers and transmits the influences of all the points of the material universe, whereas our consciousness only attains to certain parts and to certain aspects of those parts. Consciousness – in regard to external perception – lies in just this choice. But there is, in this necessary poverty of our conscious perception, something that is positive, that foretells spirit: it is, in the etymological sense of the word, discernment.

The whole difficulty of the problem that occupies us comes from the fact that we imagine perception to be a kind of photographic view of things, taken from a fixed point by that special apparatus which is called an organ of perception – a photograph which would then be developed in the brain-matter by some unknown chemical and psychical process of elaboration. But is it not obvious that the photograph, if photograph there be, is already taken, already developed in the very heart of things and at all the points of space? No metaphysics, no physics even, can escape this conclusion. Build up the universe with atoms: each of them is subject to the action, variable in quantity and quality according to the distance, exerted on it by all material atoms. Bring in Faraday's centers of force: the lines of force emitted in every direction from every center bring to bear upon each the influences of the whole material world. Call up the Leibnizian monads: each is the mirror of the universe. All philosophers, then, agree on this point. Only if, when we consider any other given place in the universe, we can regard the acton of all matter as passing through it without resistance and without loss, and the photograph of the whole as

cortex than in the spinal cord do the nervous elements work with a view to knowledge: they do but indicate a number of possible actions at once, or organize one of them.

That is to say that the nervous system is in no sense an apparatus which may serve to fabricate, or even to prepare, representations. Its function is to receive stimulation, to provide motor apparatus, and to present the largest possible number of these apparatuses to a given stimulus. The more it develops, the more numerous and the more distant are the points of space which it brings into relation with ever more complex motor mechanisms. In this way the scope which it allows to our action enlarges: its growing perfection consists in nothing else. But, if the nervous system is thus constructed, from one end of the animal series to the other, in view of an action which is less and less necessary, must we not think that perception, of which the progress is regulated by that of the nervous system, is also entirely directed toward action, and not toward pure knowledge? And, if this be so, is not the growing richness of this perception likely to symbolize the wider range of indetermination left to the choice of the living being in its conduct with regard to things? Let us start, then, from this indetermination as from the true principle, and try whether we cannot deduce from it the possibility, and even the necessity, of conscious perception. In other words, let us posit that system of closely-linked images which we call the material world, and imagine here and there, within the system, *centers of real action*, represented by living matter: what we mean to prove is that *there must* be, ranged round each one of these centers, images that are subordinated to its position and variable with it; that conscious perception is *bound* to occur, and that, moreover, it is possible to understand how it arises.

We note, in the first place, that a strict law connects the amount of conscious perception with the intensity of action at the disposal of the living being. If our hypothesis is well founded, this perception appears at the precise moment when a stimulation received by matter is not prolonged into a necessary action. In the case of a rudimentary organism, it is true that immediate contact with the object which interests it is necessary to produce the stimulation and that reaction can then hardly be delayed. Thus, in the lower organisms, touch is active and passive at one and the same time, enabling them to recognize their prey and seize it, to feel a danger and make the effort to avoid it. The various prolongations of the protozoa, the ambulacra of the echinodermata, are organs of movement as well as of tactile perception; the stinging apparatus of the coelenterata is an instrument of perception as well as a means of defence. In a word, the more immediate the reaction is compelled to be, the more must perception resemble a mere contact; and the complete process of perception and of reaction can then hardly be distinguished from a mechanical impulsion followed by a necessary movement. But in the measure that the reaction becomes more uncertain, and allows more room for suspense, does the distance increase at which the animal is sensible of the action of that which interests it. By sight, by hearing, it enters into relation with an ever greater number of things, and is subject to more and more distant influences; and, whether these objects promise an advantage or threaten a danger, both promises and threats defer the date of their fulfillment. The degree of independence of which a living being is master, or, as we shall say, the zone of indetermination which surrounds its activity, allows, then, of an a priori estimate of the number and the distance of the things with which it is in relation. Whatever this relation may be, whatever be the inner nature of perception, we can affirm that its amplitude gives the exact measure of the indetermination of the act which is to follow. So that we can formulate this law: *perception is master of space in the exact measure in which action is master of time*.

But why does this relation of the organism to more or less distant objects take the particular form of conscious perception? We have examined what takes place in the organized body, we have seen movements transmitted or inhibited, metamorphosed into accomplished actions or broken up into nascent actions. These movements appear to us to concern action, and action alone; they remain absolutely foreign to the process of representation. We then considered action itself, and the indetermination which surrounds it and is implied in the structure of the nervous system — an indetermination to which this system seems to point much more than to representation. From this indetermination, accepted as a fact, we have been able to infer the necessity of a perception, that is to say, a *variable* relation between the living being and the more-or-less distant influence of the objects which interest it. How is it that this perception is consciousness, and why does everything happen *as if* this consciousness were born of the internal movements of the cerebral substance?

To answer this question, we will first simplify considerably the conditions under which conscious perception takes place. In fact, there is no perception which is not full of memories. With the immediate and present data of our senses, we mingle a thousand details out of our past experience. In most cases these memories supplant our actual perceptions, of which we then retain only a few hints, thus using them merely as "signs" that recall to us former images. The convenience and the rapidity of perception are bought at this price; but hence also springs every kind of illusion. Let us, for the purposes of study, substitute for this perception, impregnated with our past, a perception that a consciousness would have if it were supposed to be ripe and full-grown, yet confined to the present and absorbed, to the exclusion of all else, in the task of molding itself upon the external object. It may be urged that this is an arbitrary hypothesis, and that such an ideal perception, obtained by the elimination of individual accidents, has no correspondence with reality. But we hope to show that the individual accidents are merely grafted on to this impersonal perception, which is at the very root of our knowledge of things; and that just because philosophers have overlooked it, because they have not distinguished it from that which memory adds to or subtracts from it, they have taken perception as a whole for a kind of *interior* and *subjective* vision, which would then differ from memory only by its greater intensity. This will be our first hypothesis. But it leads naturally to another. However brief we suppose any perception to be, it always occupies a certain duration, and involves, consequently, an effort of memory which prolongs, one into another, a plurality of moments. As we shall endeavor to show, even the "subjectivity" of sensible qualities consists above all else in a kind of contraction of the real, effected by our memory. In short, memory in these two forms, covering as it does with a cloak of recollections a core of immediate perception, and also contracting a number of external moments into a single internal moment, constitutes the principal share of individual consciousness in perception, the subjective side of the knowledge of things; and, since we must neglect this share in order to make our idea clearer, we shall go too far along the path we have chosen. But we shall only have to retrace our steps and to correct, especially by bringing memory back again, whatever may be excessive in our conclusions. What follows, therefore, must be regarded as only a schematic rendering, and we ask that perception should be provisionally understood to mean not my concrete and complex perception – that which is enlarged by memories and offers always a certain breadth of duration – but a *pure* perception. By this I mean a perception which exists in theory rather than in fact and would be possessed by a being placed where I am, living as I live, but absorbed in the present and capable, by giving up every form of memory, of obtaining a vision of matter both immediate and instantaneous. Adopting this hypoth-

34

esis, let us consider how conscious perception may be explained.

To deduce consciousness would be, indeed, a bold undertaking; but it is really not necessary here, because by positing the material world we assume an aggregate of images, and, moreover, because it is impossible to assume anything else. No theory of matter escapes this necessity. Reduce matter to atoms in motion: these atoms, though denuded of physical qualities, are determined only in relation to an eventual vision and an eventual contact, the one without light and the other without materiality. Condense atoms into centers of force, dissolve them into vortices revolving in a continuous fluid: this fluid, these movements, these centers, can themselves be determined only in relation to an impotent touch, an ineffectual impulsion, a colorless light; they are still images. It is true that an image may *be* without *being perceived* − it may be present without being represented − and the distance between these two terms, presence and representation, seems just to measure the interval between matter itself and our conscious perception of matter. But let us examine the point more closely and see in what this difference consists. If there were *more* in the second term than in the first, if, in order to pass from presence to representation, it were necessary to add something, the barrier would indeed be insuperable, and the passage from matter to perception would remain wrapped in impenetrable mystery. It would not be the same if it were possible to pass from the first term to the second by way of diminution, and if the representation of an image were *less* than its presence; for it would then suffice that the images present should be compelled to abandon something of themselves in order that their mere presence should convert them into representations. Now, here is the image which I call a material object; I have the representation of it. How then does it not appear to be in itself that which it is for me? It is because, being bound up with all other images, it is continued in those which follow it,

35

just as it prolonged those which preceded it. To transform its existence into representation, it would be enough to suppress what follows it, what precedes it, and also all that fills it, and to retain only its external crust, its superficial skin. That which distinguishes it as a *present* image, as an objective reality, from a *represented* image is the necessity which obliges it to act through every one of its points upon all the points of all other images, to transmit the whole of what it receives, to oppose to every action an equal and contrary reaction, to be, in short, merely a road by which pass, in every direction, the modifications propagated throughout the immensity of the universe. I should convert it into representation if I could isolate it, especially if I could isolate its shell. Representation is there, but always virtual — being neutralized, at the very moment when it might become actual, by the obligation to continue itself and to lose itself in something else. To obtain this conversion from the virtual to the actual, it would be necessary, not to throw more light on the object, but, on the contrary, to obscure some of its aspects, to diminish it by the greater part of itself, so that the remainder, instead of being encased in its surroundings as a *thing*, should detach itself from them as a *picture*. Now, if living beings are, within the universe, just "centers of indetermination," and if the degree of this indetermination is measured by the number and rank of their functions, we can conceive that their mere presence is equivalent to the suppression of all those parts of objects in which their functions find no interest. They allow to pass through them, so to speak, those external influences which are indifferent to them; the others isolated, become "perceptions" by their very isolation. Everything thus happens for us as though we reflected back to surfaces the light which emanates from them, the light which, had it passed on unopposed, would never have been revealed. The images which surround us will appear to turn toward our body the side, emphasized by the light upon it, which interests our body.

They will detach from themselves that which we have arrested on its way, that which we are capable of influencing. Indifferent to each other because of the radical mechanism which binds them together, they present each to the others all their sides at once: which means that they act and react mutually by all their elements, and that none of them perceives or is perceived consciously. Suppose, on the contrary, that they encounter somewhere a certain spontaneity of reaction: their action is so far diminished, and this diminution of their action is just the representation which we have of them. Our representation of things would thus arise from the fact that they are thrown back and reflected by our freedom.

When a ray of light passes from one medium into another, it usually traverses it with a change of direction. But the respective densities of the two media may be such that, for a given angle of incidence, refraction is no longer possible. Then we have total reflection. The luminous point gives rise to a *virtual* image which symbolizes, so to speak, the fact that the luminous rays cannot pursue their way. Perception is just a phenomenon of the same kind. That which is given is the totality of the images of the material world, with the totality of their internal elements. But, if we suppose centers of real, that is to say of spontaneous, activity, the rays which reach it, and which interest that activity, instead of passing through those centers, will appear to be reflected and thus to indicate the outlines of the object which emits them. There is nothing positive here, nothing added to the image, nothing new. The objects merely abandon something of their real action in order to manifest their virtual influence of the living being upon them. Perception therefore resembles those phenomena of reflexion which result from an impeded refraction; it is like an effect of mirage.

This is as much as to say that there is for images merely a difference of degree, and not of kind, between *being* and *being consciously perceived*. The reality of matter consists in the totality of its ele-

37

ments and of their actions of every kind. Our representation of matter is the measure of our possible action upon bodies: it results from the discarding of what has no interest for our needs, or more generally, for our functions. In one sense we might say that the perception of any unconscious material point whatever, in its instantaneousness, is infinitely greater and more complete than ours, since this point gathers and transmits the influences of all the points of the material universe, whereas our consciousness only attains to certain parts and to certain aspects of those parts. Consciousness — in regard to external perception — lies in just this choice. But there is, in this necessary poverty of our conscious perception, something that is positive, that foretells spirit: it is, in the etymological sense of the word, discernment.

The whole difficulty of the problem that occupies us comes from the fact that we imagine perception to be a kind of photographic view of things, taken from a fixed point by that special apparatus which is called an organ of perception — a photograph which would then be developed in the brain-matter by some unknown chemical and psychical process of elaboration. But is it not obvious that the photograph, if photograph there be, is already taken, already developed in the very heart of things and at all the points of space? No metaphysics, no physics even, can escape this conclusion. Build up the universe with atoms: each of them is subject to the action, variable in quantity and quality according to the distance, exerted on it by all material atoms. Bring in Faraday's centers of force: the lines of force emitted in every direction from every center bring to bear upon each the influences of the whole material world. Call up the Leibnizian monads: each is the mirror of the universe. All philosophers, then, agree on this point. Only if, when we consider any other given place in the universe, we can regard the acton of all matter as passing through it without resistance and without loss, and the photograph of the whole as translucent: here there is wanting behind the plate the black screen on which the image could be shown. Our "zones of indetermination" play in some sort the part of the screen. They add nothing to what is there; they effect merely this: that the real action passes through, the virtual action remains.

This is no hypothesis. We content ourselves with formulating data with which no theory of perception can dispense. For no philosopher can begin the study of external perception without assuming the possibility at least of a material world, that is to say, in the main, the virtual perception of all things. From this merely possible material mass he will then isolate the particular object which I call my body, and, in this body, centers of perception: he will show me the disturbance coming from a certain point in space, propagating itself along the nerves, and reaching the centers. But here I am confronted by a transformation scene from fairyland. The material world, which surrounds the body; the body, which shelters the brain; the brain, in which we distinguish centers; he abruptly dismisses, and, as by a magician's wand, he conjures up, as a thing entirely new the representation of what he began by postulating. This representation he drives out of space, so that it may have nothing in common with the matter from which he started. As for matter itself, he would fain go without it, but cannot, because its phenomena present relatively to each other an order so strict and so indifferent as to the point of origin chosen, that this regularity and this indifference really constitute an independent existence. So he must resign himself to retaining at least the phantasm of matter. But then he manages to deprive it of all the qualities which give it life. In an amorphous space he carves out moving figures; or else (and it comes to nearly the same thing), he imagines relations of magnitude which adjust themselves one to another, mathematical functions which go on evolving and developing their own content: representation, laden with the spoils of

matter, thenceforth displays itself freely in an unextended consciousness. But it is not enough to cut out, it is necessary to sew
the pieces together. You must now explain how those qualities
which you have detached from their material support can be joined
to it again. Each attribute which you take away from matter widens the interval between representation and its object. If you make
matter unextended, how will it acquire extension? If you reduce
it to homogeneous movements, whence arises quality? Above all,
how are we to imagine a relation between a thing and its image,
between matter and thought, since each of these terms possesses,
by definition, only that which is lacking to the other? Thus difficulties spring up beneath our feet; and every effort that you make
to dispose of one of them does but resolve it into many more.
What then do we ask of you? Merely to give up your magician's
wand, and to continue along the path on which you first set out.
You showed us external images reaching the organs of sense, modifying the nerves, propagating their influence in the brain. Well,
follow the process to the end. The movement will pass through
the cerebral substance (although not without having tarried there),
and will then expand into voluntary action. There you have the
whole mechanism of perception. As for perception itself, in so far
as it is an image, you are not called upon to retrace its genesis,
since you posited it to begin with, and since, moreover, no other
course was open to you. In assuming the brain, in assuming the
smallest portion of matter, did you not assume the totality of
images? *What you have to explain, then, is not how perception arises,
but how it is limited, since it should be the image of the whole, and is in
fact reduced to the image of that which interests you.* But if it differs
from the mere image, precisely in that its parts range themselves
with reference to a variable center, its limitation is easy to understand: unlimited de jure, it confines itself de facto to indicating
the degree of indetermination allowed to the acts of the special

image which you call your body. And, inversely, it follows that the indetermination of the movements of your body, such as it results from the structure of the grey matter of the brain, gives the exact measure of the extent of your perception. It is no wonder, then, that everything happens *as though* your perception were a result of the internal motions of the brain and issued in some sort from the cortical centers. It could not actually come from them, since the brain is an image like others, enveloped in the mass of other images, and it would be absurd that the container should issue from the content. But since the structure of the brain is like the detailed plan of the movements among which you have the choice, and since that part of the external images which appears to return upon itself in order to constitute perception includes precisely all the points of the universe which these movements could affect, conscious perception and cerebral movement are in strict correspondence. The reciprocal dependence of these two terms is therefore simply due to the fact that both are functions of a third, which is the indetermination of the will.

Take, for example, a luminous point P, of which the rays impinge on the different parts *a, b, c,* of the retina. At this point P, science localizes vibrations of a certain amplitude and duration. At the same point P, consciousness perceives light. We propose to show, in the course of this study, that both are right; and that there is no essential difference between the light and the movements, provided we restore to movement the unity, indivisibility, and qualitative heterogeneity denied to it by abstract mechanics; provided also that we see in sensible qualities *contractions* effected by our memory. Science and consciousness would then coincide in the instantaneous. For the moment all we need say, without examining too closely the meaning of the words, is that the point P sends to the retina vibrations of light. What happens then? If the visual image of the point P were not already given, we should indeed have to seek the manner in which it had been engendered, and should soon be confronted by an insoluble problem. But, whatever we do, we cannot avoid assuming it to begin with: the sole question is, then, to know how and why this image *is chosen* to form part of my perception, while an infinite number of other images remain excluded from it. Now I see that the vibrations transmitted from the point P to the various parts of the retina are conducted to the subcortical and cortical optic centers, often to other centers as well, and that these centers sometimes transmit them to motor mechanisms, sometimes provisionally arrest them. The nervous elements concerned are, therefore, what give efficacy to the disturbance received; they symbolize the indetermination of the will; on their soundness this indetermination depends; consequently, any injury to these elements, by diminishing our possible action, diminishes perception in the same degree. In other words, if there exist in the material world places where the vibrations received are not mechanically transmitted, if there are, as we said, zones of indetermination, these zones must occur along the path of what is termed the sensori-motor process; and hence all must happen as though the rays P*a*, P*b*, P*c* were *perceived* along this path and afterwards *projected* into P. Further, while the indetermination is something which escapes experiment and calculation, this is not the case with the nervous elements by which the impression is received and transmitted. These elements are the special concern of the physiologist and the psychologist; on them all the details of external perception would seem to depend and by them they may be explained. So we may say, if we like, that the disturbance, after having travelled along these nervous elements, after having gained the center, there changes into a conscious image which is subsequently exteriorized at the point P. But, when we so express ourselves, we merely bow to the exigencies of the scientific method; we in no way describe the real process. There is

42

not, in fact, an unextended image which forms itself in conscious-ness and then projects itself into P. The truth is that the point P, the rays which it emits, the retina and the nervous elements affected, form a single whole; that the luminous point P is a part of this whole; and that it is really in P, and not elsewhere, that the image of P is formed and perceived.

When we represent things to ourselves in this manner, we do but return to the simple convictions of common sense. We all of us began by believing that we grasped the very object, that we perceived it in itself and not in us. When philosophers disdain an idea so simple and so close to reality, it is because the intracerebral process – that diminutive part of perception – appears to them the equivalent of the whole of perception. If we suppress the object perceived and keep the internal process, it seems to them that the image of the object remains. And their belief is easily explained: there are many conditions, such as hallucination and dreams, in which images arise that resemble external perception in all their details. Because as, in such cases, the object has disappeared while the brain persists, he holds that the cerebral phenomenon is suffi-cient for the production of the image. But it must not be forgot-ten that in all psychical states of this kind memory plays the chief part. We shall try to show later that, when perception, as we under-stand it, is once admitted, memory *must* arise, and that this memory has not, any more than perception itself, a cerebral state as its true and complete condition. But, without as yet entering upon the examination of these two points, we will content ourselves with a very simple observation which has indeed no novelty. In many people who are blind from birth, the visual centers are intact; yet they live and die without having formed a single visual image. Such an image, therefore, cannot appear unless the external object has, at least, once played its part: it must, once at any rate, have been part and parcel with representation. Now this is what we claim

43

and for the moment all that we require, for we are dealing here with *pure* perception, and not with perception complicated by memory. Reject then the share of memory, consider perception in its unmixed state, and you will be forced to recognize that there is no image without an object. But, from the moment that you thus posit the intracerebral processes in addition to the external object which causes them, we can clearly see how the image of that object is given with it and in it: how the image should arise from the cerebral movement we shall never understand.

When a lesion of the nerves or of the centers interrupts the passage of the nerve vibration, perception is to that extent diminished. Need we be surprised? The office of the nervous system is to utilize that vibration, to convert it into practical deeds, really or virtually accomplished. If, for one reason or another, the disturbance cannot pass along, it would be strange if the corresponding perception still took place, since this perception would then connect our body with points of space which no longer directly invite it to make a choice. Sever the optic nerve of an animal: the vibrations issuing from the luminous point can no longer be transmitted to the brain and thence to the motor nerves; the thread, of which the optic nerve is a part and which binds the external object to the motor mechanisms of the animal, is broken: visual perception has therefore become impotent, and this very impotence is unconsciousness. That matter should be perceived without the help of a nervous system and without organs of sense, is not theoretically inconceivable; but it is practically impossible because such perception would be of no use. It would suit a phantom, not a living, and, therefore, acting, being. We are too much inclined to regard the living body as a world within a world, the nervous system as a separate being, of which the function is, first, to elaborate perceptions, and, then, to create movements. The truth is that my nervous system, interposed between the objects which affect my body and those which I can influence, is a mere conductor, transmitting, sending back or inhibiting movement. This conductor is composed of an enormous number of threads which stretch from the periphery to the center, and from the center to the periphery. As many threads as pass from the periphery to the center, so many points of space are there able to make an appeal to my will and to put, so to speak, an elementary question to my motor activity. Every such question is what is termed a perception. Thus perception is diminished by one of its elements each time one of the threads termed sensory is cut because some part of the external object then becomes unable to appeal to activity; and it is also diminished whenever a stable habit has been formed, because this time the ready-made response renders the question unnecessary. What disappears in either case is the apparent reflection of the stimulus upon itself, the return of the light on the image whence it comes; or rather that dissociation, that *discernment*, whereby the perception is disengaged from the image. We may therefore say that while the detail of perception is molded exactly upon that of the nerves termed sensory, perception as a whole has its true and final explanation in the tendency of the body to movement.

The cause of the general illusion on this point lies in the apparent indifference of our movements to the stimulation which excites them. It seems that the movement of my body in order to reach and to modify an object is the same, whether I have been told of its existence by the ear or whether it has been revealed to me by sight or touch. My motor activity thus appears as a separate entity, a sort of reservoir whence movements issue at will, always the same for the same action, whatever the kind of image which has called it into being. But the truth is that the character of movements which are externally identical is internally different, according as they respond to a visual, an auditory or a tactile impression. Suppose I perceive a multitude of objects in space; each of them,

inasmuch as it is a visual form, solicits my activity. Now I suddenly lose my sight. No doubt I still have at my disposal the same
quantity and the same quality of movements in space; but these
movements can no longer be coordinated to visual impressions;
they must in future follow tactile impressions, for example, and a
new arrangement will take place in the brain. The protoplasmic
expansions of the motor nervous elements in the cortex will now
be in relation with a much smaller number of the nervous elements termed sensory. My activity is then really diminished, in
the sense that although I can produce the same movements, the
occasion comes more rarely from the external objects. Consequently, the sudden interruption of optical continuity has brought
with it, as its essential and profound effect, the suppression of a
large part of the queries or demands addressed to my activity. Now
such as query or demand is, as we have seen, a perception. Here
we put our finger on the mistake of those who maintain that perception springs from what is properly called the sensory vibration, and not from a sort of question addressed to motor activity.
They sever this motor activity from the perceptive process; and,
as it appears to survive the loss of perception, they conclude that
perception is localized in the nervous elements termed sensory.
But the truth is that perception is no more in the sensory centers
than in the motor centers; it measures the complexity of their
relations, and is, in fact, where it appears to be.

Psychologists who have studied infancy are well aware that our
representation is at first impersonal. Only little by little, and as a
result of experience, does it adopt our body as a center and become
our representation. The mechanism of this process is, moreover,
easy to understand. As my body moves in space, all the other images
vary, while that image, my body, remains invariable. I must, therefore, make it a center, to which I refer all the other images. My
belief in an external world does not come, cannot come, from the

46

fact that I project outside myself sensations that are unextended: how could these sensations ever acquire extension, and whence should I get the notion of exteriority? But, if we allow that, as experience testifies, the aggregate of images is given to begin with, I can see clearly how my body comes to occupy, within this aggregate, a privileged position. And I understand also whence arises the notion of interiority and exteriority, which is, to begin with, merely the distinction between my body and other bodies. For, if you start from my body, as is usually done, you will never make me understand how impressions received on the surface of my body, impressions which concern that body alone, are able to become for me independent objects and form an external world. But if, on the contrary, all images are posited at the outset, my body will necessarily end by standing out in the midst of them as a distinct thing, since they change unceasingly, and it does not vary. The distinction between the inside and the outside will then be only a distinction between the part and the whole. There is, first of all, the aggregate of images; and, then, in this aggregate, there are "centers of action," from which the interesting images appear to be reflected: thus perceptions are born and actions made ready. *My body* is that which stands out as the center of these perceptions; *my personality* is the being to which these actions must be referred. The whole subject becomes clear if we travel thus from the periphery to the center, as the child does, and as we ourselves are invited to do by immediate experience and by common sense. On the contrary everything becomes obscure, and problems are multiplied on all sides, if we attempt, with the theorists, to travel from the center to the periphery. Whence arises, then, this idea of an external world constructed artificially, piece by piece, out of unextended sensations, though we can neither understand how they come to form an extended surface, nor how they are subsequently projected outside our body? Why insist, in spite of appearances, that I should go from my conscious self to my body, then from my body to other bodies, whereas in fact I place myself at once in the material world in general, and then gradually cut out within it the center of action which I shall come to call my body and to distinguish from all others? There are so many illusions gathered round this belief in the originally unextended character of our external perception; there are, in the idea that we project outside ourselves states which are purely internal, so many misconceptions, so many lame answers to badly stated questions, that we cannot hope to throw light on the whole subject at once. We believe that light will increase, as we show more clearly, behind these illusions, the metaphysical error which confounds "pure perception" with memory. But these illusions are, nevertheless, connected with real facts, which we may here indicate in order to correct their interpretation.

The first of these facts is that our senses require education. Neither sight nor touch is able at the outset to localize impressions. A series of comparisons and inductions is necessary, whereby we gradually coordinate one impression with another. Hence philosophers may jump to the belief that sensations are in their essence inextensive and that they constitute extensity by their juxtaposition. But is it not clear that, upon the hypothesis just advanced, our senses are equally in need of education — not, of course, in order to accommodate themselves to each other? Here, in the midst of all the images, there is a certain image which I term my body and of which the virtual action reveals itself by an apparent reflection of the surrounding images upon themselves. Suppose there are so many kinds of possible action for my body: there must be an equal number of systems of reflection for other bodies; each of these systems will be just what is perceived by one of my senses. My body, then, acts like an image which reflects others, and which, in so doing, analyzes them along lines corresponding to the differ-

48

ent actions which it can exercise upon them. And, consequently, each of the qualities perceived in the same object by my different senses symbolizes a particular direction of my activity, a particular need. Now, will all these perceptions of a body by my different senses give me, when united, the complete image of that body? Certainly not, because they have been gathered from a larger whole. To perceive all the influences from all the points of all bodies would be to descend to the condition of a material object. Conscious perception signifies choice, and consciousness mainly consists in this practical discernment. The diverse perceptions of the same object, given by my different senses, will not, then, when put together, reconstruct the *complete* image of the object; they will remain separated from each other by intervals which measure, so to speak, the gaps in my needs. It is to fill these intervals that an education of the senses is necessary. The aim of this education is to harmonize my senses with each other, to restore between their data a continuity which has been broken by the discontinuity of the needs of my body, in short, to reconstruct, as nearly as may be, the whole of the material object. This, on our hypothesis, explains the need for an education of the senses. Now let us compare it with the preceding explanation. In the first, unextended sensations of sight combine with unextended sensations of touch and of the other senses to give, by their synthesis, the idea of a material object. But, to begin with, it is not easy to see how these sensations can acquire extension, nor how, above all, when extension in general has been acquired, we can explain in particular the preference of a given one of these sensations for a given point of space. And then we may ask: by what happy agreement, in virtue of what preestablished harmony, do these sensations of different kinds coordinate themselves to form a stable object, henceforth solidified, common to my experience and to that of all men, subject, in its relation to other objects, to those inflexible rules which

49

we call the laws of nature? In the second, "the data of our different senses" are, on the contrary, the very qualities of things, perceived first in the things rather than in us: is it surprising that they come together, since abstraction alone has separated them? On the first hypothesis, the material object is nothing of all that we perceive: you put, on one side, the conscious principle with the sensible qualities and, on the other, a matter of which you can predicate nothing, which you define by negations because you have begun by despoiling it of all that reveals it to us. On the second hypothesis, an ever-deepening knowledge of matter becomes possible. Far from depriving matter of anything perceived, we must on the contrary, bring together all sensible qualities, restore their relationship, and reestablish among them the continuity broken by our needs. Our perception of matter is, then, no longer either relative or subjective, at least in principle, and apart, as we shall see presently, from affection and especially from memory; it is merely dissevered by the multiplicity of our needs. On the first hypothesis, spirit is as unknowable as matter, for (we) attribute to it the undefinable power of evoking sensations we know not whence, and of projecting them, we know not why, into a space where they will form bodies. On the second, the part played by consciousness is clearly defined: consciousness means virtual action, and the forms acquired by mind, those which hide the essence of spirit from us, should, with the help of this second principle, be removed as so many concealing veils. Thus, on our hypothesis, we begin to see the possibility of a clearer distinction between spirit and matter, and of a reconciliation between them. But we will leave this first point and come to the second.

The second fact brought forward consists of what was long termed the "specific energy of the nerves." We know that stimulation of the optic nerve by an external shock or by an electric current will produce a visual sensation and that this same electric current applied to the acoustic or to the glosso-pharyngeal nerve will cause a sound to be heard or a taste to be perceived. From these very particular facts have been deduced two very general laws: that different causes acting on the same nerve excite the same sensation and that the same cause, acting on different nerves, provokes different sensations. And from these laws it has been inferred that our sensations are merely signals and that the office of each sense is to translate into its own language homogeneous and mechanical movements occurring in space. Hence, as a conclusion, the idea of cutting our perception into two distinct parts, thenceforth incapable of uniting: on the one hand, homogeneous movements in space and, on the other hand, unextended sensations in consciousness. Now it is not our part to enter into an examination of the physiological problems raised by the interpretation of the two laws: in whatever way these laws are understood, whether the specific energy is attributed to the nerves or whether it is referred to the centers, insurmountable difficulties arise. But the very existence of the laws themselves appears more and more problematical. Lotze himself already suspected a fallacy in them. He awaited, before putting faith in them, "sound waves which should give to the eye the sensation of light, or luminous vibrations which should give to the ear a sound."[2] The truth is that all the facts alleged can be brought back to a single type: the one stimulus capable of producing different sensations, the multiple stimuli capable of inducing the same sensation, are either an electric current or a mechanical cause capable of determining in the organ a modification of electrical equilibrium. Now we may well ask whether the electrical stimulus does not include different *components*, answering objectively to sensations of different kinds, and whether the office of each sense is not merely to extract from the whole the component that concerns it. We should then have, indeed, the same stimuli giving the same sensations and different stimuli provoking different sensations. To speak more precisely, it is difficult to admit, for instance, that applying an electrical stimulus to the tongue would not occasion chemical changes, and these changes are what, in all cases, we term tastes. Yet, while the physicist has been able to identify light with an electromagnetic disturbance, we may say, inversely, that what he calls here an electromagnetic disturbance *is* light, so that it is really light that the optic nerve perceives objectively when subject to electrical stimulus. The doctrine of specific energy appears to be nowhere more firmly based than in the case of the ear: nowhere also has the real existence of the thing perceived become more probable. We will not insist on these facts because they will be found stated and exhaustively discussed in a recent work.[3] We will only remark that the sensations here spoken of are not images perceived by us outside our body, but rather affections localized within the body. Now it results from the nature and use of our body, as we shall see, that each of its so-called sensory elements has its own *real* action, which must be of the same kind as its *virtual* action on the external objects which it usually perceives; and thus we can understand how it is that each of the sensory nerves appears to vibrate according to a fixed manner of sensation. But to elucidate this point we must consider the nature of affection. Thus we are led to the third and last argument which we have to examine.

This third argument is drawn from the fact that we pass by insensible degrees from the representative state, which occupies space, to the affective state which appears to be unextended.

Hence it is inferred that all sensation is naturally and necessarily unextended, so that extensity is superimposed upon sensation, and the process of perception consists in an exteriorization of internal states. The psychologist starts, in fact, from his body, and, as the impressions received at the periphery of this body seem to him sufficient for the reconstitution of the entire material universe, to his body he at first reduces the universe. But this first position is not tenable; his body has not, and cannot have, any more or any less reality than all other bodies. So he must go farther, follow to the end the consequences of his principle, and, after having narrowed the universe to the surface of the living body, contract this body itself into a center which he will end by supposing unextended. Then, from this center will start unextended sensations, which will swell, so to speak, will grow into extensity, and will end by giving extension first to his body and afterwards to all other material objects. But this strange supposition would be impossible if there were not, in point of fact, between images and ideas — the former extended and the latter unextended — a series of intermediate states, more or less vaguely localized, which are the *affective* states. Our understanding, yielding to its customary illusion, poses the dilemma that a thing either is or is not extended, and as the affective state participates vaguely in extension, is in fact imperfectly localized, we conclude that this state is absolutely unextended. But then the successive degrees of extension, and extensity itself, will have to be explained by I know not what acquired property of unextended states; the history of perception will become that of internal unextended states which acquire extension and project themselves without. Shall we put the argument in another form? There is hardly any perception which may not, by the increase of the action of its object upon our body, become an affection, and, more particularly, pain. Thus we pass insensibly from the contact with a pin to its prick. Inversely the decreasing pain coincides with the lessening perception of its cause, and exteriorizes itself, so to speak, into a representation. So it does seem, then, as if there were a difference of degree and not of nature between affection and perception. Now the first is intimately bound up with my personal existence: what, indeed, would be a pain detached from the subject that feels it? It seems, there-

fore, that it must be so with the second and that external perception is formed by projecting into space an affection which has
become harmless. Realists and idealists are agreed in this method
of reasoning. The latter see in the material universe nothing but a
synthesis of subjective and unextended states; the former add that,
behind this synthesis, there is an independent reality corresponding to it, but both conclude, from the gradual passage of affection
to representation, that our representation of the material universe
is relative and subjective and that it has, so to speak, emerged
from us, rather than that we have emerged from it.

Before criticizing this questionable interpretation of an unques-
tionable fact, we may show that it does not succeed in explaining,
or even in throwing light upon, the nature either of pain or of
perception. That affective states, essentially bound up with my
personality, and vanishing if I disappear, should acquire extensity
by losing intensity, should adopt a definite position in space, and
build up a firm, solid experience, always in accord with itself and
with the experience of other men — is very difficult to realize.
Whatever we do, we shall be forced to give back to sensations, in
one form or another, first the extension and then the independence which we have tried to do without. But, what is more, affection, on this hypothesis, is hardly clearer than representation. For
if it is not easy to see how affections, by diminishing in intensity,
become representations, neither can we understand how the same
phenomenon, which was given at first as perception, becomes affection by an increase of intensity. There is in pain something positive and active, which is ill explained by saying, as do some
philosophers, that it consists in a *confused* representation. But still
this is not the principal difficulty. That the gradual augmentation
of the stimulus ends by transforming perception into pain, no one
will deny; it is none the less true that this change arises at a definite moment: why at this moment rather than at another? And

what special reason causes a phenomenon of which I was at first only an indifferent spectator to suddenly acquire for me a vital interest? Therefore, on this hypothesis I fail to see either why, at a given moment, a diminution of intensity in the phenomenon confers on it a right to extension and to an apparent independence, or why an increase of intensity should create, at one moment rather than at another, this new property, the source of positive action, which is called pain.

Let us return now to our hypothesis and show that affection *must*, at a given moment, arise out of the image. We shall thus understand how it is that we pass from a perception, which has extensity, to an affection which is believed to be unextended. But some preliminary remarks on the real significance of pain are indispensable.

When a foreign body touches one of the prolongations of the amoeba, that prolongation is retracted; every part of the protoplasmic mass is equally able to receive a stimulation and to react against it; perception and movement being here blended in a single property — contractility. But, as the organism grows more complex, there is a division of labor; functions become differentiated, and the anatomical elements thus determined forego their independence. In such an organism as our own, the nerve fibres termed sensory are exclusively empowered to transmit stimulation to a central region whence the vibration will be passed on to motor elements. It would seem then that they have abandoned individual action to take their share, as outposts, in the maneuvers of the whole body. But nonetheless they remain exposed, singly, to the same causes of destruction which threaten the organism as a whole, and while this organism is able to move — and thereby to escape a danger or to repair a loss — the sensitive element retains the relative immobility to which the division of labor condemns it. Thence arises pain, which, in our view, is nothing but the effort of the damaged element to set things right — a kind of motor tendency in a sensory nerve. Every pain, then, must consist in an effort — an effort which is doomed to be unavailing. Every pain is a *local* effort, and in its very isolation lies the cause of its impotence, because the organism, by reason of the solidarity of its parts, is able to move only as a whole. It is also because the effort is local that pain is entirely disproportioned to the danger incurred by the living being. The danger may be mortal and the pain slight; the pain may be unbearable (as in a toothache) and the danger insignificant. There is then, there must be, a precise moment when pain intervenes: it is when the interested part of the organism, instead of accepting the stimulation, repels it. And it is not merely a difference of degree that separates perception from affection but a difference in kind.

Now we have considered the living body as a kind of center whence is reflected on the surrounding objects the action which these objects exercise upon it: in that reflection external perception consists. But this center is not a mathematical point; it is a body, exposed, like all natural bodies, to the action of external causes which threaten to disintegrate it. We have just seen that it resists the influence of these causes. It does not merely reflect action received from without; it struggles, and thus absorbs some part of this action. Here is the source of affection. We might therefore say, metaphorically, that while perception measures the reflecting power of the body, affection measures its power to absorb.

But this is only a metaphor. We must consider the matter more carefully in order to understand clearly that the necessity of affection follows from the very existence of perception. Perception, understood as we understand it, measures our possible action upon things, and thereby, inversely, the possible action of things upon us. The greater the body's power of action (symbolized by a higher degree of complexity in the nervous system), the wider is the field that perception embraces. The distance which separates our body from an object perceived really measures, therefore, the greater or less imminence of a danger, the nearer or more remote fulfillment of a promise. And, consequently, our perception of an object distinct from our body, separated from our body by an interval, never expresses anything but a *virtual* action. But the more distance decreases between this object and our body (the more, in other words, the danger becomes urgent or the promise immediate), the more does virtual action tend to pass into *real* action. Suppose the distance reduced to zero, that is to say that the object to be perceived coincides with our body, that is to say again, that our body is the object to be perceived. Then it is no longer virtual action, but real action, that this specialized perception will express, and this is exactly what affection is. Our sensations are, then, to our perceptions that which the real action of our body is to its possible, or virtual, action. Its virtual action concerns other objects and is manifested within those objects; its real action concerns itself, and is manifested within its own substance. Everything then will happen as if, by a true return of real and virtual actions to their points of application or of origin, the external images were reflected by our body into surrounding space and the real actions arrested by it within itself. And that is why its surface, the common limit of the external and the internal, is the only portion of space which is both perceived and felt.

That is to say once more, that my perception is outside my body and my affection within it. Just as external objects are perceived by me where they are, in themselves and not in me, so my affective states are experienced where they occur, that is, at a given point in my body. Consider the system of images which is called the material world. My body is one of them. Around this image is grouped the representation, i.e., its eventual influence on the others. Within it occurs affection, i.e., its actual effort upon itself. Such is indeed the fundamental difference which every one of us

57

naturally makes between an image and a sensation. When we say that the image exists outside us, we signify by this that it is external to our body. When we speak of sensation as an internal state, we mean that it arises within in our body. And this is why we affirm that the totality of perceived images subsists, even if our body disappears, whereas we know that we cannot annihilate our body without destroying our sensations.

Hence we begin to see that we must correct, at least in this particular, our theory of pure perception. We have argued as though our perception were a part of the images, detached, as such, from their entirety, as though, expressing the virtual action of the object upon our body, or of our body upon the object, perception merely isolated from the total object that aspect of it which interests us. But we have to take into account the fact that our body is not a mathematical point in space, that its virtual actions are complicated by, and impregnated with, real actions, or, in other words, that there is no perception without affection. Affection is, then, that part or aspect of the inside of our body which we mix with the image of external bodies; it is what we must first of all subtract from perception to get the image in its purity. But the psychologist who shuts his eyes to the difference of function and nature between perception and sensation – the latter involving a real action, and the former a merely possible action – can only find between them a difference of degree. Because sensation (on account of the *confused* effort which it involves) is only vaguely localized, he declares it unextended, and thence makes sensation in general the simple element from which we obtain by composition all external images. The truth is that affection is not the primary matter of which perception is made; it is rather the impurity with which perception is alloyed.

Here we grasp, at its origin, the error which leads the psychologist to consider sensation as unextended and perception as an aggregate of sensations. This error is reinforced, as we shall see, by illusions derived from a false conception of the role of space and of the nature of extensity. But it has also the support of misinterpreted facts, which we must now examine.

It appears, in the first place, as if the localization of an affective sensation in one part of the body were a matter of gradual training. A certain time elapses before the child can touch with the finger the precise point where it has been pricked. The fact is indisputable, but all that can be concluded from it is that some tentative essays are required to coordinate the painful impressions on the skin, which has received the prick, with the impressions of the muscular sense, which guides the movement, of arm and hand. Our internal affections, like our external perceptions, are of different kinds. These kinds of affections, like those of perception, are discontinuous, separated by intervals which are filled up in the course of education. But it does not at all follow that there is not, for each affection, an immediate localization of a certain kind, a local color which is proper to it. We may go further: if the affection has not this local color at once, it will never have it. For all that education can do is to associate with the actual affective sensation the idea of a certain potential perception of sight and touch, so that a definite affection may evoke the image of a visual or tactile impression, equally definite. There must be, therefore, in this affection itself, something which distinguishes it from other affections of the same kind and permits of its reference to this or that potential datum of sight or touch rather than to any other. But is not this equivalent to saying that affection possesses, from the outset, a certain determination of extensity?

Again, it is alleged that there are erroneous localizations, for example, the illusion of those who have lost a limb (an illusion which requires, however, further examination). But what can we conclude from this beyond the fact that education, once acquired, persists and that such data of memory as are more useful in practical life supplant those of immediate consciousness? It is indispensable, in view of action, that we should translate our affective experience into eventual data of sight, touch and muscular sense. When this translation is made, the original pales, but it never could have been made if the original had not been there to begin with, and if sensation had not been, from the beginning, localized by its own power and in its own way.

But the psychologist has much difficulty in accepting this idea from common sense. Just as perception, in his view, could be in the things perceived only if they had perception, so a sensation cannot be in the nerve unless the nerve feels. Now it is evident that the nerve does not feel. So he takes sensation away from the point where common sense localizes it, carries it toward the brain, on which, more than on the nerve, it appears to depend, and logically should end by placing it *in* the brain. But it soon becomes clear that if it is not at the point where it appears to arise, neither can it be anywhere else: if it is not in the nerve, neither is it in the brain; for to explain its projection from the center to the periphery a certain force is necessary, which must be attributed to a consciousness that is to some extent active. Therefore, he must go further, and, after having made sensations converge toward the cerebral center, must push them out of the brain and thereby out of space. So he has to imagine, on the one hand, sensations that are absolutely unextended, and, on the other hand, an empty space indifferent to the sensations which are projected into it: henceforth he will exhaust himself in efforts of every kind to make us understand how unextended sensations acquire extensity and why they choose for their abode this or that point of space rather than any other. But this doctrine is not only incapable of showing us clearly how the unextended takes on extension; it renders affection, extension and representation equally inexplicable. It must assume affective states as so many absolutes, of which it is impossible to say why they appear in or disappear from consciousness at definite moments. The passage from affection to representation remains wrapped in an equally impenetrable mystery because, once again, you will never find in internal states, which are supposed to be simple and unextended, any reason why they should prefer this or that particular order in space. And, finally, representation itself must be posited as an absolute: we cannot guess either its origin or its goal.

Everything becomes clearer, on the other hand, if we start from representation itself, that is to say, from the totality of perceived images. My perception, in its pure state, isolated from memory, does not go on from my body to other bodies; it is, to begin with, in the aggregate of bodies, then gradually limits itself and adopts my body as a center. And it is led to do so precisely by experience of the double faculty, which this body possesses, of performing actions and feeling affections; in a word, it is led to do so by experience of the sensori-motor power of a certain image, privileged among other images. For, on the one hand, this image always occupies the center of representation, so that the other images range themselves round it in the very order in which they might be subject to its action; on the other hand, I know it from within, by sensations which I term affective, instead of knowing only, as in the case of the other images, its outer skin. There is, then, in the aggregate of images, a privileged image, perceived in its depths and no longer only on the surface — the seat of affection and, at the same time, the source of action: it is this particular image which I adopt as the center of my universe and as the physical basis of my personality.

But before we go on to establish the precise relation between the personality and the images in which it dwells, let us briefly sum up, contrasting it with the analyses of current psychology,

61

the theory of pure perception which we have just sketched out.

We will return, for the sake of simplicity, to the sense of sight, which we chose as our example. Psychology has accustomed us to assume the elementary sensations corresponding to the impressions received by the rods and cones of the retina. With these sensations it goes on to reconstitute visual perception. But, in the first place, there is not one retina, there are two; so that we have to explain how two sensations, held to be distinct, combine to form a single perception corresponding to what we call a point in space.

Suppose this problem is solved. The sensations in question are unextended; how will they acquire extension? Whether we see in extensity a framework ready to receive sensations, or an effect of the mere simultaneity of sensations coexisting in consciousness without coalescing, in either case something new is introduced with extensity, something unaccounted for: the process by which sensation arrives at extension, and the choice by each elementary sensation of a definite point in space, remain alike unexplained.

We will leave this difficulty, and suppose visual extension constituted. How does it in its turn reunite with tactile extension? All that my vision perceives in space is verified by my touch. Shall we say that objects are constituted by just the cooperation of sight and touch and that the agreement of the two senses in perception may be explained by the fact that the object perceived is their common product? But how could there be anything common, in the matter of quality, between an elementary visual sensation and a tactile sensation, since they belong to two different genera? The correspondence between visual and tactile extension can only be explained, therefore, by the parallelism of the *order* of the visual sensations with the order of the tactile sensations. So we are now obliged to suppose, over and above visual sensations, over and above tactile sensations, a certain order which is common to both and which, consequently, must be independent of either. We may go further: this order is independent of our individual perception, since it is the same for all men and constitutes a material world in which effects are linked with causes, in which phenomena obey laws. We are thus led at last to the hypothesis of an *objective* order, independent of ourselves, that is to say, of a material world distinct from sensation.

We have had, as we advanced, to multiply our irreducible data and to complicate more and more the simple hypothesis from which we started. But have we gained anything by it? Though the matter which we have been led to posit is indispensable in order to account for the marvellous accord of sensations among themselves, we still know nothing of it, since we must refuse to it all the qualities perceived, all the sensations of which it has only to explain the correspondence. It is not, then, it cannot be, anything of what we know, anything of what we imagine. It remains a mysterious entity.

But our own nature, the office and the function of our personality, remain enveloped in equal mystery. For these elementary unextended sensations which develop themselves in space, whence do they come, how are they born, what purpose do they serve? We must posit them as so many absolutes, of which we see neither the origin nor the end. And even supposing that we must distinguish, in each of us, between the spirit and the body, we can know nothing either of body or of spirit or of the relation between them.

Now in what does this hypothesis of ours consist, and at what precise point does it part company with the other? Instead of starting from *affection*, of which we can say nothing, since there is no reason why it should be what it is rather than anything else, we start from *action*, that is to say from our faculty of effecting changes in things, a faculty attested to by consciousness and toward which all the powers of the organized body are seen to converge. So we place ourselves at once in the midst of extended images, and in

this material universe we perceive centers of indetermination, characteristic of life. In order that actions may radiate from these centers, the movements or influences of the other images must be,
on the one hand, received and, on the other hand, utilized. Living
matter, in its simplest form and in a homogeneous state, accomplishes this function simultaneously with those of nourishment
and repair. The progress of such matter consists in sharing this
double labor between two categories of organs, the purpose of
the first, called organs of nutrition, being to maintain the second:
the second, in their turn, are made for *action*; they have as their
simple type a chain of nervous elements, connecting two extremities, of which the one receives external impressions and the other
executes movements. Thus, to return to the example of visual
perception, the office of the rods and cones is merely to receive
excitations which will be subsequently elaborated into movements,
either accomplished or nascent. No perception can result from
this, and nowhere in the nervous system are there conscious centers, but perception arises from the same cause which has brought
into being the chain of nervous elements, with the organs which
sustain them and with life in general. It expresses and measures
the power of action in the living being, the indetermination of
the movement or of the action which will follow the receipt of
the stimulus. This indetermination, as we have shown, will express
itself in a reflection upon themselves or, better, in a division, of
the images which surround our body, and, as the chain of nervous
elements which receives, arrests and transmits movements is the
seat of this indetermination and gives its measure, our perception
will follow all the detail and will appear to express all the variations of the nervous elements themselves. Perception, in its pure
state, is, then, in very truth, a part of things. And, as for affective
sensation, it does not spring spontaneously from the depths of
consciousness to extend itself, as it grows weaker, in space; it is

one with the necessary modifications to which, in the midst of the surrounding images that influence it, the particular image that each one of us terms his body is subject.

Such is our simplified, schematic theory of external perception. It is the theory of *pure* perception. If we went no further, the part of consciousness in perception would thus be confined to threading on the continuous string of memory an uninterrupted series of instantaneous visions, which would be a part of things rather than of ourselves. That this *is* the chief office of consciousness in external perception is indeed what we may deduce a priori from the very definition of living bodies. For though the function of these bodies is to receive stimulations in order to elaborate them into unforeseen reactions, still the choice of the reaction cannot be the work of chance. This choice is likely to be inspired by past experience, and the reaction does not take place without an appeal to the memories which analogous situations may have left behind them. The indetermination of acts to be accomplished requires, then, if it is not to be confounded with pure caprice, the preservation of the images perceived. It may be said that we have no grasp of the future without an equal and corresponding outlook over the past, that the onrush of our activity makes a void behind it into which memories flow, and that memory is thus the reverberation, in the sphere of consciousness, of the indetermination of our will. But the action of memory goes further and deeper than this superficial glance would suggest. The moment has come to reinstate memory in perception, to correct in this way the element of exaggeration in our conclusions, and so to determine with more precision the point of contact between consciousness and things, between the body and the spirit.

We assert, at the outset, that if there be memory, that is, the survival of past images, these images must constantly mingle with our perception of the present and may even take its place. For if they have survived it is with a view to utility; at every moment they complete our present experience, enriching it with experience already acquired, and, as the latter is ever increasing, it must end by covering up and submerging the former. It is indisputable that the basis of real, and so to speak instantaneous, intuition, on which our perception of the external world is developed, is a small matter compared with all that memory adds to it. Just because the recollection of earlier analogous intuitions is more useful than the intuition itself, being bound up in memory with the whole series of subsequent events and capable thereby of throwing a better light on our decision, it supplants the real intuition of which the office is then merely — we shall prove it later — to call up the recollection, to give it a body, to render it active and thereby actual. We had every right, then, to say that the coincidence of perception with the object perceived exists in theory rather than in fact. We must take into account that perception ends by being merely an occasion for remembering, that we measure in practice the degree of reality by the degree of utility, and, finally, that it is our interest to regard as mere signs of the real those immediate intuitions which are, in fact, part and parcel of reality. But here we discover the mistake of those who say that to perceive is to project externally unextended sensations, which have been drawn from our own depths, and then to develop them in space. They have no difficulty in showing that our *complete* perception is filled with images which belong to us personally, with exteriorized (that is to say, recollected) images, but they forget that an impersonal basis remains in which perception coincides with the object perceived and which is, in fact, externality itself.

The capital error, the error which, passing over from psychology into metaphysic, shuts us out in the end from the knowledge both of body and spirit, is that which sees only a difference of intensity instead of a difference of nature, between pure perception and memory. Our perceptions are undoubtedly interlaced with memories, and, inversely, a memory, as we shall show later, only becomes actual by borrowing the body of some perception into which it slips. These two acts, perception and recollection, always interpenetrate each other, are always exchanging something of their substance as by a process of endosmosis. The proper office of psychologists would be to dissociate them, to give back to each its natural purity; in this way many difficulties raised by psychology, and perhaps also by metaphysics, might be lessened. But they will have it that these mixed states, compounded, in unequal proportions, of pure perception and pure memory, are simple. And so we are condemned to an ignorance both of pure memory and of pure perception; to knowing only a single kind of phenomenon which will be called now memory and now perception, according to the predominance in it of one or other of the two aspects; and, consequently, to finding between perception and memory only a difference in degree, and not in kind. The first effect of this error, as we shall see in detail, is to vitiate profoundly the theory of memory; for, if we make recollection merely a weakened perception, we misunderstand the essential difference between the past and the present, we abandon all hope of understanding the phenomena of recognition, and, more generally, the mechanism of the unconscious. But, inversely, if recollection is regarded as a weakened perception, perception must be regarded as a stronger recollection. We are driven to argue as though it was given to us after the manner of a memory, as an internal state, a mere modification of our personality; and our eyes are closed to the primordial and fundamental act of perception — the act, constituting pure perception, whereby we place ourselves in the very heart of things. And thus the same error, which manifests itself in psychology by a radical incapacity to explain the mechanism of memory, will in metaphysics profoundly influence the idealistic and realistic conceptions of matter.

For realism, in fact, the invariable order of the phenomena of nature lies in a cause distinct from our perceptions, whether this cause must remain unknowable, or whether we can reach it by an effort (always more or less arbitrary) of metaphysical construction. For the idealist, on the contrary, these perceptions are the whole of reality, and the invariable order of the phenomena of nature is but the symbol whereby we express, alongside of real perceptions, perceptions that are possible. But, for realism as for idealism, perceptions are "veridical hallucinations," states of the subject, projected outside himself, and the two doctrines differ merely in this: that, in the one, these states constitute reality; in the other, they are sent forth to unite with it.

But behind this illusion lurks yet another that extends to the theory of knowledge in general. We have said that the material world is made up of objects, or, if you prefer it, of images, of which all the parts act and react upon each other by movements. And that which constitutes our pure perception, is our dawning action, in so far as it is prefigured in those images. The *actuality* of our perception thus lies in its *activity*, in the movements which prolong it, and not in its greater intensity: the past is only idea, the present is ideo-motor. But this is what our opponents are determined not to see because they regard perception as a kind of contemplation, attribute to it always a purely speculative end, and maintain that it seeks some strange disinterested knowledge, as though, by isolating it from action, and thus severing its links with the real, they were not rendering it both inexplicable and useless. But thenceforward all difference between perception and recollection is abolished, since the past is essentially *that which acts no longer*, and since, by misunderstanding this characteristic of the

68

past, they become incapable of making a real distinction between it and the present, i.e., *that which is acting*. No difference but that of mere degree will remain between perception and memory and neither in the one nor in the other will the subject be acknowledged to pass beyond himself. Restore, on the contrary, the true character of perception; recognize in pure perception a system of nascent acts which plunges roots deep into the real; and at once perception is seen to be radically distinct from recollection; the reality of things is no more constructed or reconstructed, but touched, penetrated, lived, and the problem at issue between realism and idealism, instead of giving rise to interminable metaphysical discussions, is solved, or rather, dissolved, by intuition.

In this way also we shall plainly see what position we ought to take up between idealism and realism, which are both condemned to see in a matter only a construction or a reconstruction executed by the mind. For if we follow to the end the principle according to which the subjectivity of our perception consists, above all, in the share taken by memory, we shall say that even the sensible qualities of matter would be known *in themselves*, from within and not from without, could we but disengage them from that particular rhythm of duration which characterizes our consciousness. Pure perception, in fact, however rapid we suppose it to be, occupies a certain depth of duration, so that our successive perceptions are never the real moments of things, as we have hitherto supposed, but are moments of our consciousness. Theoretically, we said, the part played by consciousness in external perception would be to join together, by the continuous thread of memory, instantaneous visions of the real. But, in fact, there is for us nothing that is instantaneous. In all that goes by that name there is already some work of our memory, and consequently, of our consciousness, which prolongs into each other, so as to grasp them in one relatively simple intuition, an endless number of moments of

69

an endlessly divisible time. Now what is, in truth, the difference between matter as the strictest realism might conceive it and the perception which we have of it? Our perception presents us with a series of pictorial, but discontinuous, views of the universe; from our present perceptions we could not deduce subsequent perceptions because there is nothing in an aggregate of sensible qualities which foretells the new qualities into which they will change. On the contrary, matter, as realism usually posits it, evolves in such a manner that we can pass from one moment to the next by a mathematical deduction. It is true that, between this matter and this perception, scientific realism can find no point of contact because it develops matter into homogeneous changes in space, while it contracts perception into unextended sensations within consciousness. But, if our hypothesis is correct, we can easily see how perception and matter are distinguished and how they coincide. The qualitative heterogeneity of our successive perceptions of the universe results from the fact that each, in itself, extends over a certain depth of duration and that memory condenses in each an enormous multiplicity of vibrations which appear to us all at once, although they are successive. If we were only to divide, ideally, this undivided depth of time, to distinguish in it the necessary multiplicity of moments, in a word, to eliminate all memory, we should pass thereby from perception to matter, from the subject to the object. Then matter, becoming more and more homogeneous as our extended sensations spread themselves over a greater number of moments, would tend more and more toward that system of homogeneous vibrations of which realism tells us, although it would never coincide entirely with them. There would be no need to assume, on the one hand, space with unperceived movements, and, on the other, consciousness with unextended sensations. Subject and object would unite in an extended perception, the subjective side of perception being the contraction effected by memory, and the objective reality of matter fusing with the multitudinous and successive vibrations into which this perception can be internally broken up. Such at least is the conclusion which, we hope, will issue clearly from the last part of this essay. *Questions relating to subject and object, to their distinction and their union, should be put in terms of time rather than of space.*

But our distinction between "pure perception" and "pure memory" has yet another aim. Just as pure perception, by giving us hints as to the nature of matter, allows us to take an intermediate position between realism and idealism, so pure memory, on the other hand, by opening to us a view of what is called spirit should enable us to decide between those other two doctrines, materialism and spiritualism.[4] Indeed, it is this aspect of the subject which will first occupy our attention in the two following chapters because it is in this aspect that our hypothesis allows some degree of experimental verification.

For it is possible to sum up our conclusions as to pure perception by saying that *there is in matter something more than, but not something different from, that which is actually given.* Undoubtedly, conscious perception does not compass the whole of matter, since it consists, in as far as it is conscious, in the separation, or the "discernment," of that which, in matter, interests our various needs. But between this perception of matter and matter itself there is but a difference of degree and not of kind, pure perception standing toward matter in the relation of the part to the whole. This amounts to saying that matter cannot exercise powers of any kind other than those which we perceive. It has no mysterious virtue; it can conceal none. To take a definite example, one, moreover, which interests us most nearly, we may say that the nervous system, a material mass presenting certain qualities of color, resistance, cohesion, etc., may well possess unperceived physical properties, but physical properties only. And hence it can have no other office than to receive, inhibit or transmit movement.

Now the essence of every form of materialism is to maintain the contrary, since it holds that consciousness, with all its functions, is born of the mere interplay of material elements. Hence it is led to consider even the perceived qualities of matter — sensible, and consequently felt, qualities — as so many phosphorescences which follow the track of the cerebral phenomena in the act of perception. Matter, thus supposed capable of creating elementary facts of consciousness, might therefore just as well engender intellectual facts of the highest order. It is, then, the essence of materialism to assert the perfect relativity of sensible qualities, and it is not without good reason that this thesis, which Democritus has formulated in precise terms, is as old as materialism.

But spiritualism has always followed materialism along this path. As if everything lost to matter *must* be gained by spirit, spiritualism has never hesitated to despoil matter of the qualities with which it is invested in our perception, and which, on this view, are subjective appearances. Matter has thus too often been reduced to a mysterious entity which, just because all we know of it is an empty show, might as well engender thought as well as any other phenomenon.

The truth is that there is one, and only one, method of refuting materialism: it is to show that matter is precisely that which it appears to be. Thereby we eliminate all virtuality, all hidden power, from matter and establish the phenomena of spirit as an independent reality. But to do this we must leave to matter those qualities which materialists and spiritualists alike strip from it: the latter that they may make of them representations of the spirit, the former that they may regard them only as the accidental garb of space.

This, indeed, is the attitude of common sense with regard to matter, and for this reason common sense believes in spirit. It seems to us that philosophy should here adopt the attitude of common sense, although correcting it in one respect. Memory, inseparable in practice from perception, imports the past into the present, contracts into a single intuition many moments of duration, and thus by a twofold operation compels us, de facto, to perceive matter in ourselves, whereas we, de jure, perceive matter within matter.

Hence the capital importance of the problem of memory. If it is memory above all that lends to perception its subjective character, the philosophy of matter must aim, in the first instance, we said, at eliminating the contributions of memory. We must now add that, as pure perception gives us the whole or at least the essential part of matter (since the rest comes from memory and is superadded to matter), it follows that memory must be, in principle, a power absolutely independent of matter. If, then, spirit is a reality, it is here, in the phenomenon of memory, that we may come into touch with it experimentally. And hence any attempt to derive pure memory from an operation of the brain should reveal on analysis a radical illusion.

Let us put the same statement in clearer language. We maintain that matter has no occult or unknowable power and that it coincides, in essentials, with pure perception. Therefore we conclude that the living body in general, and the nervous system in particular, are only channels for the transmission of movements, which, received in the form of stimulation, are transmitted in the form of action, reflex or voluntary. That is to say, it is vain to attribute to the cerebral substance the property of engendering representations. Now the phenomena of memory, in which we believe that we can grasp spirit in its most tangible form, are precisely those of which a superficial psychology is most ready to find the origin in cerebral activity alone; just because they are at the point of contact between consciousness and matter, and because even the adversaries of materialism have no objection to treating the brain as a storehouse of memories. But if it could be positively established that the cerebral process answers only to a very small part of memory, that it is rather the effect than the cause, that matter is here as elsewhere the vehicle of an *action* and not the substratum of a *knowledge*, then the thesis which we are maintaining would be demonstrated by the very example which is commonly supposed to be most unfavorable to it, and the necessity might arise of erecting spirit into an independent reality. In this way also, perhaps some light would be thrown on the nature of what is called spirit and on the possibility of the interaction of spirit and matter. For a demonstration of this kind could not be purely negative. Having shown what memory is not, we should have to try to discover what it is. Having attributed to the body the sole function of preparing actions, we are bound to enquire why memory appears to be one with this body, how bodily lesions influence it, and in what sense it may be said to mold itself upon the state of the brain matter. It is, moreover, impossible that this enquiry should fail to give us some information as to the psychological mechanism of memory and the various mental operations connected therewith. And, inversely, if the problems of pure psychology seem to acquire some light from our hypothesis, this hypothesis itself will thereby gain in certainty and weight.

But we must present this same idea in yet a third form, so as to make it quite clear why the problem of memory is in our eyes a privileged problem. From our analysis of pure perception issue two conclusions, which are in some sort divergent, one of them going beyond psychology in the direction of psycho-physiology and the other in that of metaphysics, but neither allowing of immediate verification. The first concerns the office of the brain in perception: we maintain that the brain is an instrument of action, and not of representation. We cannot demand from facts the direct

confirmation of this thesis because pure perception bears, by definition, upon *present* objects, acting on our organs and our nerve
centers; and because everything always happens, in consequence,
as though our perceptions emanated from our cerebral state and
were subsequently projected upon an object which differs absolutely from them. In other words, with regard to external perception, the thesis which we dispute and that which we substitute
for it lead to precisely the same consequence, so that it is possible
to invoke in favor of either the one or the other its greater intelli-
gibility, but not the authority of experience. On the contrary, the
empirical study of memory may and must decide between them.
For pure recollection is, by hypothesis, the representation of an
absent object. If the necessary and sufficient cause of perception
lies in a certain activity of the brain, this same cerebral activity,
repeating itself more or less completely in the absence of the
object, will suffice to reproduce perception: memory will be
entirely explicable by the brain. But if we find that the cerebral
mechanism does indeed in some sort condition memories, but is
in no way sufficient to ensure their survival; if it concerns, in remembered perception, our action rather than our representation; we
shall be able to infer that it plays an analogous part in perception
itself and that its office is merely to ensure our effective action on
the object present. Our first conclusion may thus find its verification. There would still remain this second conclusion, which is
of a more metaphysical order — viz.: that in pure perception we
are actually placed outside ourselves; we touch the reality of the
object in an immediate intuition. Here also an experimental verification is impossible, since the practical results are absolutely
the same whether the reality of the object is intuitively perceived
or whether it is rationally constructed. But here again a study of
memory may decide between the two hypotheses. For, in the second, there is only a difference of intensity, or more generally, of

degree, between perception and recollection, since they are both self-sufficient phenomena of representation. But if, on the contrary, we find that the difference between perception and recollection is not merely in degree, but is a radical difference in kind, the presumption will be in favor of the hypothesis which finds in perception something which is entirely absent from memory, a reality intuitively grasped. Thus the problem of memory is in very truth a privileged problem, in that it must lead to the psychological verification of two theses which appear to be insusceptible to proof, and of which the second, being of a metaphysical order, appears to go far beyond the borders of psychology.

The road which we have to follow, then, lies clear before us. We shall first review evidence of various kinds borrowed from normal and from pathological psychology, by which philosophers might hold themselves justified in maintaining a physical explanation of memory. This examination must needs be minute or it would be useless. Keeping as close as possible to facts, we must seek to discover where, in the operations of memory, the office of the body begins and where it ends. And should we, in the course of this inquiry, find confirmation of our own hypothesis, we shall not hesitate to go further and, considering in itself the elementary work of the mind, complete the theory thereby sketched out, of the relation of spirit with matter.

CHAPTER II

Of The Recognition of Images.

Memory and The Brain

We pass now to the consideration of the consequences for the theory of memory, which might ensue from the acceptance of the principles we have laid down. We have said that the body, placed between the objects which act upon it and those which it influences, is only a conductor, the office of which is to receive movements and to transmit them (when it does not arrest them) to certain motor mechanisms, determined if the action is reflex, chosen if the action is voluntary. Everything, then, must happen as if an independent memory gathered images as they successively occur along the course of time; and as if our body, together with its surroundings, was never more than one among these images, the last is that which we obtain at any moment by making an instantaneous section in the general stream of becoming. In this section our body occupies the center. The things which surround it act upon it, and it reacts upon them. Its reactions are more or less complex, more or less varied, according to the number and nature of the apparatus which experience has set up within it. Therefore, in the form of motor contrivances, and of motor contrivances only, it can store up the action of the past. Whence it results that past images, properly so called, must be otherwise preserved; and we may formulate this first hypothesis:

77

I. *The past survives under two distinct forms: first, in motor mechanisms; secondly, in independent recollections.*

But then the practical, and, consequently, the usual function of memory, the utilizing of past experience for present action — recognition, in short — must take place in two different ways. Sometimes it lies in the action itself and in the automatic setting in motion of a mechanism adapted to the circumstances; at other times it implies an effort of the mind which seeks in the past, in order to apply them to the present, those representations which are best able to enter into the present situation. Whence our second proposition:

II. *The recognition of a present object is effected by movements when it proceeds from the object, by representations when it issues from the subject.*

It is true that there remains yet another question: how these representations are preserved, and what are their relations with the motor mechanisms. We shall go into this subject thoroughly in our next chapter, after we have considered the unconscious and shown where the fundamental distinction lies between the past and the present. But already we may speak of the body as an ever advancing boundary between the future and the past, as a pointed end, which our past is continually driving forward into our future. Whereas my body, taken at a single moment, is but a conductor interposed between the objects which influence it and those on which it acts, it is, nevertheless, when replaced in the flux of time, always situated at the very point where my past expires in a deed. And, consequently, those particular images, which I call cerebral mechanisms, terminate at each successive moment the series of my past representations, being the extreme prolongation of those representations into the present, their link with the real, that is, with action. Sever that link — and you do not necessarily destroy the past image, but you deprive it of all means of acting upon the real and, consequently, as we shall show, of being realized. It is in this sense, and in this sense only, that an injury to the brain can abolish any part of memory. Hence our third, and last, proposition:

III. *We pass, by imperceptible stages, from recollections strung out along the course of time to the movements which indicate their nascent or possible action in space. Lesions of the brain may affect these movements, but not these recollections.*

We have now to see whether experience verifies these three propositions.

I. *The two forms of memory.* I study a lesson, and in order to learn it by heart I read it a first time, accentuating every line; I then repeat it a certain number of times. At each repetition there is progress; the words are more and more linked together and at last make a continuous whole. When that moment comes, it is said that I know my lesson by heart, that it is imprinted on my memory.

I consider now how the lesson has been learned, and picture to myself the successive phases of the process. Each successive reading then recurs to me with its own individuality; I can see it again with the circumstances which attended it then and still form its setting. It is distinguished from those which preceded or followed it by the place which it occupied in time; in short, each reading stands out in my mind as a definite event in my history. Again it will be said that these images are recollections, that they are imprinted on my memory. The same words, then, are used in both cases. Do they mean the same thing?

The memory of the lesson, which is remembered in the sense

of learned by heart, has *all* the marks of a habit. Like a habit, it is acquired by the repetition of the same effort. Like a habit, it demands first a decomposition and then a recomposition of the whole action. Lastly, like every habitual bodily exercise, it is stored up in a mechanism which is set in motion as a whole by an initial impulse, in a closed system of automatic movements which succeed each other in the same order and, together, take the same length of time.

The memory of each successive reading, on the contrary, the second or the third for instance, has *none* of the marks of a habit. Its image was necessarily imprinted at once on the memory, since the other readings form, by their very definition, other recollections. It is like an event in my life; its essence is to bear a date, and, consequently, to be unable to occur again. All that later readings can add to it will only alter its original nature; though my effort to recall this image becomes more and more easy as I repeat it, the image, regarded in itself, was necessarily at the outset what it always will be.

It may be urged that these two recollections, that of the reading and that of the lesson, differ only as the less from the more, and that the images successively developed by each repetition overlie each other, so that the lesson once learned is but the composite image in which all readings are blended. And I quite agree that each of the successive readings differs from the preceding mainly in the fact that the lesson is better known. But it is no less certain that each of them, considered as a new reading and not as a lesson better known, is entirely sufficient to itself, subsists exactly as it occurred, and constitutes with all its concomitant perceptions an original moment of my history. We may even go further and aver that consciousness reveals to us a profound difference, a difference in kind, between the two sorts of recollection. The memory of a given reading is a representation, and only a representation; it is embraced in an intuition of the mind which I may lengthen or shorten at will; I assign to it any duration I please; there is nothing to prevent my grasping the whole of it instantaneously, as in one picture. On the contrary, the memory of the lesson I have learned, even if I repeat this lesson only mentally, requires a definite time, the time necessary to develop one by one, were it only in imagination, all the articulatory movements that are necessary: it is no longer a representation; it is an action. And, in fact, the lesson once learned bears upon it no mark which betrays its origin and classes it in the past; it is part of my present, exactly like my habit of walking or of writing; it is lived and acted, rather than represented: I might believe it innate, if I did not choose to recall at the same time, as so many representations, the successive readings by means of which I learned it. Therefore, these representations are independent of it, and, just as they preceded the lesson as I now possess and know it, so that lesson once learned can do without them.

Following to the end this fundamental distinction, we are confronted by two different memories theoretically independent. The first records, in the form of memory-images, all the events of our daily life as they occur in time; it neglects no detail; it leaves to each fact, to each gesture, its place and date. Regardless of utility or of practical application, it stores up the past by the mere necessity of its own nature. By this memory is made possible the intelligent, or rather intellectual, recognition of perception already experienced; in it we take refuge every time that, in the search for a particular image, we remount the slope of our past. But every perception is prolonged into a nascent action; and while the images are taking their place and order in this memory, the movements which continue them modify the organism and create in the body new dispositions toward action. Thus is gradually formed an experience of an entirely different order, which accumulates within the body, a series of mechanisms would up and ready, with reactions to external stimuli ever more numerous and more varied and answers ready prepared to an ever growing number of possible solicitations. We become conscious of these mechanisms as they come into play; this consciousness of a whole past of efforts stored up in the present is indeed also a memory, but a memory profoundly different from the first, always bent upon action, seated in the present and looking only to the future. It has retained from the past only the intelligently coordinated movements which represent the accumulated efforts of the past; it recovers those past efforts, not in the memory-images which recall them, but in the definite order and systematic character with which the actual movements take place. In truth it no longer *represents* our past to us, it *acts* it; and if it still deserves the name of memory, it is not because it conserves bygone images, but because it prolongs their useful effect into the present moment.

Of these two memories, of which the one *imagines* and the other *repeats*, the second may supply the place of the first and even sometimes be mistaken for it. When a dog welcomes his master, barking and wagging his tail, he certainly recognizes him; but does this recognition imply the evocation of a past image and the comparison of that image with the present perception? Does it not rather consist in the animal's consciousness of a certain special attitude adopted by his body, an attitude which has been gradually built up by his familiar relations with his master, and which the mere perception of his master now calls forth in him mechanically? We must not go too far; even in the animal it is possible that vague images of the past overflow into the present perception; we can even conceive that its entire past is virtually indicated in its consciousness; but this past does not interest the animal enough to detach it from the fascinating present, and its recognition must be rather lived than thought. To call up the past in the form of an image, we must be able to withdraw ourselves from the action of the moment, we must have the power to value the useless, we must have the will to dream. Man alone is capable of such an effort. But even in him the past to which he returns is fugitive, ever on the point of escaping him, as though his backward turning memory were thwarted by the other, more natural, memory, of which the forward movement bears him on to action and to life.

When psychologists talk of recollection as of a fold in a material, as of an impress graven deeper by repetition, they forget that the immense majority of our memories bear upon events and details of our life of which the essence is to have a date, and, consequently, to be incapable of being repeated. The memories which we acquire voluntarily by repetition are rare and exceptional. On the contrary, the recording, by memory, of facts and images unique in their kind takes place at every moment of duration. But inasmuch as *learned* memories are more useful, they are more remarked. And as the acquisition of these memories by a repetition of the same effort resembles the well-known process of habit, we prefer to set this kind of memory in the foreground, to erect it into the model memory, and to see in spontaneous recollection only the same phenomenon in a nascent state, the beginning of a lesson learned by heart. But how can we overlook the radical difference between that which must be built up by repetition and that which is essentially incapable of being repeated? Spontaneous recollection is perfect from the outset; time can add nothing to its image without disfiguring it; it retains in memory its place and date. On the contrary, a learned recollection passes out of time in the measure that the lesson is better known; it becomes more and more impersonal, more and more foreign to our past life. Repetition, therefore, in no sense effects the conversion of the first into the last; its office is merely to utilize more and more the movements by which the first was continued, in order to organize them together and, by setting up a mechanism, to create a bodily habit. Indeed, this habit could not be called a remembrance were it not that I remember that I have acquired it, and I remember its acquisition only because I appeal to that memory which is spontaneous, which dates events and records them but once. Of the two memories, then, which we have just distinguished, the first appears to be memory par excellence. The second, that generally studied by psychologists, is *habit interpreted by memory* rather than memory itself.

It is true that the example of a lesson learned by heart is to some extent artificial. Yet our whole life is passed among a limited number of objects, which pass more or less often before our eyes: each of them, as it is perceived, provokes on our part movements, at least nascent, whereby we adapt ourselves to it. These movements, as they recur, contrive a mechanism for themselves, grow into a habit, and determine in us attitudes which automatically follow our perception of things. This, as we have said, is the main office of our nervous system. The afferent nerves bring to the brain a disturbance, which, after having intelligently chosen its path, transmits itself to motor mechanisms created by repetition. Thus is ensured the appropriate reaction, the correspondence to environment — adaptation, in a word — which is the general aim of life. And a living being which did nothing but live would need no more than this. But, simultaneously with this process of perception and adaptation which ends in the record of the past in the form of motor habits, consciousness, as we have seen, retains the image of the situations through which it has successively traveled, and lays them side by side in the order in which they took place. Of what use are these memory-images? Preserved in memory, reproduced in consciousness, do they not distort the practical character of life, mingling dream with reality? They would, no doubt, if our actual consciousness, a consciousness which reflects the exact adaptation of our nervous system to the present situation, did not set aside all those among the past images which cannot be coordinated with the present perception and are unable to form with it a *useful* combination. At most, certain confused recollections, unrelated to the present circumstances, may overflow the usefully associated images, making around these a less illuminated fringe which fades away into an immense zone of obscurity. But suppose an accident which upsets the equilibrium maintained by the brain between the external stimulation and the motor reaction, relax for a moment the tension of the threads which go from the periphery to the periphery by way of the center, and immediately these darkened images come forward into the full light: it is probably the latter condition which is realized in any sleep wherein we dream. Of these two memories that we have distinguished, the second, which is active, or motor, will, then, constantly inhibit the first, or at least only accept from it that which can throw light upon and complete in a useful way the present situation: thus, as we shall see later, could the laws of the association of ideas be explained. But, besides the services which they can render by associating with the present perception, the images stored up in the spontaneous memory have yet another use. No doubt they are dream-images; no doubt they usually appear and disappear independently of our will; this is why, when we really wish to *know* a thing, we are obliged to learn it by heart, that is to say, to substitute for the spontaneous image a motor mechanism which can serve in its stead. But there is a certain effort *sui generis* which permits us to retain the image itself, for a limited time, within the field of our consciousness; thanks to this faculty, we have no need to await at the hands of chance the accidental repetition of the same situations in order to organize into a habit concomitant movements; we make use of the fugitive image to construct a stable mechanism which takes its place. Either, then, our distinction of the two independent memories is unsound, or, if it corresponds to facts, we shall find an exaltation of spontaneous memory in most cases where the sensori-motor equilibrium of the nervous system is disturbed; an inhibition, on the contrary, in the normal state, of all spontaneous recollections which do not serve to consolidate the present equilibrium; and lastly, in the operation by means of which we acquire the habit-memory, a latent intervention of the image-memory. Let us see whether the facts confirm this hypothesis.

For the moment we will insist on neither point; we hope to throw ample light upon both when we study the disturbances of memory and the laws of the association of ideas. We shall be content for the present to show, in regard to things which are learned, how the two memories run side by side and lend to each other a mutual support. It is a matter of everyday experience that lessons committed to the motor memory can be automatically repeated, but observation of pathological cases proves that automatism extends much further in this direction than we think. In cases of dementia, we sometimes find that intelligent answers are given to a succession of questions which are not understood: language here works after the manner of a reflex.[1] Aphasics, incapable of uttering a word spontaneously, can recollect without a mistake the words of an air which they sing.[2] Or again, they will fluently repeat a prayer, a series of numbers, the days of the week or the months of the year.[3] Thus extremely complex mechanisms, subtle enough to imitate intelligence, can work by themselves when once they have been built up, and, in consequence, usually obey a mere initial impulse of the will. But what takes place while they are being built up? When we strive to learn a lesson, for instance, is not the visual or auditory image which we endeavor to reconstitute by movements already in our mind, invisible though present? Even in the very first recitation, we recognize, by a vague feeling of uneasiness, any error we have made, as though from the obscure depths of consciousness we received a sort of warning.[4] Concentrate your mind on that sensation, and you will feel that the complete image is there, but evanescent, a phantasm that disappears just at the moment when motor activity tries to fix its outline. During some recent experiments (which, however, were undertaken with quite a different purpose),[5] the subjects averred that they felt just such an impression. A series of letters, which they were asked to remember, was held before their eyes for a few seconds. But, to prevent any accentuating of the letters so perceived by appropriate movements of articulation, they were asked to repeat continuously a given syllable while their eyes were fixed on the image. From this resulted a special psychical state; the subjects felt themselves to be in complete possession of the visual image, although unable to produce any part of it on demand: to their great surprise the line disappeared. "According to one observer, the basis was a *Gesammtvorstellung*, a sort of all-embracing complex idea in which the parts have an indefinitely felt unity."[6]

This spontaneous recollection, which is masked by the acquired recollection, may flash out at intervals, but it disappears at the least movement of the voluntary memory. If the subject sees the series of letters, of which he thought he retained the image, vanish from before his eyes, this happens mainly when he begins to repeat it: the effort seems to drive the rest of the image out of his consciousness.[7] Now, analyze many of the imaginative methods of mnenomics and you will find that the object of this science is to bring into the foreground the spontaneous memory which was hidden, and to place it, as an active memory, at our service; to this end every attempt at motor memory is, to begin with, suppressed. The faculty of mental photography, says one author,[8] belongs rather to subconsciousness than to consciousness; it answers with difficulty to the summons of the will. In order to exercise it, we should accustom ourselves to retaining, for instance, several arrangements of points at once, without even thinking of counting them[9]: we must imitate in some sort the instantaneity of this memory in order to attain to its mastery. Even so it remains capricious in its manifestations; as the recollections which it brings us are akin to dreams, its more regular intrusion into the life of the mind may seriously disturb intellectual equilibrium.

What this memory is, whence it is derived and how it works will be shown in the next chapter. For the moment, the schematic conception will be enough. So we shall merely sum up the preceding paragraphs and say that the past appears indeed to be stored up, as we had surmised, under two extreme forms: on the one hand, motor mechanisms which make use of it; on the other, personal memory-images which picture all past events with their outline, their color and their place in time. Of these two memories the first follows the direction of nature; the second, left to itself, would rather go the contrary way. The first, conquered by effort, remains dependent upon our will; the second, entirely spontaneous, is as capricious in reproducing as it is faithful in preserving. The only regular and certain service which the second memory can render to the first is to bring before it images of what preceded or followed situations similar to the present situation, so as to guide its choice: in this consists the association of ideas. There is no other case in which the memory which recalls is sure to obey the memory which repeats. Everywhere else, we prefer to construct a mechanism which allows us to sketch the image again, at need, because we are well aware that we cannot count upon its reappearance. These are the two extreme forms of memory in their *pure* state.

Now we may say at once that it is because philosophers have concerned themselves only with the intermediate and, so to speak, impure forms that they have misunderstood the true nature of memory. Instead of dissociating the two elements, memory-image and movement, in order to discover subsequently by what series of operations they come, having each abandoned some part of its original purity to fuse one with the other, they are apt to consider only the mixed phenomenon which results from their coalescence. This phenomenon, being mixed, presents on the one side the aspect of a motor habit, and, on the other side, that of an image more or less consciously localized. But they will have it that the phenomenon is a simple one. So they must assume that the cerebral mechanism, whether of the brain or of the medulla oblongata or of the cord, which serves as the basis of the motor habit, is at the same time the substratum of the conscious image. Hence the strange hypothesis of recollections stored in the brain, which are supposed to become conscious as though by a miracle and bring us back to the past by a process that is left unexplained. True, some observers do not make so light of the conscious aspect of the operation and see in it something more than an epiphenomenon. But, as they have not begun by isolating the memory which retains and sets out the successive repetitions side by side in the form of memory images, since they confound it with the habit which is perfected by use, they are led to believe that the effect of repetition is brought to bear upon one and the same single and indivisible phenomenon which merely grows stronger by recurrence: and, as this phenomenon clearly ends by being merely a motor habit corresponding to a mechanism, cerebral or other, they are led, whether they will it or not, to suppose that some mechanism of this kind was from the beginning behind the image and that the brain is an organ of representation. We are now about to consider these intermediate states and distinguish in each of them the part which belongs to nascent action, that is to say of the brain, and the part of independent memory, that is to say of memory-images. What are these states? Being partly motor they must, on our hypothesis, prolong a present perception; but, on the other hand, inasmuch as they are images, they reproduce past perceptions. Now the concrete process by which we grasp the past in the present is *recognition*. Recognition, therefore, is what we have to study, to begin with.

II. *Of recognition in general: memory-images and movements.* There are two ways in which it is customary to explain the feeling of "having seen a thing before." On one theory, the recognition of a present perception consists in inserting it mentally in its former surroundings. I encounter a man for the first time: I simply perceive him. If I meet him again, I recognize him, in the sense that the concomitant circumstances of the original perception, returning to my mind, surround the actual image with a setting which is not a setting actually perceived. To recognize, then, according to this theory, is to associate with a present perception the images which were formerly given in connection with it.[10] But, as it has been justly observed, a renewed perception cannot suggest the concomitant circumstances of the original perception unless the latter is evoked, to begin with, by the present state which resembles it.[11] Let A be the first perception; the accompanying circumstances B, C, D, remain associated with it by contiguity. If I call the same perception renewed A', as it is not with A', but with A that the terms B, C, D are bound up, it is necessary, in order to evoke the terms B, C, D, that A' should be first called up by some association of resemblance. And it is of no use to assert that A' is identical with A. For the two terms, though similar, are numerically distinct, and differ at least by this simple fact that A' is a perception, whereas A is but a memory. Of the two interpretations of which we have spoken, the first, then, melts into the second, which we will now examine.

It is alleged that the present perception dives into the depths of memory in search of the remembrance of the previous perception which resembles it: the sense of recognition would thus come from a bringing together, or a blending, or perception and memory. No doubt, as an acute thinker[12] has already pointed out, resemblance is a relation established by the mind between terms which it compares and consequently already possesses; so the perception of a resemblance is rather an effect of association than its cause. But, along with this definite and perceived resemblance which consists in the common element seized and disengaged by the mind, there is a vague and in some way objective resemblance, spread over the surface of the images themselves, which might act perhaps like a physical cause of reciprocal attraction.[13] And should we ask how it is, then, that when we often recognize an object without being able to identify it with a former image, refuge is sought in the convenient hypothesis of cerebral tracks which coincide with each other, of cerebral movements made easier by practice,[14] or of perceptive cells communicating with cells where memories are stored.[15] In truth, all such theories of recognition are bound to melt away, in the end, into physiological hypotheses of this kind. What they were aiming at, first, was to make all recognition issue from a bringing together of perception and memory; but experience stands over against them, testifying that in most cases recollection emerges only after the perception is recognized. So they are sooner or later forced to relegate to the brain, in the form of a combination between movements or of a connection between cells, that which they had first declared to be an association of ideas; and to explain the fact of recognition — very clear on our view — by the hypothesis, which seems to us very obscure, of a brain which stores up ideas.

But the fact is that the association of a perception with a memory is not enough to account for the process of recognition. For, if recognition took place in this way, it would always be obliterated when the memory images had disappeared and always happen when these images are retained. Psychic blindness, or the inability to recognize perceived objects, would, then, never occur without an inhibition of visual memory, and, above all, the inhibition of visual memory would invariably produce psychic blindness. But neither consequence is borne out by facts. In a case studied by Wilbrand,[16] the patient could describe with her eyes shut the town she lived in and, in imagination, walk through its streets; yet, once in the street, she felt like a complete stranger: she recognized nothing and could not find her way. Facts of the same kind have been observed by Fr. Müller[17] and Lissauer:[18] the patients can summon up the mental picture of an object named to them; they describe it very well; but they cannot recognize it when it is shown to them. The retention, even the conscious retention, of a visual memory is, therefore, not enough for the recognition of a similar perception. Inversely, in Charcot's case, which has become the classic example of a complete eclipse of visual images,[19] not all recognition of perceptions was obliterated. A careful study of the report of the case is conclusive on this point. No doubt the patient failed to recognize the streets and houses of his native town, to the extent of being unable to name them or to find his way about them; yet he knew that they were streets and houses. He no longer recognized his wife and children; yet, when he saw them, he could say that this was a woman, that those were children. None of this would have been possible had there been psychic blindness in the absolute sense of the word. A certain kind of recognition, then, which we shall need to analyze, was obliterated, not the general faculty of recognition. So we must conclude that not every recognition implies the intervention of a memory image, and, conversely, that we may still be able to call up such images when we have lost the power of identifying perceptions with them. What, then, is recognition, and how shall we define it?

There is, in the first place, if we carry the process to the extreme, an *instantaneous* recognition, of which the body is capable by itself, without the help of any explicit memory-image. It consists in action and not in representation. For instance, I take a walk in a town seen for the first time. At every street corner I hesitate, uncertain where I am going. I am in doubt, I mean by this that alternatives are offered to my body, that my movement as a whole is discontinuous, that there is nothing in one attitude which foretells and prepares future attitudes. Later, after prolonged sojourn in the town, I shall go about it mechanically, without having any distinct perception of the objects which I am passing. Now, between these two extremes, the one in which perception has not yet organized the definite movements which accompany it and the other in which these accompanying movements are organized to a degree which renders perception useless, there is an intermediate state in which the object is perceived, yet provokes movements which are connected, continuous and called up by one another. I began by a state in which I distinguished only by my perception; I shall end in a state in which I am hardly conscious of anything but automatism: in the interval there is a mixed state, a perception followed step by step by automatism just impending. Now, if the later perceptions differ from the first perception in the fact that they guide the body toward the appropriate mechanical reaction, and if, on the other hand, those renewed perceptions appear to the mind under that special aspect which characterizes familiar or recognized perceptions, must we not assume that the consciousness of a well-regulated motor accompaniment, of an organized motor reaction, is here the foundation of the sense of familiarity? At the basis of recognition there would thus be a phenomenon of a motor order.

To recognize a common object is mainly to know how to use it. This is so true that early observers gave the name *apraxia* to that failure of recognition which we call psychic blindness.[20] But to know how to use a thing is to sketch out the movements which adapt themselves to it; it is to take a certain attitude or at least to have a tendency to do so through what the Germans call motor impulses (*Bewegungsantriebe*). The habit of using the object has, then, resulted in organizing together movements and perceptions; the consciousness of these nascent movements, which follow perception after the manner of a reflex, must be here also at the bottom of recognition.

There is no perception which is not prolonged into movement. Ribot[21] and Maudsley[22] have long since drawn attention to this point. The training of the senses consists in just the sum of the connections established between the sensory impression and the movement which makes use of it. As the impression is repeated, the connection is consolidated. Nor is there anything mysterious in the mechanism of the operation. Our nervous system is evidently arranged with a view to the building up of motor apparatus linked, through the intermediary of centers, with sense stimuli; the discontinuity of the nervous elements, the multiplicity of their terminal branches, which are probably capable of joining in various ways, make possible an unlimited number of connections between impressions and the corresponding movements. But the mechanism in course of construction cannot appear to consciousness in the same form as the mechanism already constructed. There is something which profoundly distinguishes and clearly manifests those systems of movements which are consolidated in the organism; that is, we believe, the difficulty we have in modifying their order. It is, again, the performance of the movements which follow in the movements which precede, a performance whereby the part virtually contains the whole, as when each note of a tune learned by heart seems to lean over the next to watch its execution.[23] If, then, every perception has its organized motor accompaniment, the ordinary feeling of recognition has its root in the consciousness of this organization.

In fact, we commonly act our recognition before we think it. Our daily life is spent among objects whose very presence invites us to play a part: in this the familiarity of their aspect consists. Motor tendencies would, then, be enough by themselves to give us the feeling of recognition. But we hasten to add that in most cases there is something else besides.

For, while motor apparatus are built up under the influence of perceptions that are analyzed with increasing precision by the body, our past psychical life is there: it survives – as we shall try to prove – with all the detail of its events localized in time. Always inhibited by the practical and useful consciousness of the present moment, that is to say, by the sensori-motor equilibrium of a nervous system connecting perception with action, this memory merely awaits the occurrence of a rift between the actual impression and its corresponding movement to slip in its images. As a rule, when we desire to go back along the course of the past and discover the known, localized, personal memory-image which is related to the present, an effort is necessary, whereby we draw back from the act to which perception inclines us: the latter would urge us toward the future; we have to go backwards into the past. In this sense, movement rather tends to drive away the image. Yet, in one way, it contributes to its approach. For, though the whole series of our past images remains present within us, still the representation which is analogous to the present perception has to be *chosen* from among all possible representations. Movements, accomplished or merely nascent, prepare this choice or at the very least mark out the field in which we shall seek the image we need. By the very constitution of our nervous system, we are beings in whom present impressions find their way to appropriate movements: if it so happens that former images can just as well be prolonged in these movements, they take advantage of the opportunity to slip into the actual perception and get themselves adopted by it. They then appear, in fact, to our consciousness, though it seems as if they ought, by right, to remain concealed by the present state. So we may say that the movements which bring about mechanical recognition hinder in one way, and encourage in another, recognition by images. In principle, the present supplants the past. But, just because the disappearance of former images is due to their inhibition by our present attitude, those whose shape might fit into this attitude encounter less resistance than the others; if, then, any one of them is indeed able to overcome the obstacle, it is the image most similar to the present perception that will actually do so.

If our analysis is correct, the diseases which affect recognition will be of two widely differing forms, and facts will show us two kinds of psychic blindness. For we may presume that, in some cases, it is the memory-image which can no longer reappear, and that, in other cases, it is merely the bond between perception and the accompanying habitual movements which is broken — perception provoking *diffused* movements, as though it were wholly new. Do the facts confirm this hypothesis?

There can be no dispute as to the first point. The apparent abolition of visual memory in psychic blindness is so common a fact that it served, for a time, as a definition of that disorder. We shall have to consider how far, and in what sense, memories can really disappear. What interests us for the moment is that cases occur in which there is no recognition, and yet visual memory is not altogether lost. Have we here then, as we maintain, merely a disturbance of motor habits or at most an interruption of the chain which unite them to sense perceptions? As no observer has considered a question of this nature, we should be hard put for an answer to it if we had not noticed here and there in their descriptions certain facts which appear to us significant.

The first of these facts is the loss of the sense of direction. All those who have treated the subject of psychic blindness have been struck by this peculiarity. Lissauer's patient had completely lost the faculty of finding his way about his own house.[24] Fr. Müller insists on the fact that, while blind men soon learn to find their way, the victim of psychic blindness fails, even after months of practice, to find his way about his own room.[25] But is not this faculty of orientation the same thing as the faculty of coordinating the movements of the body with the visual impression, and of mechanically prolonging perceptions in useful reactions?

There is a second, and even more characteristic fact, and that is the manner in which these patients draw. We can conceive two fashions of drawing. In the first, we manage, by tentative efforts, to set down here and there on the paper a certain number of points, and we then connect them together, verifying continually the resemblance between the drawing and the object. This is what is known as "point to point" drawing. But our habitual method is quite different. We draw with a continuous line, after having looked at, or thought of, our model. How shall we explain such a faculty, except by our habit of discovering at once the *organization* of the outlines of common objects, that is to say, by a motor tendency to draft their diagram in one continuous line? But if it is just such habits or correspondences which are lost in certain forms of psychic blindness, the patient may still perhaps be able to draw bits of a line which he will connect together more or less well; but he will no longer be able to draw at a stroke because the tendency to adopt and reproduce the general *movement* of the outline is no longer present in his hand. Now this is just what experiment verifies. Lissauer's observations are instructive on this head.[26] His patient had the greatest difficulty in drawing simple objects; if he tried to draw them from memory, he traced detached portions of them chosen at random and was unable to unite these into a whole. Cases of complete psychic blindness are, however, rare. Those of

97

word-blindness are much more numerous — cases of a loss, that is, of visual recognition limited to the characters of the alphabet. Now it is a fact of common observation that the patient in such cases is unable to seize what may be called the *movement* of the letters when he tries to copy them. He begins to draw them at any point, passing back and forth between the copy and the original to make sure that they agree. And this is the more remarkable in that he often retains unimpaired the faculty of writing from dictation or spontaneously. What is lost is clearly the habit of distinguishing the articulations of the object perceived, that is to say, of completing the visual perception by a motor tendency to sketch its diagram. Whence we may conclude that such is indeed the primordial condition of recognition.

But we must pass now from automatic recognition, which is mainly achieved through movements, to that which requires the regular intervention of memory-images. The first is recognition by *in*attention; the second, as we shall see, is attentive recognition.

This form also begins by movements. But, whereas, in automatic recognition, our movements prolong our perception in order to draw from it useful effects and thus *take us away* from the object perceived, here, on the contrary, they *bring us back* to the object, to dwell upon its outlines. Thus is explained the preponderant, and no longer merely accessory, part taken here by memory-images. For, if we suppose that the movements forego their practical end, and that motor activity, instead of continuing perception by useful reactions, turns back to mark out its more striking features, then the images which are analogous to the present perception — images of which these movements have already sketched out, so to speak, the form — will come regularly, and no longer accidentally, to flow into this mold, though they may have to give up much of their detail in order to get in more easily.

III. *Gradual passage of recollections into movements. Recognition and attention.* Here we come to the essential point of our discussion. In those cases where recognition is attentive, i.e., where memory-images are *regularly* united with the present perception, is it the perception which determines mechanically the appearance of the memories, or is it the memories which spontaneously go to meet the perception?

On the answer to this question will depend the nature of the relation which philosophers will have to establish between the brain and memory. For in every perception there is a disturbance communicated by the nerves to the perceptive centers. If the passing on of this movement to other cortical centers had, as its real effect, the springing up of images in these, then we might in strictness maintain that memory is but a function of the brain. But if we can establish that here, as elsewhere, movement produces nothing but movement, that the office of the sense-stimulation is merely to impress on the body a certain attitude into which recollections will come to insert themselves, then, as it would be clear that the whole effect of the material vibrations is exhausted in this work of motor adaptation, we should have to look for memory elsewhere. On the first hypothesis, the disorders of memory occasioned by a cerebral lesion would result from the fact that the recollections occupied the damaged region and were destroyed with it. On the second hypothesis, these lesions would affect our nascent or possible action, but our action alone. Sometimes they would hinder the body from taking, in regard to the object, the attitude that may call back its memory-image; sometimes they would sever the bonds between remembrance and the present reality; that is, by suppressing the last phase of the realization of a memory — the phase of action — they would thereby hinder the memory from becoming actual. But in neither case would a lesion of the brain really destroy memories.

99

The second hypothesis is ours; but, before we attempt to verify it, we must briefly state how we understand the general relations of perception, attention and memory. In order to show how a memory may, by gradual stages, come to graft itself on an attitude or a movement, we shall have to anticipate in some degree the conclusions of our next chapter.

What is attention? In one point of view, the essential effect of attention is to render perception more intense and to spread out its details; regarded in its *content*, it would resolve itself into a certain magnifying of the intellectual state.[27] But, on the other hand, consciousness testifies to an irreducible difference of *form* between this increase of intensity and that which is owing to a higher power of the external stimulus: it seems indeed to come from within and to indicate a certain *attitude* adopted by the intellect. But it is just here that the difficulty begins, for the idea of an intellectual attitude is not a clear idea. Psychologists will here speak of a "concentration of the mind,"[28] or again of an "apperceptive"[29] effort to bring perception into the field of distinct intelligence. Some of them, materializing this idea, will suppose a higher tension of cerebral energy,[30] or even the setting free of a certain amount of central energy which reinforces the stimulation received.[31] But either the fact observed psychologically is merely translated thereby into a physiological symbolism which seems to us even less clear, or else we always come back to a metaphor.

Stage by stage we shall be led on to define attention as an adaptation of the body rather than of the mind and to see in this attitude of consciousness mainly the consciousness of an attitude. Such is the position assumed by Ribot[32] in the discussion, and, though it has been attacked,[33] it appears to have retained all its strength, provided, however, that we are content to see, in the movements described by Ribot, only the negative condition of the phenomenon. For, even if we suppose that the accompanying movements of voluntary attention are mainly movements of arrest, we still have to explain the accompanying work of the mind, that is to say, the mysterious operation by which the same organ, perceiving in the same surroundings the same object, discovers in it a growing number of things. But we may go farther and maintain that the phenomena of inhibition are merely a preparation for the actual movements of voluntary attention. Suppose for a moment that attention, as we have already suggested, implies a backward movement of the mind which thus gives up the pursuit of the useful effect of a present perception: there will indeed be, first, an inhibition of movement, an arresting action. But, upon this general attitude, more subtle movements will soon graft themselves, some of which have been already remarked and described,[34] and all of which combine to retrace the outlines of the object perceived. With these movements the positive, no longer merely negative, work of attention begins. It is continued by memories.

For, while external perception provokes on our part movements which retrace its main lines, our memory directs upon the perception received the memory-images which resemble it and which are already sketched out by the movements themselves. Memory thus creates anew the present perception, or rather it doubles this perception by reflecting upon it either its own image or some other memory-image of the same kind. If the retained or remembered image will not cover all the details of the image that is being perceived, an appeal is made to the deeper and more distant regions of memory, until other details that are already known come to project themselves upon those details that remain unperceived. And the operation may go on indefinitely — memory strengthening and enriching perception, which, in its turn becoming wider, draws into itself a growing number of complementary recollections. So let us no longer think of a mind which disposes of some fixed quantity of light, now diffusing it around, now concentrating it on a single point. Metaphor for metaphor, we would rather compare the elementary work of attention to that of the telegraph clerk who, on receipt of an important dispatch, sends it back again, word for word, in order to check its accuracy.

But, to send a telegram, we must know how to use the machine. And, in the same way, in order to reflect upon a perception the image which we have received from it, we must be able to reproduce it, i.e., to reconstruct it by an effort of synthesis. It has been said that attention is a power of analysis, and it is true; but it has not been sufficiently shown how an analysis of this kind is possible, nor by what process we are able to discover in a perception that which could not be perceived in it at first. The truth is that this analysis is effected by a series of attempts at a synthesis, i.e., by so many hypotheses: our memory chooses, one after the other, various analogous images which it launches in the direction of the new perception. But the choice is not made at random. What suggests the hypotheses, what presides, even from afar, over the choice is the movement of imitation, which continues the perception, and provides for the perception and for the images a common framework.

But, if this be so, the mechanism of distinct perception must be different from what it is usually thought to be. Perception does not consist merely in impressions gathered, or even elaborated, by the mind. This is the case, at most, with the perceptions that are dissipated as soon as received, those which we disperse in useful actions. But every *attentive* perception truly involves a *reflection*, in the etymological sense of the word, that is to say the projection, outside ourselves, of an actively created image, identical with, or similar to, the object on which it comes to mold itself. If, after having gazed at any object, we turn our eyes abruptly away, we obtain an "afterimage" of it: must we not suppose that this image existed already while we were looking? The recent discovery of centrifugal fibers of perception inclines us to think that this is the usual course of things and that, beside the afferent process which carries the impression to the center, there is another process, of contrary direction, which brings back the image to the periphery. It is true that we are dealing here with images photographed upon the object itself, and with memories following immediately upon the perception of which they are but the echo. But, behind these images, which are identical with the object, there are others, stored in memory, which merely resemble it, and others, finally, which are only more or less distantly akin to it. All these go out to meet the perception, and, feeding on its substance, acquire sufficient vigor and life to abide with it in space. The experiments of Münsterberg[35] and of Külpe[36] leave no doubt as to this latter point: any memory-image that is capable of interpreting our actual perception inserts itself so thoroughly into it that we are no longer able to discern what is perception and what is memory. The ingenious experiments of Goldscheider and Müller on the mechanism of reading are most interesting in this regard.[37] Arguing against Grashey, who, in a well-known essay,[38] maintained that we read words letter by letter, these observers proved by experiments that rapid reading is a real work of divination. Our mind notes here and there a few characteristic lines and fills all the intervals with memory-images which, projected on the paper, take the place of the real printed characters and may be mistaken for them. Thus we are constantly creating or reconstructing. Our distinct perception is really comparable to a closed circle, in which the perception-image, going toward the mind, and the memory-image, launched into space, careen the one behind the other.

We must emphasize this latter point. Attentive perception is often represented as a series of processes which make their way in single file; the object exciting sensations, the sensations causing ideas to start up before them, each idea setting in motion, one in front of the other, points more and more remote of the intellectual mass. Thus there is supposed to be a rectilinear progress, by which the mind goes further and further from the object, never to return to it. We maintain, on the contrary, that reflective perception is a *circuit*, in which all the elements, including the perceived object itself, hold each other in a state of mutual tension as in an electric circuit, so that no disturbance starting from the object can stop on its way and remain in the depths of the mind: it must always find its way back to the object from where it proceeds. Now it must not be thought that this is a mere matter of words. We have here two radically different conceptions of the intellectual process. According to the first, things happen mechanically and by a merely accidental series of successive additions. At each moment of an attentive perception, for example, new elements sent up from a deeper stratum of the mind might join the earlier elements, without thereby creating a general disturbance and without bringing about a transformation of the whole system. In the second, on the contrary, an act of attention implies such a solidarity between the mind and its object, it is a circuit so well closed that we cannot pass to states of higher concentration without creating, whole and entire, so many new circuits which envelop the first and have nothing in common between them but the perceived object. Of these different circles of memory, which later we shall study in detail, the smallest, A, is the nearest to immediate perception. It contains only the object O, with the afterimage which comes back and overlies it. Behind it, the larger and larger circles B, C, D correspond to growing efforts at intellectual expansion. It is the whole of memory, as we shall see, that passes over into each of these circuits, since memory is always present; but that memory, capable, by reason of its elasticity, of expanding more and more, reflects upon the object a growing number of suggested

Fig. 1

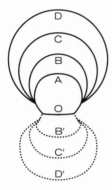

images — sometimes the details of the object itself, sometimes concomitant details which may throw light upon it. Thus, after having rebuilt the object perceived, as an independent whole, we reassemble, together with it, the more and more distant conditions with which it forms one system. If we call B′, C′, D′, these causes of growing depth, situated behind the object and virtually given with the object itself, it will be seen that the progress of attention results in creating anew not only the object perceived, but also the ever widening systems with which it may be bound up; so that in the measure in which the circles B, C, D represent a higher expansion of memory, their reflection attains in B′, C′, D′ deeper strata of reality.

The same psychical life, therefore, must be supposed to be repeated an endless number of times on the different stories of memory, and the same act of the mind may be performed at varying heights. In the effort of attention, the mind is always concerned in its entirety, but it simplifies or complicates itself according to the level on which it chooses to go to work. Usually it is the present perception which determines the direction of our mind; but, according to the degree of tension which our mind adopts and the height at which it takes its stand, the perception develops a greater or smaller number of images.

In other words, personal recollections, exactly localized, the series of which represents the course of our past existence, make up, all together, the last and largest enclosure of our memory. Essentially fugitive, they become materialized only by chance, either when an accidentally precise determination of our bodily attitude attracts them or when the very indetermination of that attitude leaves a clear field to the caprices of their manifestation. But this outermost envelope contracts and repeats itself in inner and concentric circles, which in their narrower range enclose the same recollections grown smaller, more and more removed from their personal and original form, and more and more capable, from their lack of distinguishing features, of being applied to the present perception and of determining it after the manner of a species which defines and absorbs the individual. There comes a moment when the recollection thus brought down is capable of blending so well with the present perception that we cannot say where perception ends or where memory begins. At that precise moment, memory, instead of capriciously sending in and calling back its images, follows regularly, in all their details, the movements of the body.

But, in the degree that these recollections draw nearer to movements, and so to external perception, the work of memory acquires a higher practical importance. Past images, reproduced exactly as they were, with all their details and even with their affective coloring, are the images of idle fancy or of dream: to act is just to induce this memory to shrink, or rather to become thinned and sharpened, so that it presents nothing thicker than the edge of a blade to actual experience, into which it will thus be able to penetrate. In truth, it is because psychology has failed to separate out the motor element in memory that we have sometimes overlooked and sometimes exaggerated what is automatic in the evocation of remembrances. According to our view, an appeal is made to activity at the precise moment when perception gives rise to imitative movements which scan it, as it were, automatically. A sketch is thereby furnished to us, into which we put the right details and the right coloring by projecting into it memories more or less remote. But such is not the usual way of describing the process. Sometimes the mind is supposed to be absolutely independent of circumstances, to work exactly as it likes on present or absent objects — and then we can no longer understand how it is that the normal process of attention may be seriously impaired by even a slight disturbance of the sensori-motor equilibrium. Sometimes, on the contrary, the evocation of images is supposed to be a mere mechanical effect of present perception: it is assumed that, by a necessary concatenation of processes supposed to be all alike, the object calls forth sensations and the sensations ideas which cling to them — but then, since there is no reason why the operation, which is mechanical to begin with, should change its character as it goes on, we are led to the hypothesis of a brain wherein mental states may dwell in order to slumber and to awaken. In both cases the true function of the body is misunderstood, and as neither theory teaches how and why the intervention of a mechanism is necessary, neither of them is able to show where such intervention should stop if it is once brought in.

But it is time to leave these general considerations. We must ascertain whether our hypothesis is confirmed or contradicted by the facts of cerebral localization known at the present day. The disorders of imaginative memory, which correspond to local lesions of the cortex, are always diseases of the faculty of recognition, either of visual or auditory recognition in general (psychic blindness and deafness) or of the recognition of words (word blindness, word deafness, etc.). These disorders we have now to examine.

If our hypothesis is well founded, these failures of recognition are in no sense due to the fact that the recollections occupied the injured region of the brain. They must be due to one of two causes: sometimes our body is no longer able automatically to adopt, under the influence of the external stimulus, the precise attitude by means of which a choice could be automatically made among our memories; sometimes the memories are no longer able to find a fulcrum in the body, a means of prolonging themselves in action. In the first case, the lesion affects the mechanisms which continue, in an automatically executed movement, the stimulation received: attention can no longer be fixed by the object. In the second case, the lesion involves those particular cortical centers which *prepare* voluntary movements by lending them the required sensory antecedent, centers which, rightly or wrongly, are termed image-centers: attention can no longer be fixed by the subject. But, in either case, it is actual movements, which are hindered, or future movements, which are no longer prepared: there has been no destruction of memories.

Now pathology confirms this forecast. It rereveals to us two absolutely distinct kinds of psychic blindness and deafness and word blindness and deafness. In the first kind, visual and auditory memories are still evoked, but they cannot apply themselves to the corresponding perceptions. In the second, evocation of the memories themselves is hindered. Is it true that the lesion involves, as we said, the sensori-motor mechanisms of automatic attention in the first case, and the imaginative mechanisms of voluntary attention in the second? In order to verify our hypothesis, we must limit demonstration to a definite example. No doubt we could show that visual recognition of things in general, and of words in particular, implies a semiautomatic motor process to begin with, and then an active projection of memories which engraft themselves on the corresponding attitudes. But we prefer to confine ourselves to impressions of hearing, and more particularly to the hearing of articulate language, because this example is the most comprehensive. To hear speech is, in fact, first of all to recognize a sound, then to discover its sense, and finally to interpret it more or less thoroughly: in short, it is to pass through all the stages of attention and to exercise several higher or lower powers of memory. Moreover, no disorders are more common or better studied than those of the auditive memory of words. And, lastly, acoustic verbal images are not destroyed without a serious lesion of certain determined convolutions of the cortex: so that we are provided here with an undisputed example of localization, in regard to which we can enquire whether the brain is really capable of storing up memories. We have, then, to show in the auditory recognition of words: first, an automatic sensori-motor process; secondly, an active and, so to speak, excentric projection of memory-images.

1. I listen to two people speaking in a language which is unknown to me. Do I therefore hear them talk? The vibrations which reach my ears are the same as those which strike theirs. Yet I perceive only a confused noise, in which all sounds are alike. I distinguish nothing and could not repeat anything. In this same sonorous mass, however, the two interlocutors distinguish consonants, vowels and syllables which are not at all alike, in short, separate words. Between them and me where is the difference?

The question is, how can the knowledge of a language, which is only memory, modify the material content of a present perception and cause some listeners actually to hear what others, in the same physical conditions, do not hear. It is alleged, indeed, that the auditory recollections of words, accumulated in memory, are called up by the sound-impression and come to strengthen its effect. But if the conversation to which I listen is, for me, only a noise, we may suppose the sound increased as much as we like: the noise will be none the more intelligible for being louder. I grant that the memory of a word will be called up by the sound of that word: yet it is necessary, for this, that the sound of the word should have been heard by the ear. How can the sounds perceived speak to memory, how can they choose, in the storehouse of auditory images, those which should come to rejoin them, unless they have been already separated, distinguished — in short, perceived — as syllables and as words?

This difficulty does not appear to have been sufficiently noticed by the theorists of sensory aphasia. For in word-deafness the patient finds himself, in regard to his own language, in the same position as we all are when we hear an unknown tongue. He has generally preserved intact his sense of hearing, but he has no understanding of the words spoken to him and is frequently even unable to distinguish them. The explanation generally given of the disease is that the auditory recollection of words has been destroyed in the cortex or that a lesion, sometimes transcortical, sometimes subcortical, hinders the auditive memory from evoking the idea, or the perception, from uniting with the memory. But in the latter case, at least, the psychological question has still to be answered: what is the conscious process which the lesion has abolished, and what is the intermediary process that we go through in our normal condition in order to discern words and syllables which are, at first, given to the ear as a continuity of sound?

The difficulty would be insuperable if we really had only auditory impressions on the one hand, and auditory memories, on the other hand. Not so however, if auditory impressions organize nascent movements, capable of scanning the phrase which is heard and of emphasizing its main articulations. These automatic movements of internal accompaniment, at first undecided or uncoordinated, might become more precise by repetition; they would end by sketching a simplified figure in which the listener would find, in their main lines and principal directions, the very movements of the speaker. Thus would unfold itself in consciousness, under the form of nascent muscular sensations, the *motor diagram*, as it were, of the speech we hear. To adapt our hearing to a new language would then consist, at the outset, neither in modifying the crude sound nor in supplementing the sounds with memories; it would be to coordinate the motor tendencies of the muscular apparatus of the voice to the impressions of the ear; it would be to perfect the motor accompaniment.

In learning a physical exercise, we begin by imitating the movement as a whole, as our eyes see it from without, as we think we have seen it done. Our perception of it is confused; confused, therefore, will be the movement whereby we try to repeat it. But whereas our visual perception was of a *continuous* whole, the movement by which we endeavor to reconstruct the image is *compound* and made up of a multitude of muscular contractions and tensions; our consciousness of these itself includes a number of sensations resulting from the varied play of the articulations. The confused movement which copies the image is, then, already its virtual decomposition; it bears within itself, so to speak, its own analysis. The progress which is brought about by repetition and practice consists merely in unfolding what was previously wrapped up, in bestowing one of the elementary movements that *autonomy* which ensures precision without, however, breaking up that *solidarity* with the others without which it would become useless. We are right when we say that habit is formed by the repetition of an effort; but what would be the use of repeating it, if the result were always to reproduce the same thing? The true effect of repetition is to decompose and then to recompose, and thus appeal to the intelligence of the body. At each new attempt it separates movements which were interpenetrating; each time it calls the attention of the body to a new detail which had passed unperceived; it bids the body discriminate and classify; it teaches what is the essential; it points out, one after another, within the total movement, the lines that mark off its internal structure. In this sense, a movement is learned when the body has been made to understand it.

So a motor accompaniment of speech may well break the continuity of the mass of sound. But we have now to point out in what this accompaniment consists. Is it speech itself, repeated internally? If this were so, the child would be able to repeat all the words that its ear can distinguish and we ourselves should only need to understand a foreign language to be able to pronounce it with a correct accent. The matter is far from being so simple. I may be able to catch a tune, to follow its phrasing, even to fix it in memory, without being able to sing it. I can easily distinguish the peculiarities of inflection and tone in an Englishman speaking German — I correct him therefore, mentally — but it by no means follows that I could give the right inflection and tone to the German phrase if I were to utter it. Here, moreover, the observation of everyday life is confirmed by clinical facts. It is still possible to follow and understand speech when one has become incapable of speaking. Motor aphasia does not involve word deafness.

This is because the diagram, by means of which we divide up the speech we hear, indicates only its salient outlines. It is to speech itself what the rough sketch is to the finished picture. For it is one thing to understand a difficult movement, another to be able to carry it out. To understand it, we need only to realize in it what is essential, just enough to distinguish it from all other possible movements. But to be able to carry it out, we must have also brought our *body* to understand it. Now the logic of the body admits of no tacit implications. It demands that all the constituent parts of the required movement shall be set forth one by one, and then put together again. Here a *complete* analysis is necessary, in which no detail is neglected, and an *actual* synthesis, in which nothing is curtailed. The imagined diagram, composed of a few nascent mus-

112

cular sensations, is but a sketch. The muscular sensations, really and completely experienced, give it color and life.

It remains to be considered how an accompaniment of this kind can be produced and whether it really is always produced. We know that in order effectively to pronounce a word the tongue and lips must articulate, the larynx must be brought into play for phonation, and the muscles of the chest must produce an expiratory movement of air. Thus, for every syllable uttered there corresponds the play of a number of mechanisms already prepared in the cerebral and bulbar centers. These mechanisms are joined to the higher centers of the cortex by the axis-cylinder processes of the pyramidal cells in the psycho-motor zone. Along this path the impulse of the will travels. So, when we desire to articulate this or that sound, we transmit the order to act to this or that group of motor mechanisms selected from among them all. But, while the ready-made mechanisms which correspond to the various possible movements of articulation and phonation are connected with the causes (whatever these may be) which set them to work in voluntary speech, there are facts which put beyond all doubt the linkage of these same mechanisms with the auditory perception of words. First of all, among the numerous varieties of aphasia described in clinical reports, we know of two (Lichtheim's fourth and sixth forms) which appear to imply a relation of this kind. Thus, in a case observed by Lichtheim himself, the subject had lost, as the result of a fall, the memory of the articulation of words and, consequently, the faculty of spontaneous speech; yet he repeated quite correctly what was said to him.[39] On the other hand, in cases where spontaneous speech is unaffected, but where word deafness is absolute and the patient no longer understands what is said to him, the faculty of repeating another person's words may still be completely retained.[40] It may be said, with Bastian, that these phenomena merely point to a fatigue of the articulatory or auditive memory of words, the acoustic impressions only serving to awaken that memory from its torpor.[41] We may have to allow for this hypothesis, but it does not appear to us to account for the curious phenomena of *echolalia*, long since pointed out by Romberg,[42] Voisin[43] and Forbes Winslow,[44] which are termed by Kussmaul[45] (probably with some exaggeration) acoustic reflexes. Here the subject repeats mechanically, and perhaps unconsciously, the words he hears, as though the auditory sensations converted themselves automatically into movements of articulation. From these facts some have inferred that there is a special mechanism which unites a so-called acoustic center of words with an articulatory center of speech.[46] The truth appears to lie between these two hypotheses. There is more in these various phenomena than absolutely mechanical actions but less than an appeal to voluntary memory. They testify to a *tendency* of verbal auditory impressions to prolong themselves in movements of articulation; a tendency which assuredly does not escape, as a rule, the control of the will, and perhaps even implies a rudimentary discrimination, and expresses itself, in the normal state, by an internal repetition of the striking features of the words that are heard. Now our motor diagram is nothing else.

Considering this hypothesis more closely, we shall perhaps find in it the psychological explanation, which we were just now seeking, of certain forms of word deafness. A few cases of word deafness are known where there was a complete survival of acoustic memory. The patient had retained, unimpaired, both the auditive memory of words and the sense of hearing; yet he recognized no word that was said to him.[47] A subcortical lesion is here supposed, which prevents the acoustic impressions from going to join the verbal auditory images in the cortical centers where they are supposed to be deposited. But, in the first place, the question is whether the brain *can* store up images. And, secondly, even if it were proved that there is some lesion in the paths that the acoustic impressions have to follow, we should still be compelled to seek a psychological interpretation of the final result. For, by hypothesis, the auditory memories can still be recalled to consciousness; by hypothesis also, the auditory impressions still reach consciousness; there must therefore be in consciousness itself a gap, a solution of continuity, something, whatever it is, which hinders the perception from joining the memories. Now we may throw some light on the case if we remember that crude auditory perception is really that of a continuity of sound, and that the sensori-motor connections established by habit must have as their office, in the normal state, to decompose this continuity. A lesion of these conscious mechanisms, by hindering the decomposition, might completely check the upsurge of memories which tend to alight upon the corresponding perceptions. Therefore, the "motor diagram" might be what is injured by the lesion. If we pass in review the cases (which are, indeed, not very numerous) of word-deafness, where acoustic memories were retained, we notice certain details that are interesting in this respect. Adler notes, as a remarkable fact in word-deafness, that the patients no longer react even to the loudest sounds, though their hearing has preserved all its acuteness.[48] In other words, sound no longer finds in them its motor echo. A patient of Charcot's, attacked by a passing word-deafness, relates that he heard his clock strike but that he could not count the strokes.[49] Probably he was unable to separate and distinguish them. Another patient declares that he perceives the words of a conversations, but as a confused noise.[50] Lastly, the patient who has lost the understanding of the spoken word recovers it if the word is repeated to him several times, and especially if it is pronounced with marked divisions, syllable by syllable.[51] This last fact, observed in several cases of word-deafness, where acoustic memories were unimpaired, is particularly significant.

Stricker's[52] mistake was to believe in a complete internal repetition of the words that are heard. His assertion is already
contradicted by the simple fact that we do not know of a single
case of motor aphasia which brought out word-deafness. But all
the facts combine to prove the existence of a motor tendency to
separate the sounds and to establish their diagram. This automatic
tendency is not without (as we said above) a certain elementary
mental effort: how otherwise could we identify with each other,
and, consequently, follow with the same diagram, similar words
pronounced on different notes and by different qualities of voice?
These inner movements of repeating and recognizing are like a
prelude to voluntary attention. They mark the limit between the
voluntary and the automatic. By them, as we hinted before, the
characteristic phenomena of intellectual recognition are first prepared and then determined. But what is this complete and fully
conscious recognition?

2. We come to the second part of our subject: from movements
we pass to memories. We have said that attentive recognition is a
kind of *circuit* in which the external object yields to us deeper and
deeper parts of itself, as our memory adopts a correspondingly
higher degree of tension in order to project recollections toward
it. In the particular case we are now considering, the object is an
interlocutor whose ideas develop within his consciousness into
auditory representations which are then materialized into uttered
words. So, if we are right, *the hearer places himself at once in the midst
of the corresponding ideas*, and then develops them into acoustic
memories which go out to overlie the crude sounds perceived,
while fitting themselves into the motor diagram. To follow an arith-
metical addition is to do it over again for ourselves. To understand
another's words is, in like manner, to reconstruct intelligently,
starting from the ideas, the continuity of sound which the ear per-

ceives. And, more generally, to attend, to recognize intellectu-
ally, to interpret, may be summed up in a single operation whereby
the mind, having chosen its level, having selected within itself,
with reference to the crude perceptions, the point that is exactly
symmetrical with their more or less immediate cause, allows to
flow toward them the memories that will go out to overlie them.

Such, however, is certainly not the usual way of looking at the
matter. The associationist habit is there; in accordance with it,
we find men maintaining that, by the mere effect of contiguity,
the perception of a sound brings back the memory of the sound,
and memories bring back the corresponding ideas. And then, we
have the cerebral lesions which seem to bring about a destruction
of memories; more particularly, in the case we are studying, there
are the lesions of the brain found in word deafness. Thus psychological observations and clinical facts seem to conspire. Together
they seem to point to the existence, within the cortex, of auditory memories slumbering whether as a physico-chemical modification of certain cells or under some other form. A sensory
stimulation is then supposed to awaken them; finally, by an
intracerebral process, perhaps by transcortical movements that
go to find the complementary representations, they are supposed
to evoke ideas.

Now consider for a moment the amazing consequences of an
hypothesis of this kind. The auditory image of a word is not an
object with well-defined outlines, for the same word pronounced
by different voices, or by the same voice on different notes, gives a
different sound. So, if you adopt the hypothesis of which we have
been speaking, you must assume that there are as many auditory
images of the same word as there are pitches of sound and qualities of voice. Do you mean that *all* these images are treasured up
in the brain? Or is it that the brain chooses? If the brain chooses
one of them, where does its preference come from? Suppose, even,

117

that you can explain why the brain chooses one or the other; how is it that this same word, uttered by a new person, gives a sound which, although different, is still able to rejoin the same memory? For you must bear in mind that this memory is supposed to be an inert and passive thing and consequently, incapable of discovering, beneath external differences, an internal similitude. You speak of the auditory image of a word as if it were an entity or a genus: such a genus can, indeed, be constructed by an active memory which extracts the resemblance of several complex sounds and only retains, as it were, their common diagram. But for a brain that is supposed – nay, is bound – to record only the materiality of the sounds perceived, there must be, of one and the same word, thousands of distinct images. Uttered by a new voice, it will constitute a new image which will simply be added to the others.

But there is something still more perplexing: a word has an individuality for us only from the moment that we have been taught to abstract it. What we first hear are short phrases, not words. A word is always continuous with the other words which accompany it and takes different aspects according to the cadence and movement of the sentences in which it is set: just as each note of a melody vaguely reflects the whole musical phrase. Suppose, then, that there are indeed model auditory memories, consisting in certain intracerebral arrangements, and lying in what for analogous impressions of sound: these impressions may come, but they will pass unrecognized. How could there be a common measure; how could there be a point of contact, between the dry, inert, isolated image and the living reality of the word organized with the rest of the phrase? I understand clearly enough that beginning of automatic recognition which would consist, as I have said above, in emphasizing inwardly the principal division of the sentence that is heard, and so in adopting its movement. But, unless we are to suppose in all men identical voices pronouncing in the same tone the same stereotyped phrases, I fail to see how the words we hear are able to rejoin their images in the brain.

Now, if memories are really deposited in the cortical cells, we should find in sensory aphasia, for instance, the irreparable loss of certain determined words, the integral conservation of others. But, as a matter of fact, things happen quite differently. Sometimes it is the whole set of memories that disappears, the faculty of mental hearing being purely and simply abolished; sometimes there is a general weakening of the function, but it is usually the function which is diminished and not the number of recollections. It seems as if the patient had no longer strength to grasp his acoustic memories, as if he turned round about the verbal image without being able to hit upon it. To enable him to recover a word, it is often enough to put him on the track of it by giving him its first syllable,[53] or even by merely encouraging him.[54] An emotion may produce the same effect.[55] There are, however, cases in which it does indeed seem that definite groups of representations have disappeared from memory. I have passed in review a large number of these facts, and it has seemed that they could be referred to two absolutely distinct categories. In the first, the loss of memories is usually abrupt; in the second, it is progressive. In the first, the recollections detached from memory are arbitrarily and even *capriciously* chosen: they may be certain words, certain figures, or often all the words of an acquired language. In the second, the disappearance of the words is governed by a methodical and grammatical order, that which is indicated by Ribot's law: proper names go first, then common nouns, and lastly verbs.[56] Such are the external differences. Now this, I believe, is the internal difference. In the amnesias of the first type, which are nearly always the result of a violent shock, I incline to think that the memories which are apparently destroyed are really present, and not only present but acting. To take an example frequently borrowed from Forbes Winslow,[57] that of a patient who had forgotten the letter F, and the letter F only, I wonder how it is possible to subtract a given letter wherever met with — to detach it, that is, from the spoken or written words in which it occurs — if it were not first implicitly recognized. In another case cited by the same author,[58] the patient had forgotten languages he had learnt and poems he had written. Having begun to write again, he reproduced nearly the same lines. Moreover, in such cases the patient may often recover the lost memories. Without wishing to be too dogmatic on a question of this kind, we cannot avoid noticing the analogy between these phenomena and that dividing of the self of which instances have been described by Pierre Janet:[59] some of them bear a remarkable resemblance to the "negative hallucinations," and suggestions with *point de repère*, induced by hypnotizers.[60] Entirely different are the aphasias of the second kind, which are indeed the true aphasias. These are due, as we shall try to show presently, to the progressive diminution of a well-localized function, the faculty of actualizing the recollection of words. How are we to explain the fact that amnesia here follows a methodical course, beginning with proper nouns and ending with verbs? We could hardly explain it if the verbal images were really deposited in the cells of the cortex: it would be wonderful indeed that disease should always attack these cells in the same order.[61] But the fact can be explained, if we admit that memories need, for their actualization, a motor ally, and that they require for their recall a kind of mental attitude which must itself be engrafted upon an attitude of the body. If such be the case, verbs in general, which essentially express *imitable actions*, are precisely the words that a bodily effort might enable us to recapture when the function of language has all but escaped us: proper names, on the other hand, being of all words the most remote from those impersonal actions which our body can sketch out, are those which a weakening of the function will earliest affect. It is a noteworthy fact that the aphasic patient, who has become as a rule incapable of finding the noun he seeks, may replace it by an appropriate periphrasis into which other nouns,[62] and perhaps even the evasive noun itself, enter. Unable to think of the precise word, he has thought of the corresponding action, and this attitude has determined the general direction of a movement from which the phrase then springs. So likewise it may happen to any of us that, having retained the initial of a forgotten name, we recover the name by repeating the initial.[63] Therefore, in facts of the second kind, it is the function that is attacked as a whole, and in those of the first kind the forgetting, though in appearance more complete, is never really final. Neither in the one case nor in the other do we find memories localized in certain cells of the cerebral substance and abolished by their destruction.

But let us question our own consciousness, and ask of it what happens when we listen to the words of another person with the desire to understand them. Do we passively wait for the impressions to go in search of their images? Do we not rather feel that we are adopting a certain disposition, which varies with our interlocutor, with the language he speaks, with the nature of the ideas which he expresses – and varies, above all, with the general movement of his phrase, as though we were choosing the key in which our own intellect is called upon to play? The motor diagram, emphasizing his utterance, following through all its windings the curve of his thought, shows our thought the road. It is the empty vessel, which determines, by its form, the form which the fluid mass, rushing into it, already tends to take.

But psychologists may be unwilling to explain in this way the mechanism of interpretation because of the invincible tendency which impels us to think on all occasions of *things* rather than of movements. We have said that we start from the idea, and that we develop it into auditory memory-images capable of inserting themselves in the motor diagram, so as to overlie the sounds we hear. We have here a continuous movement, by which the nebulosity of the idea is condensed into distinct auditory images, which, still fluid, will be finally solidified as they coalesce with the sounds materially perceived. At no moment is it possible to say with precision that the idea or the memory-image or the sensation begins. And, in fact, where is the dividing line between the confusion of sounds perceived in the lump and the clearness which the remembered auditory images add to them, between the discontinuity of these remembered images themselves and the continuity of the original idea which they dissociate and refract into distinct words? But scientific thought, analyzing this unbroken series of changes, and yielding to an irresistible need of symbolic presentment, arrests and solidifies into finished things the principal phases of this development. It erects the crude sounds heard into separate and complete words, then the remembered auditory images into entities independent of the idea they develop: these three terms, crude perception, auditory image and idea, are thus made into distinct wholes of which each is supposed to be self-sufficing. And while, if we really confined ourselves to pure experience, the idea is what we should start from — since it is to the idea that the auditory memories owe their connection and since it is by the memories that the crude sounds become completed. On the contrary, when once we have arbitrarily supposed the crude sound to be by itself complete and arbitrarily also assumed the memories to be connected together, we see no harm in reversing the real order of the processes, and in asserting that we go from the perception to the memories and from the memories to the idea. Nevertheless, we cannot help feeling that we must bring back again, under one form or another, at one moment or another, the continuity which we have thus broken between the perception, the memory and the idea. So we make out that these three things, each lodged in a

certain portion of the cortex or of the medulla, intercommuni-
cate, the perceptions going to awaken the auditory memories, and
the memories going to rouse up the ideas. As we have begun by
solidifying into distinct and independent things what were only
phases – the main phases – of a continuous development, we go on
materializing the development itself into lines of communication,
contacts and impulsions. But not with impunity can we thus invert
the true order, and as a necessary consequence, introduce into each
term of the series elements which are only realized by those that
follow. Not with impunity, either, can we congeal into distinct
and independent things the fluidity of a continuous undivided process. This symbolism may indeed suffice as long as it is strictly
limited to the facts which have served to invent it: but each new
fact will force us to complicate our diagram, to insert new stations along the line of the movement; yet all those stations laid
side by side will never be able to reconstitute the movement itself.

Nothing is more instructive in this regard than the history of
the diagrams of sensory aphasia. In the early period, marked by the
work of Charcot,[64] Broadbent,[65] Kussmaul[66] and Lichtheim,[67]
the theorists confined themselves to the hypothesis of an "ide-
ational center" linked by transcortical paths to the various speech
centers. But, as the analysis of cases was pushed further, this center for ideas receded and finally disappeared. For, while the physiology of the brain was more and more successful in localizing
sensations and movements, but never ideas, the diversity of sensory aphasias obliged clinicians to break up the intellectual center into a growing multiplicity of image centers – a center for
visual representations, for tactile representations, for auditory representations, etc. – nay, to divide sometimes into two different
tracks, the one ascending and the other descending, the line of
communication between any two of them.[68] This was the characteristic feature of the diagrams of the later period, those of

Wysman,[69] of Moeli,[70] of Freud,[71] etc. Thus the theory grew more and more complicated, yet without ever being able to grasp the full complexity of reality. And, as the diagrams became more complicated, they figured and suggested the possibility of lesions which, just because they were more diverse, were more special and more simple, the complication of the diagram being due precisely to that dissociation of centers which had at first been confounded. Experience, however, was far from justifying the theory at this point, since it nearly always showed, in partial and diverse combinations, several of those simple psychical lesions which the theory isolated. The complication of the theories of aphasia being thus self-destructive, it is no wonder that modern pathology, becoming more and more sceptical with regard to diagrams, is returning purely and simply to the description of facts.[72]

But how could it be otherwise? To hear some theorists discourse on sensory aphasia, we might imagine that they had never considered with any care the structure of a sentence. They argue as if a sentence were composed of nouns which call up the images of things. What becomes of those parts of speech, of which the precise function is to establish, between images, relations and shades of meaning of every kind? Is it said that each of such words still expresses and evokes a material image, more confused, no doubt, but yet determined? Consider then the host of different relations which can be expressed by the same word, according to the place it occupies and the terms which it unites. Is it urged that these are the refinements of a highly developed language, but that speech is possible with concrete nouns that all summon up images of things? No doubt it is, but the more primitive the language you speak with me and the poorer in words which express relations, the more you are bound to allow for my mind's activity, since you compel me to find out the relations which you leave unexpressed: which amounts to saying that you abandon more and more the hypothesis that each verbal image goes up and fetches down its corresponding idea. In truth, there is here only a question of degree: every language, whether elaborated or crude, leaves many more things to be understood than it is able to express. Essentially discontinuous, since it proceeds by juxtaposing words, speech can only indicate by a few guideposts placed here and there the chief stages in the movement of thought. That is why I can indeed understand your speech if I start from a thought analogous to your own and follow its windings by the aid of verbal images which are so many signposts that show me the way from time to time. But I shall never be able to understand it if I start from the verbal images themselves, because between two consecutive verbal images there is a gulf which no amount of concrete representations can ever fill. For images can never be anything but things, and thought is a movement.

It is vain, therefore, to treat memory-images and ideas as ready-made things, and then assign to them an abiding place in problematical centers. Nor is it of any avail to disguise the hypothesis under the cover of a language borrowed from anatomy and physiology; it is nothing but the association theory of mind; it has nothing in its favor but the constant tendency of discursive intellect to cut up all progress into *phases* and afterwards to solidify these phases into *things*; and since it is born a priori from a kind of metaphysical prepossession, it has neither the advantage of following the movement of consciousness nor that of simplifying the explanation of the facts.

But we must follow this illusion up to the point where it issues in a manifest contradiction. We have said that ideas — pure recollections summoned from the depths of memory — develop into memory-images more and more capable of inserting themselves into the motor diagram. To the degree that these recollections take the form of a more complete, more concrete and more con-

125

scious representation, they tend to confound themselves with the perception which attracts them or of which they adopt the outline. Therefore, there is not, there cannot be in the brain a region in which memories congeal and accumulate. The alleged destruction of memories by an injury to the brain is but a break in the continuous progress by which they actualize themselves. And, consequently, if we insist on localizing the auditory memory of words, for instance, in a given part of the brain, we shall be led by equally cogent reasons to distinguish this image-center from the perceptive center or to confound the two in one. Now this is just what experience teaches.

For notice the strange contradiction to which this theory is led by psychological analysis on the one hand, by pathological facts, on the other hand. One the one hand, it would seem that if perception, once it has taken place, remains in the brain in the state of a stored-up memory, this can only be as an acquired disposition of the very elements that perception has affected: how, at what precise moment, can it go in search of others? This is, indeed, the most natural hypothesis, and Bain[73] and Ribot[74] are content to rest upon it. But, on the other hand, there is pathology, which tells us that *all* the recollections of a certain kind may have gone while the corresponding faculty of perception remains unimpaired. Psychic blindness does not hinder seeing, any more than psychic deafness hinders hearing. More particularly, in regard to the loss of the auditory memory of words – the only one we are now considering – there are a number of facts which show it to be regularly associated with a destructive lesion of the first and second left temporo-sphenoidal convolutions,[75] though not a single case is on record in which this lesion was the cause of deafness properly so-called: it has even been produced experimentally in the monkey without determining anything but psychic deafness, that is to say, a loss of the power to interpret the sounds which it was still able to hear.[76] So we must attribute to perception and to memory separate nervous elements. But then this hypothesis will be contradicted by the most elementary psychological observation; for we see that a memory, as it becomes more distinct and more intense, tends to become a perception, though there is no precise moment at which a radical transformation takes place, nor, consequently, a moment when we can say that it moves forward from imaginative elements to sensory elements. Thus these two contrary hypotheses, the first identifying the elements of perception with the elements of memory, the second distinguishing among them, are of such a nature that each sends us back to the other without allowing us to rest in either.

How should it be otherwise? Here again distinct perception and memory-image are taken in the static condition, as *things* of which the first is supposed to be already complete without the second; whereas we ought to consider the dynamic *progress* by which the one passes into the other.

For, on the one hand, complete perception is only defined and distinguished by its coalescence with a memory-image, which we send forth to meet it. Only thus is attention secured, and without attention there is but a passive juxtapositing of sensations, accompanied by a mechanical reaction. But, as we shall show later, the memory-image itself, if it remained pure memory, would be ineffectual. Virtual, this memory can only become actual by means of the perception which attracts it. Powerless, it borrows life and strength from the present sensation in which it is materialized. Does not this amount to saying that distinct perception is brought about by two opposite currents, of which the one, centripetal, comes from the external object, and the other, centrifugal, has for its point of departure that which we term "pure memory"? The first current, alone, would only give a passive perception with the mechanical reactions which accompany it. The second, left to itself, tends to give a recollection that is actualized — more and more actual as the current becomes more marked. Together, these two currents make up, at their point of confluence, the perception that is distinct and recognized.

This is the witness of introspection. But we have no right to stop there. Undoubtedly, there is considerable risk in venturing, without sufficient evidence, into the obscure problems of cerebral localization. But we have said that to separate from one another the completed perception and the memory image is to bring clinical observation into conflict with psychological analysis and that the result is a serious antinomy in the theory of the localization of memories. We are bound to consider what becomes of the known facts when we cease to regard the brain as a storehouse of memories.[77]

Let us admit, for the moment, in order to simplify the argument, that stimuli from without give birth, either in the cortex or in other cerebral centers, to elementary sensations. In fact, every perception includes a considerable number of such sensations, all coexisting and arranged in a determined order. Where does this order come from, and what ensures this coexistence? In the case of a present material object, there is no doubt as to the answer: order and coexistence come from an organ of sense, receiving the impression of an external object. This organ is constructed precisely with a view to allowing a plurality of simultaneous excitants to impress it in a certain order and in a certain way, by distributing themselves, all at one time, over selected portions of its surface. It is like an immense keyboard, on which the external object executes at once its harmony of a thousand notes, thus calling forth in a definite order, and at a single moment, a great multitude of elementary sensations corresponding to all the points of the sensory center that are concerned. Now suppress the external object or the organ of sense or both: the same elementary sensations may be excited, for the same strings are there, ready to vibrate in the same way; but where is the keyboard which permits thousands of them to be struck at once, and so many single notes to unite in one accord? In our opinion the "region of images," if it exists, can only be a keyboard of this nature. Certainly, it is in no way inconceivable that a purely psychical cause should directly set in action all the strings concerned. But, in the case of mental hearing — which we are considering alone now — the localization of the function appears certain, since a definite injury of the temporal lobe abolishes it; yet we have set forth the reasons which make it impossible for us to admit, or even to conceive, traces of images deposited in any region of the cerebral substance. Hence only one plausible hypothesis remains, namely, that this region occupies with regard to the center of hearing itself the place that is exactly symmetrical with the organ of sense. It is, in this case, a mental ear.

But then the contradiction we have spoken of disappears. We see, on the one hand, that the auditory image called back by memory must set in motion the same nervous elements as the first perception and that recollection must thus change gradually into perception. And we see also, on the other hand, that the faculty of recalling to memory complex sounds, such as words, may concern other parts of the nervous substance than does the faculty of perceiving them. This is why in psychic deafness real hearing survives mental hearing. The strings are still there, and to the influence of external sounds they vibrate still; it is the internal keyboard which is lacking.

In other terms, the centers in which the elementary sensations seem to originate may be actuated, in some way, from two different sides, from the front and from behind. From the front they receive impressions sent in by the sense-organs, and, consequently, by a *real object*; from behind they are subject, through successive intermediaries, to the influence of a *virtual object*. The centers of images, if these exist, can only be the organs that are exactly symmetrical with the organs of the senses in reference to the sensory centers. They are no more the depositories of pure memories, that is, of virtual objects, than the organs of the senses are depositories of real objects.

We would add that this is but a much abridged version of what may happen in reality. The various sensory aphasias are sufficient proof that the calling up of an auditory image is not a single act. Between the intention, which is what we call the pure memory, and the auditory memory-image properly so called, intermediate memories are commonly intercalated which must first have been realized as memory-images in more or less distant centers. It is, then, by successive degrees that the idea comes to embody itself in that particular image which is the verbal image. Thereby mental hearing may depend upon the integrity of the various centers and of the paths which lead to them. But these complications change nothing at the root of things. Whatever be the number and the nature of the intervening processes, we do not go from the perception to the idea, but from the idea to the perception; the essential process of recognition is not centripetal, but centrifugal.

Here, indeed, the question arises how stimulation from within can give birth to sensations, either by its action on the cerebral cortex or on other centers. But it is clear enough that we have here only a convenient way of expressing ourselves. Pure memories, as they become actual, tend to bring about, within the body, all the corresponding sensations. But these virtual sensations themselves, in order to become real, must tend to urge the body to action and to impress upon it those movements and attitudes of which they are the habitual antecedent. The modifications in the centers called sensory, modifications which usually precede movements accomplished or sketched out by the body and of which the normal office is to prepare them while they begin them, are, then, less the real cause of the sensation than the mark of its power and the condition of its efficacy. The progress by which the virtual image realizes itself is nothing else than the series of stages by which this image gradually obtains from the body useful actions or useful attitudes. The stimulation of the so-called sensory centers is the last of these stages: it is the prelude to a motor reaction, the beginning of an action in space. In other words, the virtual image evolves toward the virtual sensation and the virtual sensation toward real movement: this movement, in realizing itself, realizes both the sensation of which it might have been the natural continuation and the image which has tried to embody itself in the sensation. We must now consider these virtual states more carefully, and, penetrating further into the internal mechanism of psychical and psycho-physical actions, show by what continuous progress the past tends to reconquer, by actualizing itself, the influence it had lost.

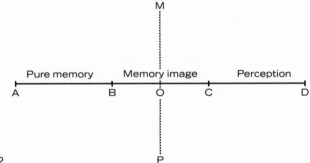

Fig. 2

CHAPTER III

Of The Survival of Images.

Memory and Mind.

To sum up briefly the preceding chapters: we have distinguished three processes, pure memory, memory-image and perception, of which none of them in fact, occurs apart from the others. Perception is never a mere contact of the mind with the object present; it is impregnated with memory-images which complete it as they interpret it. The memory-image, in its turn, partakes of the "pure memory," which it begins to materialize, and of the perception in which it tends to embody itself: regarded from the latter point of view, it might be defined as a nascent perception. Lastly, pure memory, though independent in theory, manifests itself as a rule only in the colored and living image which reveals it. Symbolizing these three terms by the consecutive segments AB, BC, CD, of the same straight line AD, we may say that our thought describes this line in a single movement, which goes from A to D, and that is impossible to say precisely where one of the terms ends and another begins.

In fact, this is just what consciousness bears witness to whenever, in order to analyze memory, it follows the movement of memory at work. Whenever we are trying to recover a recollection, to call up some period of our history, we become conscious of an act *sui generis* by which we detach ourselves from the present in order to replace ourselves, first, in the past in general, then, in a certain region of the past — a work of adjustment, something like the focusing of a camera. But our recollection still remains virtual; we simply prepare ourselves to receive it by adopting the appropriate attitude. Little by little it comes into view like a condensing cloud; from the virtual state it passes into the actual; and as its outlines become more distinct and its surface takes on color, it tends to imitate perception. But it remains attached to the past by its deepest roots, and if, when once realized, it did not retain something of its original virtuality, if, being a present state, it were not also something which stands out distinct from the present, we should never know it for a memory.

The capital error of associationism is that it substitutes for this continuity of becoming, which is the living reality, a discontinuous multiplicity of elements, inert and juxtaposed. Just because each of the elements so constituted contains, by reason of its origin, something of what precedes and also of what follows, it must take to our eyes the form of a mixed and, so to speak, impure state. But the principle of associationism requires that each psychical state should be a kind of atom, a simple element. Hence the necessity for sacrificing, in each of the phases we have distinguished, the unstable to the stable, that is to say, the beginning to the end. If we are dealing with perception, we are asked to see in it nothing but the agglomerated sensations which color it and to overlook the remembered images which form its dim nucleus. If it is the remembered image that we are considering, we are bidden to take it already made, realized in a weak perception, and to shut our eyes to the pure memory which this image has progressively developed. In the rivalry which associationism thus sets up between the stable and the unstable, perception is bound to expel the memory-image, and the memory-image to expel pure memory.

And thus the pure memory disappears altogether. Associationism, cutting in two by a line MO, the totality of the progress AD, sees, in the part OD, only the sensations which terminate it and which have been supposed to constitute the whole of perception; yet it also reduces the part AO to the realized image which pure memory attains to as it expands. Psychical life, then, is entirely summed up in these two elements, sensation and image. And as, on the one hand, this theory drowns in the image the pure memory, which makes the image into an original state, and, on the other hand, brings the image yet closer to perception by putting into perception, in advance, something of the image itself, it ends up by finding between these two states only a difference of degree, or of intensity. Hence the distinction between *strong states* and *weak states*, of which the first are supposed to be set up by us as perceptions of the present, and the second (why, no man knows) as representations of the past. But the truth is that we shall never reach the past unless we frankly place ourselves within it. Essentially virtual, it cannot be known as something past unless we follow and adopt the movement by which it expands into a present image, thus emerging from obscurity into the light of day. In vain do we seek its trace in anything actual and already realized: we might as well look for darkness beneath the light. This is, in fact, the error of associationism: placed in the actual, it exhausts itself in vain attempts to discover in a realized and present state the mark of its past origin, to distinguish memory from perception, and to erect into a difference in kind that which it condemned in advance to be but a difference of magnitude.

To *picture* is not to *remember*. No doubt a recollection, as it becomes actual, tends to live in an image; however, the converse is not true, and the image, pure and simple, will not be referred to the past unless, indeed, it was in the past that I sought it, thus following the continuous progress which brought it from darkness into light. This is what psychologists too often forget when they conclude, from the fact that a remembered sensation becomes more actual the more we dwell upon it, that the memory of the sensation is the sensation itself beginning to be. The fact which they allege is undoubtedly true: the more I strive to recall a past pain, the nearer I come to feeling it in reality. But this is easy to understand, since the progress of a memory precisely consists, as we have said, in its becoming materialized. The question is: was the memory of a pain, when it began, really pain? Because the hypnotized subject ends by feeling hot when he is repeatedly told that he is hot, it does not follow that the words of the suggestion were themselves hot. Neither must we conclude that, because the memory of a sensation prolongs itself into that very sensation, the memory was a nascent sensation: perhaps, indeed, this memory plays, with regard to the sensation which follows it, precisely the part of the hypnotizer who makes the suggestion. The argument we are criticizing, presented in this form, is then already of no value as proof; still, it is not yet a vicious argument because it profits by the incontestable truth that memory passes into something else by becoming actual. The absurdity becomes patent when the argument is inverted (although this ought to be legitimate on the hypothesis adopted), that is to say, when the intensity of the sensation is decreased instead of the intensity of pure memory being increased. For then, if the two states differ merely in degree, there should be a given moment at which the sensation changed into a memory. If the memory of an acute pain, for instance, is but a slight pain, inversely, an intense pain which I feel, will end, as it grows less, by being an acute pain remembered. Now the moment will come, undoubtedly, when it is impossible for me to say whether what I feel is a slight sensation, which I experience, or a slight sensation, which I imagine (and this is natural, because the memory-image is already partly sensation), but never will this weak state appear to me to be the memory of a strong state. Memory, then, is something quite different.

But the illusion which consists in establishing only a difference of degree between memory and perception is more than a mere consequence of associationism, more than an accident in the history of philosophy. Its roots lie deep. It rests, in the last analysis, on a false idea of the nature and of the object of external perception. We are bent on regarding perception as only an instruction addressed to a pure spirit, as having a purely speculative interest. Then, as memory is itself essentially a knowledge of this kind, since its object is no longer present, we can only find between perception and memory a difference of degree — perceptions being then supposed to throw memories back into the past, and thus to reserve to themselves the present simply because right is might. But there is much more between past and present than a mere difference of degree. My present is that which interests me, which lives for me, and in a word, that which summons me to action; in contrast, my past is essentially powerless. We must dwell further on this point. By contrasting it with present perception we shall better understand the nature of what we call "pure memory."

For we should endeavor in vain to characterize the memory of a past state unless we began by defining the concrete note, accepted by consciousness, of present reality. What is, for me, the present moment? The essence of time is that it goes by; time already gone by is the past, and we call the present the instant in which it goes by. But there can be no question here of a mathematical instant. No doubt there is an ideal present — a pure conception, the indivisible limit which separates past from future. But the real, concrete, live present — that of which I speak when I speak of my present perception — that present necessarily occupies a duration. Where then is this duration placed? Is it on the nearer or on the further side of the mathematical point which I determine ideally when I think of the present instant? Quite evidently, it is both on this side and on that, and what I call "my present" has one foot in my past and another in my future. In my past, first, because "the moment in which I am speaking is already far from me"; in my future, next, because this moment is impending over the future: it is to the future that I am tending, and could I fix this indivisible present, this infinitesimal element of the curve of time, it is the direction of the future that it would indicate. The psychical state, then, that I call "my present," must be both a perception of the immediate past and a determination of the immediate future. Now the immediate past, in so far as it is perceived, is, as we shall see, sensation, since every sensation translates a very long succession of elementary vibrations, and the immediate future, in so far as it is being determined, is action or movement. My present, then, is both sensation and movement; since my present forms an undivided whole, then the movement must be linked with the sensation, must prolong it in action. Whence I conclude that my present consists in a joint system of sensations and movements. My present is, in its essence, sensori-motor.

This is to say that my present consists in the consciousness I have of my body. Having extension in space, my body experiences sensations and at the same time executes movements. Sensations and movements being localized at determined points of this extended body, there can only be, at a given moment, a single system of movements and sensations. That is why my present appears to me to be a thing absolutely determined, and contrasting with my past. Situated between the matter which influences it and that on which it has influence, my body is a center of action, the place where the impressions received choose intelligently the path they will follow to transform themselves into movements accomplished. Thus it, indeed, represents the actual state of my becoming, that part of my duration which is in process of growth.

More generally, in that continuity of becoming which is reality itself, the present moment is constituted by the quasi-instantaneous section effected by our perception in the flowing mass, and this section is precisely that which we call the material world. Our body occupies its center; it is, in this material world, that part of which we directly feel the flux; in its actual state the actuality of our present lies. If matter, so far as extended in space, is to be defined (as we believe it must) as a present which is always beginning again, inversely, our present is the very materiality of our existence, that is to say, a system of sensations and movements and nothing else. And this system is determined, unique for each moment of duration, just because sensations and movements occupy space, and because there cannot be in the same place several things at the same time. Why is it that it has been possible to misunderstand so simple, so evident a truth, one which is, moreover, the very idea of common sense?

The reason lies simply in the fact that philosophers insist on regarding the difference between actual sensations and pure memory as a mere difference in degree, and not in kind. In our view the difference is radical. My actual sensations occupy definite portions of the surface of my body; pure memory, on the other hand, interests no part of my body. No doubt, it will beget sensations as it materializes, but at that very moment it will cease to be a memory and pass into the state of a present thing, something actually lived. I shall then only restore to it its character of memory by carrying myself back to the process by which I called it up, as it was virtual, from the depths of my past. It is just because I made it active that it has become actual, that is to say, a sensation capable of provoking movements. But most psychologists see in pure memory only a weakened perception, an assembly of nascent sensations. Having thus effaced, to begin with, all difference in kind between sensation and memory, they are led by the logic of their hypothesis to materialize memory and to idealize sensation. They perceive memory only in the form of an image, that is to say, already embodied in nascent sensations. Having thus attributed to it that which is essential to sensation, and refusing to see in the ideality of memory something distinct, something contrasted with sensation itself, they are forced, when they come back to pure sensation, to leave to it that ideality with which they have thus implicitly endowed nascent sensations. For if the past, which by hypothesis is no longer active, can subsist in the form of a weak sensation, there must be sensations that are powerless. If pure memory, which by hypothesis interests no definite part of the body, is a nascent sensation, then sensation is not essentially localized in any point of the body. Hence the illusion that consists in regarding sensation as an ethereal and unextended state which acquires extension and consolidates in the body by mere accident: an illusion which vitiates profoundly, as we have seen the theory of external perception and raises a great number of the questions at issue between the various metaphysics of matter. We must make up our minds to it: sensation is, in its essence, extended and localized; it is a source of movement. Pure memory, being inextensive and powerless, does not in any degree share the nature of sensation.

That which I call my present is my attitude with regard to the immediate future; it is my impending action. My present is, then, sensori-motor. Of my past, that alone becomes image and, consequently, sensation, at least nascent, which can collaborate in that action, insert itself in that attitude, in a word make itself useful; but, from the moment that it becomes image, the past leaves the state of pure memory and coincides with a certain part of my present. Memory actualized in an image differs, then, profoundly from pure memory. The image is a present state, and its sole share in the past is the memory from which it arose. Memory, on the contrary, powerless as long as it remains without utility, is pure from all admixture of sensation, is without attachment to the present, and is, consequently, unextended.

This radical powerlessness of pure memory is just what will enable us to understand how it is preserved in a latent state. Without as yet going to the heart of the matter, we will confine ourselves to the remark that our unwillingness to conceive *unconscious psychical states* is due, above all, to the fact that we hold consciousness to be the essential property of psychical states: so a psychical state cannot, it seems, cease to be conscious without ceasing to exist. But if consciousness is but the characteristic note of the *present*, that is to say, of the actually lived, in short, of the *active*, then that which does not act may cease to belong to consciousness without therefore ceasing to exist in some manner. In other words, in the psychological domain, consciousness may not be the synonym of existence, but only of real action or of immediate efficacy; limiting thus the meaning of the term, we shall have less difficulty in representing to ourselves a psychical state which is unconscious, that is to say, ineffective. Whatever idea we may frame of consciousness in itself, such as it would be if it could work untrammeled, we cannot deny that, in a being which has bodily functions, the chief office of consciousness is to preside over action and to enlighten choice. Therefore, it throws light on the immediate antecedents of the decision, and on those past recollections which can usefully combine with it; all else remains in shadow. But we find here once more, in a new form, the ever-recurrent illusion which, throughout this work, we have endeavored to dispel. It is supposed that consciousness, even when linked with bodily functions, is a faculty that is only accidentally practical and is directed essentially toward speculation. Then, since we cannot see what interest, devoted as it is supposed to be to pure knowledge, it would have in allowing any information that it possesses to escape, we fail to understand why it refuses to throw light on something that was not entirely lost to it. From this we conclude that it can possess nothing more de jure than what it holds de facto, and that, in the domain of consciousness, all that is real is actual. But restore to consciousness its true role: there will no longer be any more reason to say that the past effaces itself as soon as perceived than there is to suppose that material objects cease to exist when we cease to perceive them.

We must insist on this last point, for here we have the central difficulty, and the source of the ambiguities which surround the problem of the unconscious. The idea of an *unconscious representation* is clear, despite current prejudice; we may even say that we make constant use of it, and that there is no conception more familiar to common sense. For every one admits that the images actually present to our perception are not the whole of matter. But, on the other hand, what can be a nonperceived material object, an image not imagined, unless it is a kind of unconscious mental state? Beyond the walls of your room, which you perceive at this moment, there are the adjoining rooms, then the rest of the house, finally the street and the town in which you live. It signifies little to which theory of matter you adhere; realist or idealist, you are evidently thinking, when you speak of the town, of the street, of the other rooms in the house, of so many perceptions absent from your consciousness and yet given outside of it. They are not created as your consciousness receives them; they existed, then, in some manner, and since, by hypothesis, your consciousness did not apprehend them, how could they exist in themselves unless in the unconscious state? How comes it then that an *existence outside of consciousness* appears clear to us in the case of objects, but obscure when we are speaking of the subject? Our perceptions, actual and virtual, extend along two lines, the one horizontal, AB, which contains all simultaneous objects in space, the other vertical, CI, on which are ranged our successive recollections set out

142

Fig. 3

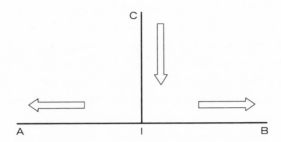

in time. The point I, at the intersection of the two lines, is the only one actually given to consciousness. Whence comes it that we do not hesitate to posit the reality of the whole line AB, although it remains unperceived, while, on the contrary, of the line CI, the present I which is actually perceived is the only point which appears to us really to exist? There are, at the bottom of this radical distinction between the two series, temporal and spatial, so many confused or half-formed ideas, so many hypotheses devoid of any speculative value, that we cannot all at once make an exhaustive analysis of them. In order to unmask the illusion entirely, we should have to seek its origin and follow through all its windings, the double movement by which we come to assume objective realities without relation to consciousness, and states of consciousness without objective reality – space thus appearing to preserve indefinitely the *things* which are there juxtaposed, while time in its advance devours the *states* which succeed each other within it. Part of this work has been done in our first chapter, where we discussed objectivity in general; another part will be dealt with in the last pages of this book, where we shall speak of the idea of matter. We confine ourselves here to a few essential points.

First, the objects ranged along the line AB represent to our eyes what we are going to perceive, while the line CI contains only that which has already been perceived. Now the past has no longer any interest for us; it has exhausted its possible action or will only recover an influence by borrowing the vitality of the present perception. The immediate future, on the contrary, consists in an impending action, in an energy not yet spent. The unperceived part of the material universe, big with promises and threats, has then for us a reality which the actually unperceived periods of our past existence cannot and should not possess. But this distinction, which is entirely relative to practical utility and to the material needs of life, takes in our minds the more and more marked form of a metaphysical distinction.

We have shown that the objects which surround us represent, in varying degrees, an action which we can accomplish upon things or which we must experience from them. The date of fulfilment of this possible action is indicated by the greater or lesser remoteness of the corresponding object, so that distance in space measures the proximity of a threat or of a promise in time. Thus space furnishes us at once with the diagram of our near future, and, as this future must recede indefinitely, space which symbolizes it has for its property to remain, in its immobility, indefinitely open. Hence the immediate horizon given to our perception appears to us to be necessarily surrounded by a wider circle, existing though unperceived, this circle itself implying yet another outside it and so on, ad infinitum. It is, then, of the essence of our actual perception, inasmuch as it is extended, to be always only a *content* in relation to a vaster, even an unlimited, experience which contains it; this experience, absent from our consciousness, since it spreads beyond the perceived horizon, nevertheless, appears to be actually given. But while we feel ourselves to be dependent upon these material objects which we thus erect into present realities, our memories, on the contrary, inasmuch as they are past, are so much dead weight that we carry with us, and by which we prefer to imagine ourselves unencumbered. The same instinct, in virtue of which we open out space indefinitely before us, prompts us to shut off time behind us as it flows. And while reality, in so far as it is extended, appears to us to overpass infinitely the bounds of our perception, in our inner life that alone seems to us to be *real* which begins with the present moment; the rest is practically abolished. Then, when a memory reappears in consciousness, it produces on us the effect of a ghost whose mysterious apparition must be explained by special causes. In truth, the adherence of this memory to our present condition is exactly comparable to the adherence of unperceived objects to those objects which we perceive; and *the unconscious* plays in each case a similar part.

But we have great difficulty in representing the matter to ourselves in this way because we have fallen into the habit of emphasizing the differences and, on the contrary, of slurring over the resemblances, between the series of *objects* simultaneously set out in space and that of *states* successively developed in time. In the first, the terms condition each other in a manner which is entirely determined, so that the appearance of each new term may be foreseen. Thus I know, when I leave my room, what other rooms I shall go through. However, my memories present themselves in an order which is apparently capricious. The order of the representations is then necessary in the one case, contingent in the other; it is this necessity which I hypostatize, as it were, when I speak of the existence of objects outside of all consciousness. If I see no inconvenience in supposing, given the totality of objects which I do not perceive, it is because the strictly determined order of these objects lends to them the appearance of a chain, of which my present perception is only one link. This link communicates its actuality to the rest of the chain. But, if we look at the matter closely, we shall see that our memories form a chain of the same kind, and that our character, always present in all our decisions, is indeed the actual synthesis of all our past states. In this epitomized form our previous psychical life exists for us even more than the external world, of which we never perceive more than a very small part, whereas, on the contrary, we use the whole of our lived experience. It is true that we possess merely a digest of it, and that our former perceptions, considered as distinct individualities, seem to us to have completely disappeared or to appear again only at the bidding of their caprice. But this semblance of complete destruction or of capricious revival is due merely to the fact that actual consciousness accepts at each moment the useful and rejects in the same breath the superfluous. Ever bent upon action, it can only materialize those of our former perceptions which can ally themselves with the present perception to take a share in the final decision. If it is necessary, when I would manifest my will at a given point of space, that my consciousness should go successively through those intermediaries or those obstacles of which the sum constitutes what we call *distance in space*, so, on the other hand, it is useful, in order to throw light on this action, that my consciousness should jump the interval of time which separates the actual situation from a former one which resembles it; and as consciousness goes back to the earlier date at a bound, all the intermediate past escapes its hold. The same reasons, then, which cause our perceptions to range themselves in strict continuity in space, cause our memories to be illumined discontinuously in time. We have not, in regard to objects unperceived in space and unconscious memories in time, to do with two radically different forms of existence, but the exigencies of action are the inverse in the one case of what they are in the other.

But here we come to the capital problem of *existence*, a problem we can only glance at, for otherwise it would lead us step by step into the heart of metaphysics. We will merely say that with regard to matters of experience — which alone concern us here — existence appears to imply two conditions taken together: (1) presentation in consciousness and (2) the logical or casual connection of that which is so presented with what precedes and with what follows. The reality for us of a psychical state or of a material object consists in the double fact that our consciousness perceives them and that they form part of a series, temporal or spatial, of which the elements determine each other. But these two conditions admit of degrees, and it is conceivable that, though both are necessary, they may be unequally fulfilled. Thus, in the case of actual internal states, the connection is less close, and the determination of the present by the past, leaving ample room for contingency, has not the character of a mathematical derivation — but then, presentation in consciousness is perfect, an actual psychical state yielding the whole of its content in the act itself, whereby we perceive it. On the contrary, if we are dealing with external objects it is the connection which is perfect, since these objects obey necessary laws; but then the other condition, presentation in consciousness, is never more than partially fulfilled, for the material object, just because of the multitude of unperceived elements by which it is linked with all other objects, appears to enfold within itself and to hide behind it infinitely more than it allows to be seen. We ought to say, then, that existence, in the empirical sense of the word, always implies conscious apprehension and regular connection; both at the same time, although in different degrees. But our intellect, of which the function is to establish clear-cut distinctions, does not so understand things. Rather than admit the presence in all cases of the two elements mingled in varying proportions, it prefers to dissociate them, and thus attribute to external objects, on the one hand, and to internal states, on the other hand, two radically different modes of existence, each characterized by the exclusive presence of the condition which should be regarded as merely preponderating. Then the existence of psychical states is assumed to consist entirely in their apprehension by consciousness, and that of external phenomena, entirely also, in the strict order of their concomitance and their succession. Whence the impossibility of leaving to material objects, existing, but unperceived, the smallest share in consciousness, and to internal unconscious states the smallest share in existence. We have shown, at the beginning of this book, the consequences of the first illusion: it ends by falsifying our representation of matter. The second illusion, complementary to the first, vitiates our conception of mind by casting over the idea of the unconscious an artificial obscurity. The whole of our past psychical life conditions our present state, without being its necessary determinant; whole, also, it reveals itself in our character, although none of its past states manifests itself explicitly in character. Taken together, these two conditions assure to each one of the past psychological states a real, though an unconscious, existence.

But we are so much accustomed to reverse, for the sake of action, the real order of things, we are so strongly obsessed by images drawn from space, that we cannot hinder ourselves from asking *where* memories are stored up. We understand that physico-chemical phenomena take place *in* the brain, that the brain is *in* the body, the body *in* the air which surrounds it, etc.; but the past, once achieved, if it is retained, where is it? To locate it in the cerebral substance, in the state of molecular modification, seems clear and simple enough because then we have a receptacle, actually given, which we have only to open in order to let the latent images flow into consciousness. But if the brain cannot serve such a purpose, in what warehouse shall we store the accumulated images? We forget that the relation of container to content borrows its apparent clearness and universality from the necessity laid upon us of always opening out space in front of us and of always closing duration behind us. Because it has been shown that one thing is within another, the phenomenon of its preservation is not thereby made any clearer. We may even go further: let us admit for a moment that the past survives in the form of a memory stored in the brain; it is then necessary that the brain, in order to preserve the memory, should preserve itself. But the brain, insofar as it is an image extended in space, never occupies more than the present moment: it constitutes, with all the rest of the material universe, an ever-renewed section of universal becoming. Either, then, you must suppose that this universe dies and is born again miraculously at each moment of duration, or you must attribute to it that continuity of existence which you deny to consciousness, and make of its past a reality which endures and is prolonged into its present. So that you have gained nothing by depositing the memories in matter, and you find yourself, on the contrary, compelled to extend to the totality of the states of the material world that complete and independent survival of the past which you have just refused to psychical states. This survival of the past *per se* forces itself upon philosophers, then, under one form or another; the difficulty that we have in conceiving it comes simply from the fact that we extend to the series of memories, in time, that obligation of *containing* and *being contained* which applies only to the collection of bodies instantaneously perceived in space. The fundamental illusion consists in transferring to duration itself, in its continuous flow, the form of the instantaneous sections which we make in it.

But how can the past, which, by hypothesis, has ceased to be, preserve itself? Have we not here a real contradiction? We reply that the question is just whether the past has ceased to exist or whether it has simply ceased to be useful. You define the present in an arbitrary manner as *that which is*, whereas the present is simply *what is being made*. Nothing *is* less than the present moment, if you understand by that the indivisible limit which divides the past from the future. When we think this present as going to be, it exists not yet, and when we think it as existing, it is already past. If, on the other hand, what you are considering is the concrete present such as it is actually lived by consciousness, we may say that this present consists, in large measure, in the immediate past. In the fraction of a second which covers the briefest possible perception of light, billions of vibrations have taken place, of which the first is separated from the last by an interval which is enormously divided. Your perception, however instantaneous, consists then in an incalculable multitude of remembered elements; in truth, every perception is already memory. *Practically, we perceive only the past*, the pure present being the invisible progress of the past gnawing into the future.

Consciousness, then, illumines, at each moment of time, that immediate part of the past which, impending over the future, seeks to realize and to associate with it. Solely preoccupied in thus determining an undetermined future, consciousness may shed a little of its light on those of our states, more remote in the past, which can be usefully combined with our present state, that is to say, with our immediate past: the rest remains in the dark. It is in this illuminated part of our history that we remain seated, in virtue of the fundamental law of life, which is a law of action: hence the difficulty we experience in conceiving memories which are preserved in the shadow. Our reluctance to admit the integral survival of the past has its origin, then, in the very bent of our psychical life – an unfolding of states wherein our interest prompts us to look at that which is unrolling, and not at that which is entirely unrolled.

So we return, after a long digression, to our point of departure. There are, we have said, two memories which are profoundly distinct: the one, fixed in the organism, is nothing else but the complete set of intelligently constructed mechanisms which ensure the appropriate reply to the various possible demands. This memory enables us to adapt ourselves to the present situation; through it the actions to which we are subject prolong themselves into reactions that are sometimes accomplished, sometimes merely nascent, but always more or less appropriate. Habit rather than memory, it acts our past experience but does not call up its image. The other is the true memory. Coextensive with consciousness, it retains and ranges alongside of each other all our states in the order in which they occur, leaving to each fact its place and, consequently, marking its date, truly moving in the past and not, like the first, in an ever renewed present. But, in marking the profound distinction between these two forms of memory, we have not shown their connecting link. Above the body, with its mechanisms which symbolize the accumulated effort of past actions, the memory which imagines and repeats has been left to hang, as it were, suspended in the void. Now, if it be true that we never perceive anything but our immediate past, if our consciousness of the present is already memory, the two terms which had been separated to begin with cohere closely together. Seen from this new point of view, indeed, our body is nothing but that part of our representation which is ever being born again, the part always present, or rather that which, at each moment, is just past. Itself an image, the body cannot store up images, since it forms a part of the images, and this is why it is a chimerical enterprise to seek to localize past or even present perceptions in the brain: they are not in it; it is the brain that is in them. But this special image which persists in the midst of the others, and which I call my body, constitutes at every moment, as we have said, a section of the universal becoming. It is then the *place of passage* of the movements received and thrown back, a hyphen, a connecting link between the things which act upon me

Fig. 4

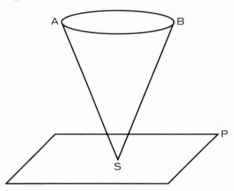

and the things upon which I act – the seat, in a word, of the sensori-motor phenomena. If I represent by a cone SAB, the totality of the recollections accumulated in my memory, the base AB, situated in the past, remains motionless, while the summit S, which indicates at all times my present, moves forward unceasingly, and unceasingly also touches the moving plane P of my actual representation of the universe. At S, the image of the body is concentrated, and, since it belongs to the plane P, this image does but receive and restore actions emanating from all the images of which the plane is composed.

The bodily memory, made up of the sum of the sensori-motor systems organized by habit, is then a quasi-instantaneous memory to which the true memory of the past serves as base. Since they are not two separate things, since the first is only, as we have said, the pointed end, ever moving, inserted by the second in the shifting plane of experience, it is natural that the two functions should lend each other a mutual support. So, on the one hand, the memory of the past offers to the sensori-motor mechanisms all the recollections capable of guiding them in their task and of giving to the motor reaction the direction suggested by the lessons of experi-

ence. It is in just this that the associations of contiguity and likeness consist. But, on the other hand, the sensori-motor apparatus
furnish to ineffective, that is unconscious, memories, the means
of taking on a body, of materializing themselves, in short of becoming present. For, that a recollection should reappear in consciousness, it is necessary that it should descend from the heights of pure
memory down to the precise point where *action* is taking place.
In other words, it is from the present that the appeal to which
memory responds comes, and it is from the sensori-motor elements of present action that a memory borrows the warmth which
gives it life.

Is it not by the constancy of this agreement, by the precision
with which these two complementary memories insert themselves
each into the other, that we recognize a "well-balanced" mind,
that is to say, in fact, a man nicely adapted to life? The characteristic of the man of action is the promptitude with which he summons to the help of a given situation all the memories which have
reference to it; yet it is also the insurmountable barrier which
encounters, when they present themselves on the threshold of his
consciousness, memories that are useless or indifferent. To live
only in the present, to respond to a stimulus by the immediate
reaction which prolongs it, is the mark of the lower animals: the
man who proceeds in this way is a man of *impulse*. But he who
lives in the past for the mere pleasure of living there, and in whom
recollections emerge into the light of consciousness without any
advantage for the present situation, is hardly better fitted for action:
here we have no man of impulse, but a *dreamer*. Between these
two extremes lives the happy disposition of memory docile enough
to follow with precision all the outlines of the present situation,
but energetic enough to resist all other appeal. Good sense, or
practical sense, is probably nothing but this.

The extraordinary development of spontaneous memory in most

children is due to the fact that they have not yet persuaded their memory to remain bound up with their conduct. They usually follow the impression of the moment, and as with them action does not bow to the suggestions of memory, so neither are their recollections limited to the necessities of action. They seem to retain with greater facility only because they remember with less discernment. The apparent diminution of memory, as intellect develops, is then due to the growing organization of recollections with acts. Thus conscious memory loses in range what it gains in force of penetration: it had at first the facility of the memory of dreams, but then it was actually dreaming. Indeed we observe this same exaggeration of spontaneous memory in men whose intellectual development hardly goes beyond that of childhood. A missionary, after preaching a long sermon to some African savages, heard one of them repeat it textually, with the same gestures, from beginning to end.[1]

But, if almost the whole of our past is hidden from us because it is inhibited by the necessities of present action, it will find strength to cross the threshold of consciousness in all cases where we renounce the interests of effective action to replace ourselves, so to speak, in the life of dreams. Sleep, natural or artificial, brings about an indifference of just this kind. It has been recently suggested that in sleep there is an interruption of the contact between the nervous elements, motor and sensory.[2] Even if we do not accept this ingenious hypothesis, it is impossible not to see in sleep a relaxing, even if only functional, of the tension of the nervous system, ever ready, during waking hours, to prolong by an appropriate reaction the stimulation received. Now the exaltation of the memory in certain dreams and in certain somnambulistic states is well known. Memories, which we believed abolished, then reappear with striking completeness; we live over again, in all their detail, forgotten scenes of childhood; we speak languages which we no longer even remember to have learned. But there is nothing more instructive in this regard than what happens in cases of sudden suffocation, in men drowned or hanged. Such a man, when brought to life again, states that he saw, in a very short time, all the forgotten events of his life passing before him with great rapidity, with their smallest circumstances and in the very order in which they occurred.[3]

A human being who should *dream* his life instead of living it would no doubt thus keep before his eyes at each moment the infinite multitude of the details of his past history. And, conversely, the man who should repudiate this memory with all that it begets would be continually acting his life instead of truly representing it to himself: a conscious automaton, he would follow the lead of useful habits which prolong into an appropriate reaction the stimulation received. The first would never rise above the particular, or even above the individual; leaving to each image its date in time and its position in space, he would see wherein it *differs* from others and not how it resembles them. The other, always swayed by habit, would only distinguish in any situation that aspect in which it practically *resembles* former situations; incapable, doubtless, of *thinking* universals, since every general idea implies the representation, at least virtual, of a number of remembered images, he would, nevertheless, move in the universal, habit being to action what generality is to thought. But these two extreme states, the one of an entirely contemplative memory which apprehends only the singular in its *vision*, the other of a purely motor memory which stamps the note of generality on its *action*, are really separate and are fully visible only in exceptional cases. In normal life they are interpenetrating, so that each has to abandon some part of its original purity. The first reveals itself in the recollection of differences, the second in the perception of resemblances: at the meeting of the two currents appears the general idea.

155

We are not concerned here to settle once for all the whole question of general ideas. Some have not originated in perception alone, and have but a very distant connection with material objects. We will leave these on one side and consider only those general ideas that are founded on what we have called the perception of similarity. We will try to follow pure memory, integral memory, in the continuous effort which it makes to insert itself into motor habit. In this way we may throw more light upon the office and nature of this memory, and perhaps make clearer, at the same time, by regarding them in this particular aspect, the two equally obscure notions of *resemblance* and of *generality*.

If we consider as closely as possible the difficulties of a psychological order which surround the problem of general ideas, we shall come, we believe, to enclose them in this circle: to generalize, it is first of all necessary to abstract, but to abstract to any purpose we must already know how to generalize. Round this circle gravitate, consciously or unconsciously, nominalism and conceptualism, each doctrine having in its favor mainly the insufficiency of the other. The nominalists, retaining of the general idea only its extension, see in it merely an open and unlimited series of individual objects. The unity of the idea can then, for them, consist only in the identity of the symbol by which we designate indifferently all these distinct objects. According to them, we begin by perceiving a thing, and then we assign to it a word: this word, backed by the faculty or the habit of extending itself to an unlimited number of other things, then sets up for a general idea. But, in order that the word should extend and yet limit itself to the objects which it designates, it is necessary that these objects should offer us resemblances which, when we compare them, shall distinguish them from all the objects to which the word does not apply. Generalization does not, consequently, occur without our taking into account qualities that have been found to be common and therefore considered in the abstract; from step to step, nominalism is thus led to define the general idea by its intention and not merely by its extension, as it set out to do. It is just from this intention that conceptualism starts; the intellect, in this theory, resolves the superficial unity of the individual into different qualities, each of which, isolated from the individual who limited it, becomes by that very isolation representative of a genus. Instead of regarding each genus as including *actually* a multiplicity of objects, it is now maintained, on the contrary, that each object involves *potentially*, and as so many qualities which it holds captive, a multiplicity of genera. But the question before us is whether individual qualities, even isolated by an effort of abstraction, do not remain individual, and whether, to make them into genera, a new effort of the mind is not required, by which it first bestows on each quality a name, and then collects under this name a multitude of individual objects. The whiteness of a lily is not the whiteness of a snowfield; they remain, even as isolated from the snow and the lily, snow-white or lily-white. They only forego their individuality if we consider their likeness in order to give them a common name; then, applying this name to an unlimited number of similar objects, we throw back upon the quality, by a sort of *ricochet*, the generality which the word went out to seek in its application to things. But, reasoning in this way, do we not return to the point of view of extension, which we just now abandoned? We are then, in truth, revolving in a circle, nominalism leading us to conceptualism, and conceptualism bringing us back to nominalism. Generalization can only be effected by extracting common qualities; however, that qualities should appear common, they must have already been subjected to a process of generalization.

Now, when we get to the bottom of these two opposite theories, we find in them a common postulate; each will have it that we start from the perception of individual objects. The first composes the genus by an enumeration; the second disengages it by an analysis; but it is upon individuals, considered as so many realities given to immediate intuition, that both analysis and enumeration are supposed to bear. This is the postulate. In spite of its apparent obviousness, we must expect to find, and we do indeed find, that experience belies it.

A priori, indeed, we may expect the clear distinction of individual objects to be a luxury of perception, just as the clear representation of general ideas is a refinement of the intellect. The full conception of genera is no doubt proper to human thought; it demands an effort of reflection, by which we expunge from a representation the details of time and place. But the reflection *on* these details — a reflection without which the individuality of objects would escape us — presupposes a faculty of noticing differences, and therefore, a memory of images, which is certainly the privilege of man and of the higher animals. It would seem, then, that we start neither from the perception of the individual nor from the conception of the genus, but from an intermediate knowledge, from a confused sense of the *striking quality* or of resemblance: this sense, equally remote from generality fully conceived and from individuality clearly perceived, begets both of them by a process of dissociation. Reflective analysis clarifies it into the general idea; discriminative memory solidifies it into a perception of the individual.

But this will be more clearly evident if we go back to the purely utilitarian origin of our perception of things. That which interests us in a given situation, that which we are likely to grasp in it first, is the side by which it can respond to a tendency or a need. But a need goes straight to the resemblance or quality; it cares little for individual differences. To this discernment of the useful we may surmise that the perception of animals is, in most cases confined. It is grass *in general* which attracts the herbivorous animal: the color and the smell of grass, felt and experienced as forces (we do not go so far as to say, thought as qualities or genera), are the sole immediate data of its external perception. On this background of generality or of resemblance the animal's memory may show up contrasts from which will issue differentiations; it will then distinguish one countryside from another, one field from another field; but this is, we repeat, the superfluity of perception, not a necessary part. It may be urged that we are only throwing the problem further back, that we are merely relegating to the unconscious the process by which similarity is discovered and genera are constituted. But we relegate nothing to the unconscious for the very simple reason that it is not, in our opinion, an effort of a psychological nature which here disengages similarity; this similarity acts objectively like a force and provokes reactions that are identical in virtue of the purely physical law which requires that the same general effects should follow the same profound causes. Hydrochloric acid always acts in the same way upon carbonate of lime whether in the form of marble or of chalk yet we do not say that the acid perceives in the various species the characteristic features of the genus. Now there is no essential difference between the process by which this acid picks out from the salt its base and the act of the plant which invariably extracts from the most diverse soils those elements that serve to nourish it. Make one more step; imagine a rudimentary consciousness such as that of an amoeba in a drop of water: it will be sensible of the resemblance, and not of the difference, in the various organic substances which it can assimilate. In short, we can follow from the mineral to the plant, from the plant to the simplest conscious beings, from the animal to man, the progress of the operation by which things and beings seize from their surroundings that which attracts them, that which interests them practically, without needing any effort of abstraction, simply because the rest of their surroundings takes no hold upon them: this similarity of reaction following actions superficially different is the germ which the human consciousness develops into general ideas.

Consider, indeed, the purpose and function of our nervous system as far as we can infer them from its structure. We see a great variety of mechanisms of perception, all bound, through the intermediary of the centers, to the same motor apparatus. Sensation is unstable; it can take the most varied shades; the motor mechanism, on the contrary, once set going, will invariably work in the same way. We may then suppose perceptions as different as possible in their superficial details: if only they are continued by the same motor reactions, if the organism can extract from them the same useful effects, if they impress upon the body the same attitude, something common will issue from them, and the general idea will have been felt and passively experienced, before being represented. Here then we escape at last from the circle in which we at first appeared to be confined. In order to generalize, we said, we have to abstract similarity, but in order to disengage similarity usefully we must already know how to generalize. There really is no circle because the similarity, from which the mind starts when it first begins the work of abstraction, is not the similarity at which the mind arrives when it consciously generalizes. That from which it starts is a similarity felt and lived, or, if you prefer the expression, a similarity which is automatically acted. That to which it returns is a similarity intelligently perceived, or thought. And it is precisely in the course of this progress that are built up, by the double effort of the understanding and of the memory, the perception of individuals and the conception of genera – memory grafting distinctions upon resemblances which have been spontaneously abstracted, the understanding disengaging from the habit of resemblances the clear idea of generality. This idea of generality was, in the beginning, only our consciousness of a likeness of attitude in a diversity of situations; it was habit itself, mounting from the sphere of movement to that of thought. But from genera so sketched out mechanically by habit we have passed by an effort of reflection upon this very process, to the *general idea of genus*; and when that idea has been once constituted, we have constructed (this time voluntarily) an unlimited number of general notions. It is not necessary here to follow the intellect into the detail of this construction. It is enough to say that the understanding, imitating the effort of nature, has also set up motor apparatuses, artificial in this case, to make a limited number of them answer to an unlimited number of individual objects: the assemblage of these mechanisms is articulate speech.

Yet these two divergent operations of the mind, the one by which it discerns individuals, the other by which it constructs genera, are far from demanding the same effort or progressing with the same rapidity. The first, requiring only the intervention of memory, takes place from the outset of our experience; the second goes on indefinitely without ever reaching its goal. The first emerges in the formation of stable images, which in their turn are stored up in memory; the second comes out in representations that are unstable and evanescent. We must dwell on this last point, for we touch here an essential problem of mental life.

The essence of the general idea, in fact, is to be unceasingly going backwards and forwards between the plane of action and that of pure memory. Let us refer once more to the diagram we traced above. At S is the present perception which I have of my body, that is to say, of a certain sensori-motor equilibrium. Over the surface of the base AB are spread, we may say, my recollections in their totality. Within the cone so determined, the general idea oscillates continually between the summit S and the base AB. In S, it would take the clearly defined form of a bodily attitude or of an uttered word; at AB, it would wear the aspect, no less

Fig. 5

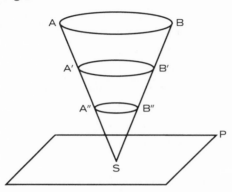

defined, of the thousand individual images into which its fragile unity would break up. And that is why a psychology which abides by the *already done*, which considers only that which is made and ignores that which is in the making, will never perceive in this movement anything more than the two extremities between which it oscillates; it makes the general idea coincide sometimes with the action which manifests it or the word which expresses it and at other times with the multitudinous images, unlimited in number, which are its equivalent in memory. But the truth is that the general idea escapes us as soon as we try to fix it at either of the two extremities. It consists in the double current which goes from the one to the other – always ready either to crystallize into uttered words or to evaporate into memories.

This amounts to saying that between the sensori-motor mechanisms figured by the point S and the totality of the memories disposed in AB there is room, as we indicated in the preceding chapter, for a thousand repetitions of our psychical life, figured by as many sections A'B',A''B'', etc., of the same cone. We tend to scatter ourselves over AB in the measure that we detach ourselves from our sensory and motor state to live in the life of dreams; we tend to concentrate ourselves in S in the measure that we attach our-selves more firmly to the present reality, responding by motor reac-tions to sensory stimulation. In point of fact, the normal self never stays in either of these extreme positions; it moves between them, adopts in turn the positions corresponding to the intermediate sections, or, in other words, gives to its representations just enough image and just enough idea for them to be able to lend useful aid to the present action.

From this conception of the lower mental life, the laws of the association of ideas can be deduced. But, before we deal with this point, we must first show the insufficiency of the current theories of association.

That every idea which arises in the mind has a relation of simi-larity or of contiguity with the previous mental state, we do not dispute; but a statement of the kind neither throws light on the mechanism of association nor, indeed, does it really tell us any-thing at all. For we should seek in vain for two ideas which have not some point of resemblance or which do not touch each other somewhere. To take similarity first: however profound are the dif-ferences which separate two images, we shall always find, if we go back high enough, a common genus to which they belong, and, consequently, a resemblance which may serve as a connecting link between them. And, in regard to contiguity, a perception A, as we said before, will not evoke "by contiguity" a former image B, unless it recalls to us first an image A', which is like it, because it is the recollection A', and not the perception A, which really touches B in memory. However distant, then, we suppose the terms A and B from each other, a relation of contiguity can always be found between them, provided that the intercalated term A' bears a sufficiently farfetched resemblance to A. This is as much as to say that between any two ideas chosen at random there is always a resemblance, and always, even, contiguity, so that, when we discover a relation of contiguity or of resemblance between two successive ideas, we have in no way explained why the one evokes the other.

What we really need to discover is how a choice is effected among an infinite number of recollections which all resemble in some way the present perception, and why only one of them — this rather than that — emerges into the light of consciousness. But this is just what associationism cannot tell us, because it has made ideas and images into independent entities floating, like the atoms of Epicurus, in an inward space, drawing near to each other when chance brings them within the sphere of mutual attraction. And if we try to get to the bottom of the doctrine on this point, we find that its error is that it overly *intellectualizes* ideas: it attributes to them a purely speculative role, believes that they exist for themselves and not for us, and overlooks the relation which they bear to the activity of the will. If memories move about indifferently in a consciousness that is both lifeless and shapeless, there is no reason why the present perception should prefer and attract any one of them: we can only, in that case, note the conjunction, when once it has taken place, and speak of similarity or of contiguity — which is merely, at bottom, to express in vague terms that our mental states have affinities for one another.

But even of this affinity, which takes the double form of contiguity and of similarity, associationism can furnish no explanation. The general tendency to associate remains as obscure for us, if we adhere to this doctrine, as the particular forms of association. Having stiffened individual memory-images into ready-made things, given cut-and-dry in the course of our mental life, associationism is reduced to bringing in, between these objects, mysterious attractions, of which it is not even possible to say beforehand, as of physical attraction, by what effects they will manifest themselves. For why should an image which is, by hypothesis, self-sufficient, seek to accrue to itself others either similar or given in contiguity with it? The truth is that this independent image is a late and artificial product of the mind. In fact, we perceive the resemblance before we perceive the individuals which resemble each other; and, in an aggregate of contiguous parts, we perceive the whole before the parts. We go on from similarity to similar objects, embroidering upon the similarity, as on their common stuff, or canvas, the variety of individual differences. And we go on also from the whole to the parts, by a process of decomposition the law of which will appear later, a process which consists in breaking up, for the greater convenience of practical life, the continuity of the real. *Association*, then, is not the primary fact: *dissociation* is what we begin with, and the tendency of every memory to gather to itself others must be explained by the natural return of the mind to the undivided unity of perception.

But here we discover the radical vice of associationsim. Given a present perception which forms by turns, with different recollections, several associations one after another, there are two ways, as we said, of conceiving the mechanism of this association. We may suppose that the perception remains identical with itself, a true psychical atom which gathers to itself others just as these happen to be passing by. This is the point of view of associationism. But there is also another — precisely the one which we have indicated in our theory of recognition. We have supposed that our entire personality, with the totality of our recollections, is present, undivided within our actual perception. Then, if this perception evokes in turn different memories, it is not by a mechanical adjunction of more and more numerous elements which, while remaining unmoved, it attracts around it, but rather by an expansion of the entire consciousness which, spreading out over a larger area, discovers the fuller detail of its wealth. So a nebulous mass, seen through more and more powerful telescopes, resolves itself into an ever greater number of stars. In the first hypothesis (in favor of which there is little but its apparent simplicity and its analogy with a misunderstood physical atomism), each recollection is a fixed and independent being, of which we can neither say why it seeks to accrue to itself others, nor how it chooses, among a thousand memories which should have equal rights, those with which to associate itself in virtue of similarity or contiguity. We must suppose that ideas jostle each other at random, or that they exert among themselves mysterious forces, and, moreover, we have against us the witness of consciousness, which never shows us psychical facts floating as independent entities. From the second point of view, we merely state a fact, viz., that psychic facts are bound up with each other, and are always given together to immediate consciousness as an undivided whole which reflection alone cuts up into distinct fragments. What we have to explain, then, is no longer the cohesion of internal states, but the double movement of contraction and expansion by which consciousness narrows or enlarges the development of its content. But this movement, we shall see, is the result of the fundamental needs of life; and we shall also see why the "associations," which we appear to form in the course of this movement, correspond to all the possible degrees of so-called contiguity and resemblance.

Let us, for a moment, suppose our psychical life reduced to sensori-motor functions alone. In other words, suppose ourselves placed in Figure 5 on page 162 at point S, which corresponds to the greatest possible simplification of our mental life. In this state every perception spontaneously prolongs itself into appropriate reactions, for analogous former perceptions have set up more or less complex motor apparatus, which only await a recurrence of the same appeal in order to enter into play. Now there is, in this mechanism, an *association of simplicity*, since the present perception acts in virtue of its likeness to past perceptions; there is also an *association of contiguity*, since the movements which followed those former perceptions reproduce themselves and may even bring in their train a vast number of actions coordinate with the first. Here then we seize association of similarity and association of contiguity at their very source, and at a point where they are almost confounded in one — not indeed thought, but acted and lived. They are not contingent forms of our psychical life; they represent the two complementary aspects of one and the same fundamental tendency, the tendency of every organism to extract from a given situation that in it which is useful, and to store up the eventual reaction in the form of a motor habit, that it may serve other situations of the same kind.

Let us jump now to the other extremity of our mental life, and, following our line of thought, go from the psychical existence which is merely "acted," to that which is exclusively "dreamed." In other words, let us place ourselves on the base AB of memory in Figure 5 on page 162, where all the events of our past life are set out in their smallest details. A consciousness which, detached from action, should thus keep in view the totality of its past, would have no reason to dwell upon one part of this past rather than upon another. In one sense, all its recollections would differ from its present perception, for, if we take them in the multiplicity of their detail, no two memories are ever precisely the same thing. But, in another sense, *any* memory may be set alongside the present situation: it would be sufficient to neglect in this perception and in this memory just enough detail for similarity alone to appear. Moreover, the moment that the recollection is linked with the perception, a multitude of events contiguous to the memory are thereby fastened to the perception — an indefinite multitude, which is only limited at the point at which we choose to stop it. The necessities of life are no longer there to regulate the effect of similarity, and, consequently, of contiguity; as, after all, everything resembles everything else, it follows that anything can be associated with anything. In the first case, the present perception continued itself in determinate movements; now it melts into an infinity of memories, all equally possible. At AB, association would provoke an arbitrary choice, and, in S, an inevitable deed.

But these are only two extreme limits, at which the psychologist must place himself alternately for convenience of study, and which are really never reached in practice. There is not, in man at least, a purely sensori-motor state, any more than there is in him an imaginative life without some slight activity beneath it. Our psychical life, as we have said, oscillates normally between these two extremes. On the one hand, the sensori-motor state S delineates the present direction of memory, being nothing else, in fact, than its actual and acting extremity; and, on the other hand, this memory itself, with the totality of our past, is continually pressing forward, so as to insert the largest possible part of itself into the present action. From this double effort result, at every moment, an infinite number of possible *states* of memory, states figured by the sections A'B', A''B'' of our diagram. These are, as we have said, so many repetitions of the whole of our past life. But each section is larger or smaller according to its nearness to the base or to the summit; moreover, each of these complete representations of the past brings to the light of consciousness only that which can fit into the sensori-motor state and, consequently, that which resembles the present perception from the point of view of the action to be accomplished. In other words, memory, laden with the whole of the past, responds to the appeal of the present state by two simultaneous movements, one of translation, by which it moves in its entirety to meet experience, thus contracting more or less, though without dividing, with a view to action; and the other of rotation upon itself, by which it turns toward the situation of the moment, presenting to it that side of itself which may prove to be the most useful. To these varying degrees of contraction correspond the various forms of association by similarity.

Everything happens, then, as though our recollections were repeated an infinite number of times in these many possible reductions of our past life. They take a more common form when memory shrinks most, more personal when it widens out, and they thus enter into an unlimited number of different "systematizations." A word from a foreign language, uttered in my hearing, may make me think of that language in general or of a voice which once pronounced it in a certain way. These two associations by similarity are not due to the accidental arrival of two different representations, which chance brought by turns within the attracting influence of the actual perception. They answer to two different mental *dispositions*, to two distinct degrees of tension of the memory; in the latter case they are nearer to the pure image, in the former, they are more disposed toward immediate response, that is to say, to action. To classify these systems, to discover the law which binds them respectively to the different "tones" of our mental life, to show how each of these tones is itself determined by the needs of the moment and also by the varying degree of our personal effort, would be a difficult task: the whole of this psychology is yet unmapped, and for the moment we do not even wish to attempt it. But every one is clearly aware of the existence of these laws, and of stable relations of this kind. We know, for instance, when we read a psychological novel, that certain associations of ideas there depicted for us are true, that they may have been lived; others offend us, or fail to give us an impression of reality, because we feel in them the effect of a connection, mechanically and artificially brought about, between different mental levels, as though

169

the author had not taken care to maintain himself on that plane of the mental life which he had chosen. Memory has then its successive and distinct degrees of tension or of vitality: they are certainly not easy to define, but the painter of mental scenery may not with impunity confound them. Pathology, moreover, here confirms — by means, it is true, of coarser examples — a truth of which we are all instinctively aware. In the "systematized amnesias" of hysterical patients, for example, the recollections which appear to be abolished are really present, but they are probably all bound up with a certain determined tone of intellectual vitality in which the subject can no longer place himself.

Just as there are these *different planes*, infinite in number, for association by similarity, so there are with association by contiguity. In the extreme plane, which represents the base of memory, there is no recollection which is not linked by contiguity with the totality of the events which precede and also with those which follow it. Yet at the point in space where our action is concentrated, contiguity brings back, in the form of movement, only the reaction which immediately followed a former similar perception. As a matter of fact, every association by contiguity implies a position of the mind intermediate between the two extreme limits. If, here again, we imagine a number of possible repetitions of the totality of our memories, each of these copies of our past life must be supposed to be cut up, in its own way, into definite parts, and the cutting up is not the same when we pass from one copy to another, each of them being in fact characterized by the particular kind of dominant memories on which the other memories lean as on supporting points. The nearer we come to action, for instance, the more contiguity tends to approximate to similarity and to be thus distinguished from a mere relation of chronological succession: thus we cannot say of the words of a foreign language, when they call each other up in memory, whether they are associated by similarity or by contiguity. On the contrary, the more we detach ourselves from action, real or possible, the more association by contiguity tends merely to reproduce the consecutive images of our past life. It is impossible to enter here into a profound study of these different systems. But it is sufficient to point out that these systems are not formed of recollections laid side by side like so many atoms. There are always some dominant memories, shining points round which the others form a vague nebulosity. These shining points are multiplied in the degree to which our memory expands. The process of localizing a recollection in the past, for instance, cannot at all consist, as has been said, in plunging into the mass of our memories, as into a bag, to draw out memories, closer and closer to each other, between which the memory to be localized may find its place. By what happy chance could we just hit upon a growing number of intercalary recollections? The work of localization consists, in reality, in a growing effort of *expansion*, by which the memory, always present in its entirety to itself, spreads out its recollections over an ever wider surface and so ends by distinguishing, in what was till then a confused mass, the remembrance which could not find its proper place. Here again, moreover, the pathology of memory is instructive. In retrogressive amnesia, the recollections which disappear from consciousness are probably preserved in remote planes of memory, and the patient can find them there by an exceptional effort like that which is effected in the hypnotic state. But, on the lower planes, these memories await, so to speak, the dominant image to which they may be fastened. A sharp shock, a violent emotion, forms the decisive event to which they cling; if this event, by reason of its sudden character, is cut off from the rest of our history, they follow it into oblivion. We can understand, then, that the oblivion which follows a physical or moral shock should include the events which immediately preceded it — a phenomenon which is very difficult to explain in all other conceptions of memory. Let us remark in passing that if we refuse to attribute some such waiting to recent, and even to relatively distant, recollections, the normal work of memory becomes unintelligible. For every event of which the recollection is now imprinted on the memory, however simple we suppose it to be, has occupied a certain time. The perceptions, which filled the first period of this interval, and now form with the later perceptions an undivided memory, were then really "loose" as long as the decisive part of the event had not occurred and drawn them along. Between the disappearance of a memory with its various preliminary details, and the abolition, in retrogressive amnesia, of a greater or less number of recollections previous to a given event, there is, then, merely a difference of degree, not of kind.

From these various considerations on the lower mental life results a certain view of intellectual equilibrium. This equilibrium will be upset only by a perturbation of the elements which serve as its matter. We cannot here go into questions of mental pathology; yet neither can we avoid them entirely, since we are endeavoring to discover the exact relation between body and mind.

We have supposed that the mind travels unceasingly over the interval comprised between its two extreme limits, the plane of action and the plane of dream. Let us suppose that we have to make a decision. Collecting, organizing the totality of its experience in what we call its character, the mind causes it to converge upon actions in which we shall afterwards find, together with the past which is their matter, the unforeseen form which is stamped upon them by personality; but the action is not able to become real unless it succeeds in encasing itself in the actual situation, that is to say, in that particular assemblage of circumstances which is due to the particular position of the body in time and space. Let us suppose that we have to do a piece of intellectual work, to form a conception, to extract a more or less general idea from the multiplicity of our recollections. A wide margin is left to fancy, on the one hand, to logical discernment on the other hand; but, if the idea is to live, it must touch present reality on some side; that is to say, it must be able, from step to step, and by progressive diminutions or contractions of itself, to be more or less acted by the body at the same time as it is thought by the mind. Our body, with the sensations which it receives on the one hand and the movements which it is capable of executing on the other hand, is then, that which fixes our mind, and gives it ballast and poise. The activity of the mind goes far beyond the mass of accumulated memories, as this mass of memories itself is infinitely more than the sensations and movements of the present hour; but these sensations and these movements condition what we may term our *attention to life*, and that is why everything depends on their cohesion in the normal work of the mind, as in a pyramid which should stand upon its apex.

If, moreover, we cast a glance at the minute structure of the nervous system as recent discoveries have revealed it to us, we see everywhere conducting lines, nowhere any centers. Threads placed end to end, of which the extremities probably touch when the current passes: this is all that is seen. And perhaps this is all there is, if it is true that the body is only a place of meeting and transfer, where stimulations received result in movements accomplished, as we have supposed it to be throughout this work. But these threads, which receive disturbances or stimulations from the external world and return them to it in the form of appropriate reactions, these threads so beautifully stretched from the periphery to the periphery, are just what ensure by the solidity of these connections and the precision of their interweaving the sensori-motor equilibrium of the body, that is to say, its adaptation to the present circumstances. Relax this tension or destroy this equilibrium: everything happens as if attention detached itself from life. Dreams and insanity appear to be little else than this.

We were speaking just now of the recent hypothesis which attributes sleep to an interruption of the solidarity among the neurons. Even if we do not accept this hypothesis (which is, however, confirmed by some curious experiments), we must suppose, in deep sleep, at least a functional break in the relation established in the nervous system between stimulation and motor reaction. So dreams would always be the state of a mind of which the attention was not fixed by the sensori-motor equilibrium of the body. And it appears more and more probable that this relaxing of tension in the nervous system is due to the poisoning of its elements by products of their normal activity accumulated in the waking state. Now, in every way, dreams imitate insanity. Not only are all the psychological symptoms of madness found in dreams – to such a degree that the comparison of the two states has become a commonplace – but insanity appears also to have its origin in an exhaustion of the brain, which is caused, like normal fatigue, by the accumulation of certain specific poisons in the elements of the nervous system.[4] We know that insanity is often a sequel to infectious diseases, and that, moreover, it is possible to reproduce experimentally, by toxic drugs, all the phenomena of madness.[5] Is it not likely, therefore, that the loss of mental equilibrium in the insane is simply the result of a disturbance of the sensori-motor relations established in the organism? This disturbance may be enough to create a sort of psychic vertigo and so cause memory and attention to lose contact with reality. If we read the descriptions given by some mad patients of the beginning of their malady, we find that they often feel a sensation of strangeness, or, as they say, of "unreality," as if the things they perceived had for them lost solidity and relief.[6] If our analyses are correct, the concrete feeling

that we have of present reality consists, in fact, of our consciousness of the actual movements whereby our organism is naturally
responding to stimulation; so that where the connecting links
between sensations and movements are slackened or tangled, the
sense of the real grows weaker, or disappears.[7]

There are here, moreover, many distinctions to be made, not
only between the various forms of insanity, but also between properly so-called insanity and that division of the personality which
recent psychology has so ingeniously compared with it.[8] In these
diseases of personality, it seems that groups of recollections detach
themselves from the central memory and forego their solidarity
with the others. But, then, it seldom occurs that the patient does
not also display accompanying scissions of sensibility and of motor
activity.[9] We cannot help seeing in these latter phenomena the
real material substratum of the former. If it be true that our intellectual life rests, as a whole, upon its apex, that is to say, upon the
sensori-motor functions by which it inserts itself into present reality, intellectual equilibrium will be differently affected as these
functions are damaged in one manner or in another. Now, besides
the lesions which affect the general vitality of the sensori-motor
functions, weakening or destroying what we have called the sense
of reality, there are others which reveal themselves in a mechanical, not a dynamical, diminution of these functions, as if certain
sensori-motor connections merely parted company with the rest.
If we are right in our hypothesis, memory is very differently affected
in the two cases. In the first, no recollection is taken away, but all
recollections are less ballasted, less solidly directed toward the
real; from this a true disturbance of the mental equilibrium arises.
In the second, the equilibrium is not destroyed, but it loses something of its complexity. Recollections retain their normal aspect,
but forego a part of their solidarity, because their sensori-motor
base, instead of being, so to speak, chemically changed, is mechani-

cally diminished. But neither in the one case nor in the other are memories directly attacked or damaged.

The idea that the body preserves memories in the mechanical form of cerebral deposits, that the loss or decrease of memory consists in their more or less complete destruction, whereas the heightening of memory and hallucination consists in an excess of their activity, is not, then, borne out either by reasoning or by facts. The truth is that there is one case, and one only, in which observation would seem at first to suggest this view: we mean aphasia, or, more generally, the disturbance of auditory or visual recognition. This is the only case in which the constant seat of the disorder is in a determined convolution of the brain; yet it is also precisely the case in which we do not find a mechanical, immediate and final destruction of certain definite recollections, but rather the gradual and functional weakening of the whole of the affected memory. And we have explained how the cerebral lesion may effect this weakening, without the necessity of supposing any sort of provision of memories stored in the brain. What the injury really attacks are the sensory and motor regions corresponding to this class of perception, and especially those adjuncts through which they may be set in motion from within, so that memory, finding nothing to catch hold of, ends by becoming practically powerless: now, in psychology, powerlessness means unconsciousness. In all other cases, the lesion observed or supposed, never definitely localized, acts by the disturbance which it causes to the whole of the sensori-motor connections, either by damaging or by breaking up this mass: whence results a breach or a simplifying of the intellectual equilibrium, and, by *ricochet*, the disorder or the disjunction of memory. The doctrine which makes of memory an immediate function of the brain – a doctrine which raises insoluble theoretical difficulties – a doctrine the complexity of which defies all imagination, and the results of which are incompatible

with the data of introspection – cannot even count upon the support of cerebral pathology. All the facts and all the analogies are in
favor of a theory which regards the brain as only an intermediary
between sensation and movement, which sees in this aggregate of
sensations and movements the pointed end of mental life – a point
ever pressed forward into the tissue of events, and, attributing thus
to the body the sole function of directing memory toward the
real and of binding it to the present, considers memory itself as
absolutely independent of matter. In this sense, the brain contributes to the recall of the useful recollection, but still more to
the provisional banishment of all the others. We cannot see how
memory could settle within matter; but we do clearly understand
how – according to the profound saying of a contemporary philosopher – materiality begets oblivion.[10]

CHAPTER IV

The Delimiting and Fixing of Images.

Perception and Matter.

Soul and Body.

One general conclusion follows from the first three chapters of this book: it is that the body, always turned toward action, has for its essential function to limit, with a view to action, the life of the spirit. In regard to representations it is an instrument of choice, and of choice alone. It can neither beget nor cause an intellectual state. Consider perception, to begin with. The body, by the place which at each moment it occupies in the universe, indicates the parts and the aspects of matter on which we can lay hold: our perception, which exactly measures our virtual action on things, thus limits itself to the objects which actually influence our organs and prepare our movements. Now let us turn to memory. The function of the body is not to store up recollections, but simply to choose, in order to bring back to distinct consciousness, by the real efficacy thus conferred on it, the useful memory, that which may complete and illuminate the present situation with a view to ultimate action. It is true that this second choice is much less strictly determined than the first, because our past experience is an individual and no longer a common experience, because we have always many different recollections equally capable of squaring with the same actual situation, and because nature cannot here,

179

as in the case of perception, have one inflexible rule for delimiting our representations. A certain margin is, therefore, necessarily left in this case to fancy; though animals scarcely profit by it, bound as they are to material needs, it would seem that the human mind ceaselessly presses with the totality of its memory against the door which the body may half open to it: hence the play of fancy and the work of imagination — so many liberties which the mind takes with nature. It is nonetheless true that the orientation of our consciousness toward action appears to be the fundamental law of our psychical life.

Strictly speaking, we might stop here, for this work was undertaken to define the function of the body in the life of the spirit. But, on the one hand, we have raised by the way a metaphysical problem which we cannot bring ourselves to leave in suspense; on the other hand, our researches, although mainly psychological, have on several occasions given us glimpses, if not of the means of solving the problem, at any rate of the side on which it should be approached.

This problem is no less than that of the union of soul and body. It comes before us clearly and with urgency because we make a profound distinction between matter and spirit. And we cannot regard it as insoluble, since we define spirit and matter by positive characters, and not by negations. It is in very truth within matter that pure perception places us, and it is really into spirit that we penetrate by means of memory. But, on the other hand, while introspection reveals to us the distinction between matter and spirit, it also bears witness to their union. Either, then, our analyses are vitiated *ab origine*, or they must help us to issue from the difficulties that they raise.

The obscurity of this problem, in all doctrines, is due to the double antithesis which our understanding establishes between the extended and the unextended on the one side and between quality and quantity on the other side. It is certain that mind, first of all, stands over against matter as a pure unity in face of an essentially divisible multiplicity; moreover, our perceptions are composed of heterogeneous qualities, whereas the perceived universe seems to resolve itself into homogeneous and calculable changes. There would thus be inextension and quality, on the one hand, extensity and quantity, on the other hand. We have repudiated materialism, which derives the first term from the second; but neither do we accept idealism, which holds that the second is constructed by the first. We maintain, as against materialism, that perception overflows infinitely the cerebral state; but we have endeavored to establish, as against idealism, that matter goes in every direction beyond our representation of it, a representation which the mind has gathered out of it, so to speak, by an intelligent choice. Of these two opposite doctrines, the one attributes to the body and the other to the intellect a true power of creation, the first insisting that our brain begets representation and the second that our understanding designs the plan of nature. And against these two doctrines we invoke the same testimony, that of consciousness, which shows us our body as one image among others and our understanding as a certain faculty of dissociating, of distinguishing, of opposing logically, but not of creating or of constructing. Thus, willing captives of psychological analysis and, consequently, of common sense, it would seem that, after having exacerbated the conflicts raised by ordinary dualism, we have closed all the avenues of escape which metaphysic might set open to us.

But, just because we have pushed dualism to an extreme, our analysis has perhaps dissociated its contradictory elements. The theory of pure perception, on the one hand, of pure memory, on the other hand, may thus prepare the way for a reconciliation between the unextended and the extended, between quality and quantity.

To take pure perception first. When we make the cerebral state the beginning of an action, and in no sense the condition of a perception, we place the perceived images of things outside the image of our body, and thus replace perception within the things themselves. But then, our perception being a part of things, things participate in the nature of our perception. Material extensity is not, cannot any longer be, that composite extensity which is considered in geometry; it indeed resembles rather the undivided extension of our own representation. That is to say, the analysis of pure perception allows us to foreshadow in the idea of *extension* the possible approach to each other of the extended and the unextended.

But our conception of pure memory should lead us, by a parallel road, to attenuate the second opposition, that of quality and quantity. For we have radically separated pure recollection from the cerebral state which continues it and renders it efficacious. Memory is, then, in no degree an emanation of matter; on the contrary, matter, as grasped in concrete perception which always occupies a certain duration, is in great part the work of memory. Now where is, precisely, the difference between the heterogeneous qualities which succeed each other in our concrete perception and the homogeneous changes which science puts at the back of these perceptions in space? The first are discontinuous and cannot be deduced one from another; the second, on the contrary, lend themselves to calculation. But, in order that they may lend themselves to calculation, there is no need to make them into pure quantities: we might as well say that they are nothing at all. It is enough that their heterogeneity should be, so to speak, sufficiently diluted to become, from our point of view, practically negligible. Now, if every concrete perception, however short we suppose it, is already a synthesis, made by memory, of an infinity of "pure perceptions" which succeed each other, must we not think that the heterogeneity of sensible qualities is due to their being contracted in our memory and the relative homogeneity of objective changes to the slackness of their natural tension? And might not the interval between quantity and quality be lessened by considerations of *tension*, as the distance between the extended and the unextended is lessened by considerations of extension?

Before entering on this question, let us formulate the general principle of the method we would apply. We have already made use of it in an earlier work and even, by implication, in the present essay.

That which is commonly called a *fact* is not reality as it appears to immediate intuition, but an adaptation of the real to the interests of practice and to the exigencies of social life. Pure intuition, external or internal, is that of an undivided continuity. We break up this continuity into elements laid side by side, which correspond in the one case to distinct *words*, in the other to independent *objects*. But, just because we have thus broken the unity of our original intuition, we feel ourselves obliged to establish between the severed terms a bond which can only then be external and superadded. For the living unity, which was one with internal continuity, we substitute the factitious unity of an empty diagram as lifeless as the parts which it holds together. Empiricism and dogmatism are, at bottom, agreed in starting from phenomena so reconstructed; they differ only in that dogmatism attaches itself more particularly to the form and empiricism to the matter. Empiricism, feeling indeed, but feeling vaguely, the artificial character of the relations which unite the terms together, holds to the terms and neglects the relations. Its error is not that it sets too high a value on experience, but that it substitutes for true experience, that experience which arises from the immediate contact of the mind with its object, an experience which is disarticulated and, therefore, most probably, disfigured — at any rate arranged for the greater facility of action and of language. Just because this parceling of the real has been effected in view of the exigencies of prac-

183

tical life, it has not followed the internal lines of the structure of things: for that very reason empiricism cannot satisfy the mind in regard to any of the great problems and, indeed, whenever it becomes fully conscious of its own principle, it refrains from putting them. Dogmatism discovers and disengages the difficulties to which empiricism is blind; however, it really seeks the solution along the very road that empiricism has marked out. It accepts, at the hands of empiricism, phenomena that are separate and discontinuous and simply endeavors to effect a synthesis of them which, not having been given by intuition, cannot but be arbitrary. In other words, if metaphysic is only a construction, there are several systems of metaphysic equally plausible, which consequently refute each other, and the last word must remain with a *critical* philosophy, which holds all knowledge to be relative and the ultimate nature of things to be inaccessible to the mind. Such is, in truth, the ordinary course of philosophic thought: we start from what we take to be experience, we attempt various possible arrangements of the fragments which apparently compose it, and when at last we feel bound to acknowledge the fragility of every edifice that we have built, we end by giving up all effort to build. But there is a last enterprise that might be undertaken. It would be to seek experience at its source, or rather above that decisive *turn* where, taking a bias in the direction of our utility, it becomes properly *human* experience. The impotence of speculative reason, as Kant has demonstrated it, is perhaps at bottom only the impotence of an intellect enslaved to certain necessities of bodily life and concerned with a matter which man has had to disorganize for the satisfaction of his wants. Our knowledge of things would thus no longer be relative to the fundamental structure of our mind, but only to its superficial and acquired habits, to the contingent form which it derives from our bodily functions and from our lower needs. The relativity of knowledge may not, then, be definitive. By

184

unmaking that which these needs have made, we may restore to intuition its original purity and so recover contact with the real.

This method presents, in its application, difficulties which are considerable and ever recurrent, because it demands for the solution of each new problem an entirely new effort. To give up certain habits of thinking, and even of perceiving, is far from easy: yet this is but the negative part of the work to be done; and when it is done, when we have placed ourselves at what we have called the *turn* of experience, when we have profited by the faint light which, illuminating the passage from the *immediate* to the *useful*, marks the dawn of our human experience, there still remains to be reconstituted, with the infinitely small elements which we thus perceive of the real curve, the curve itself stretching out into the darkness behind them. In this sense the task of the philosopher, as we understand it, closely resembles that of the mathematician who determines a function by starting from the differential. The final effort of philosophical research is a true work of integration.

We have already attempted to apply this method to the problem of consciousness;[1] and it appeared to us that the utilitarian work of the mind, in what concerns the perception of our inner life, consisted in a sort of refracting of pure duration into space, a refracting which permits us to separate our psychical states, to reduce them to a more and more impersonal form, and to impose names upon them – in short, to make them enter the current of social life. Empiricism and dogmatism assume interior states in this discontinuous form; the first confining itself to the states themselves, so that it can see in the self only a succession of juxtaposed facts; the other grasping the necessity of a bond, but unable to find this bond anywhere except in a form or in a force – an exterior form into which the aggregate is inserted, an indetermined and so to speak physical force which assures the cohesion of the elements. Hence the two opposing points of view as to the question of freedom: for determinism, the act is the resultant of a mechanical composition of the elements; for the adversaries of that doctrine, if they adhered strictly to their principle, the free decision would be an arbitrary *fiat*, a true creation ex nihilo. It seemed to us that a third course lay open. This is to replace ourselves in pure duration, of which the flow is continuous and in which we pass insensibly from one state to another: a continuity which is really lived, but artificially decomposed for the greater convenience of customary knowledge. Then, it seemed to us, we saw the action issue from its antecedents by an evolution sui generis, in such a way that we find in this action the antecedents which explain it, while it also adds to these something entirely new, being an advance upon them such as the fruit is upon the flower. Freedom is not hereby, as has been asserted, reduced to sensible spontaneity. At most, this would be the case in the animal, of which the psychical life is mainly affective. But, in man, the thinking being, the free act may be termed a synthesis of feelings and ideas and the evolution which leads to it a reasonable evolution. The artifice of this method simply consists, in short, in distinguishing the point of view of customary or useful knowledge from that of true knowledge. The duration *wherein we see ourselves acting*, and in which it is useful that we should see ourselves, is a duration whose elements are dissociated and juxtaposed. The duration *wherein we act* is a duration wherein our states melt into each other. It is within this that we should try to replace ourselves by thought, in the exceptional and unique case when we speculate on the intimate nature of action, that is to say, when we are discussing human freedom.

Is a method of this kind applicable to the problem of matter? The question is, whether, in this "diversity of phenomena" of which Kant spoke, that part which shows a vague tendency toward extension could be seized by us on the nearer side of the homogeneous space to which it is applied and through which we subdivide it —

just as that part which goes to make up our own inner life can be detached from time, empty and indefinite, and brought back to pure duration. Certainly, it would be a chimerical enterprise to try to free ourselves from the fundamental conditions of external perception. But the question is whether certain conditions, which we usually regard as fundamental, do not rather concern the use to be made of things, the practical advantage to be drawn from them, far more than the pure knowledge which we can have of them. More particularly, in regard to concrete extension, continuous, diversified and at the same time organized, we do not see why it should be bound up with the amorphous and inert space which subtends it — a space which we divide indefinitely, out of which we carve figures arbitrarily, and in which movement itself, as we have said elsewhere, can only appear as a multiplicity of instantaneous positions, since nothing there can ensure the coherence of past with present. It might, then, be possible, in a certain measure, to transcend space without stepping out from extensity; and here we should really have a return to the immediate, since we do indeed perceive extensity, whereas space is merely conceived — being a kind of mental diagram. It may be urged against this method that it arbitrarily attributes a privileged value to immediate knowledge? But what reasons should we have for doubting any knowledge — would the idea of doubting it ever occur to us — but for the difficulties and the contradictions which reflection discovers, but for the problems which philosophy poses? And would not immediate knowledge find in itself its justification and proof if we could show that these difficulties, contradictions and problems are mainly the result of the symbolic diagrams which cover it up, diagrams which have for us become reality itself, and beyond which only an intense and unusual effort can succeed in penetrating?

Let us choose immediately, among the results to which the application of this method may lead, those which concern our present enquiry. We must confine ourselves to mere suggestions; there can be no question here of constructing a theory of matter.

I. *Every movement, inasmuch as it is a passage from rest to rest, is absolutely indivisible.*

This is not an hypothesis, but a fact, generally masked by an hypothesis.

Here, for example, is my hand, placed at the point A. I carry it to the point B, passing at one stroke through the interval between them. There are two things in this movement: an image, which I see, and an act, of which my muscular sense makes my consciousness aware. My consciousness gives me the inward feeling of a single fact, for in A was rest, in B there is again rest, and between A and B is placed an indivisible or at least an undivided act, the passage from rest to rest, which is movement itself. But my sight perceives the movement in the form of a line AB, which is traversed, and this line, like all space, may be indefinitely divided. It seems then, at first sight, that I may at will take this movement to be multiple or indivisible, according as I consider it in space or in time, as an image which takes shape outside of me or as an act which I am myself accomplishing.

Yet, when I put aside all preconceived ideas, I soon perceive that I have no such choice, that even my sight takes in the movement from A to B as an indivisible whole, and that if it divides anything, it is the line supposed to have been traversed, and not the movement traversing it. It is indeed true that my hand does not go from A to B without passing through the intermediate positions, and that these intermediate points resemble stages, as numerous as you please, along the route; but there is, between the divisions so marked out and stages properly so-called, this capital difference, that at a stage we *halt*, whereas at these points the moving body *passes*. Now a passage is movement and a halt is an immobility. The halt interrupts the movement; the passage is one with the movement itself. When I see the moving body pass any point, I conceive, no doubt, that it *might* stop there; even when it does not stop there, I incline to consider its passage as an arrest, though infinitely short, because I must have at least the time to think of it; yet it is only my imagination which stops there, and what the moving body has to do is, on the contrary, to move. As every point of space necessarily appears to me fixed, I find it extremely difficult not to attribute to the moving body itself the immobility of the point with which, for a moment, I make it coincide; it seems to me, then, when I reconstitute the total movement, that the moving body has stayed an infinitely short time at every point of its trajectory. But we must not confound the data of the senses, which perceive the movement, with the artifice of the mind, which recomposes it. The senses, left to themselves, present to us the real movement, between two real halts, as a solid and undivided whole. The division is the work of our imagination, of which indeed the office is to fix the moving images of our ordinary experience, like the instantaneous flash which illuminates a stormy landscape by night.

We discover here, at its outset, the illusion which accompanies and masks the perception of real movement. Movement visibly consists in passing from one point to another and consequently, in traversing space. Now the space which is traversed is infinitely divisible; and as the movement is, so to speak, applied to the line along which it passes, it appears to be one with this line and, like it, divisible. Has not the movement itself drawn the line? Has it not traversed in turn the successive and juxtaposed points of that line? Yes, no doubt, but these points have no reality except in a line drawn, that is to say, motionless. And by the very fact that you represent the movement to yourself successively in these different points, you necessarily arrest it in each of them; your successive positions are, at bottom, only so many imaginary halts. You substitute the path for the journey, and because the journey is subtended by the path, you think that the two coincide. But how should a *progress* coincide with a *thing*, a movement with an immobility?

What facilitates this illusion is that we distinguish moments in the course of duration, like halts in the passage of the moving body. Even if we grant that the movement from one point to another forms an undivided whole, this movement, nevertheless, takes a certain time, so if we carve out of this duration an indivisible instant, it seems that the moving body must occupy, at that precise moment, a certain position, which thus stands out from the whole. The indivisibility of motion implies, then, the impossibility of real instants; indeed, a very brief analysis of the idea of duration will show us both why we attribute instants to duration and why it cannot have any. Suppose a simple movement, like that of my hand when it goes from A to B. This passage is given to my consciousness as an undivided whole. No doubt it endures; but this duration, which in fact coincides with the aspect which the movement has inwardly for my consciousness, is, like it, whole and undivided. Now while it presents itself, qua movement, as a simple movement, as a simple fact, it describes in space a trajectory which I may consider, for purposes of simplification, as a geometrical line, and the extremities of this line, considered as abstract limits, are no longer lines, but indivisible points. Now, if the line, which the moving body has described, measures for me the duration of its movement, must not the point, where the line ends, symbolize for me a terminus of this duration? And if this point is an indivisible of length, how shall we avoid terminating the duration of the movement by an indivisible of duration? If the total line represents the total duration, the parts of the line must, it seems, correspond to parts of the duration and the points of the line to moments in time. The indivisibles of duration, or moments of time, are born, then, of the need of symmetry; we come to them naturally as soon as we demand from space an integral presentment of duration. But herein, precisely, lies the error. While the line AB symbolizes the duration already lapsed of the movement from A to B already accomplished, it cannot, motionless, represent the movement in its accomplishment nor duration in its flow. And from the fact that this line is divisible into parts and that it ends in points, we cannot conclude either that the corresponding duration is composed of separate parts or that it is limited by instants.

The arguments of Zeno of Elea have no other origin than this illusion. They all consist in making time and movement coincide with the line which underlies them, in attributing to them the same subdivisions as to the line, in short, in treating them like that line. In this confusion Zeno was encouraged by common sense, which usually carries over to the movement the properties of its trajectory, and also by language, which always translates movement and duration in terms of space. But common sense and language have a right to do so and are even bound to do so, for, since they always regard the *becoming* as a *thing* to be made use of, they have no more concern with the interior organization of movement than a workman has with the molecular structure of his tools. In holding movement to be divisible, as its trajectory is, common sense merely expresses the two facts which alone are of importance in practical life: first, that every movement describes a space; second, that at every point of this space the moving body *might* stop. But the philosopher who reasons upon the inner nature of movement is bound to restore to it the mobility which is its essence, and this is what Zeno omits to do. By the first argument (the Dichotomy) he supposes the moving body to be at rest and then considers nothing but the stages, infinite in number, that are along the line to be traversed: we cannot imagine, he says, how the body could ever get through the interval between them. But, in this way, he merely proves that it is impossible to construct, a priori, movement with immobilities, a thing no man ever doubted. The sole question is whether, movement being posited as a fact, there is a sort of retrospective absurdity in assuming that an infinite number of points has been passed through. But at this we need not wonder, since movement is an undivided fact, or a series of undivided facts, whereas the trajectory is infinitely divisible. In the second argument (the Achilles) movement is indeed given; it is even attributed to two moving bodies, but, always by the same error, there is an assumption that their movement coincides with their path and that we may divide it, like the path itself, in any way we please. Then, instead of recognizing that the tortoise has the pace of a tortoise and Achilles the pace of Achilles, so that after a certain number of these indivisible acts or bounds Achilles will have outrun the tortoise, the contention is that we may disarticulate as we will the movement of Achilles and, as we will also, the movement of the tortoise: thus reconstructing both in an arbitrary way, according to a law of our own which may be incompatible with the real conditions of mobility. The same fallacy appears, yet more evident, in the third argument (the Arrow), which consists in the conclusion that, because it is possible to distinguish points on the path of a moving body, we have the right to distinguish indivisible moments in the duration of its movement. But the most instructive of Zeno's arguments is perhaps the fourth (the Stadium) which has, we believe, been unjustly disdained, and of which the absurdity is more manifest only because the postulate masked in the three others is here frankly displayed.[2] Without entering into a discussion which would be out of place here, we will content ourselves with observing that motion, as given to spontaneous perception, is a fact which is quite clear, and that the difficulties and contradictions pointed out by the Eleatic school concern far less the living movement itself than a dead and artificial reorganization of movement by the mind. But we now come to the conclusion of all the preceding paragraphs:

II. *There are* real *movements.*

The mathematician, expressing with greater precision an idea of common sense, defines position by the distance from points of reference or from axes, and movement by the variation of the distance. Of movement, then, he only retains changes in length; and as the absolute values of the variable distance between a point and an axis, for instance, express either the displacement of the axis with regard to the point or that of the point with regard to the axis, just as we please, he attributes indifferently to the same point, repose or motion. If, then, movement is nothing but a change of distance, the same object is in motion or motionless according to the points to which it is referred, and there is no absolute movement.

But things wear a very different aspect when we pass from mathematics to physics, and from the abstract study of motion to a consideration of the concrete changes occurring in the universe. Though we are free to attribute rest or motion to any material point taken by itself, it is nonetheless true that the aspect of the material universe changes, that the internal configuration of every real system varies, and that here we have no longer the choice between mobility and rest. Movement, whatever its inner nature, becomes an indisputable reality. We may not be able to say what parts of the whole are in motion; motion there is in the whole, nonetheless. Therefore, it is not surprising that the same thinkers, who maintain that every particular movement is relative, speak of the totality of movements as of an absolute. The contradiction has been pointed out in Descartes, who, after having given to the thesis of relativity its most radical form by affirming that all movement is "reciprocal,"[3] formulated the laws of motion as though motion were an absolute.[4] Leibniz and others after him have remarked this contradiction[5]: it is due simply to the fact that Descartes handles motion as a physicist after having defined it as a geometer. For the geometer all movement is relative: which signifies only, in our view, *that none of our mathematical symbols can express the fact that it is the moving body which is in motion rather than the axes or the points to which it is referred.* And this is very natural because these symbols, always meant for measurement, can express only distances. But that there is real motion no one can seriously deny: if there were not, nothing in the universe would change, and, above all, there would be no meaning in the consciousness which we have of our own movements. In his controversy with Descartes Henry More makes jesting allusion to this last point: "When I am quietly seated, and another, going a thousand paces away, is flushed with fatigue, it is certainly he who moves and I who am at rest."[6]

But if there is absolute motion, is it possible to persist in regarding movement as nothing but a change of place? We should then have to make diversity of place into an absolute difference and distinguish absolute positions in an absolute space. Newton[7] went as far as this, followed moreover by Euler[8] and by others. But can this be imagined, or even conceived? A place could be absolutely distinguished from another place only by its quality or by its relation to the totality of space: so space would become, on this hypothesis, either composed of heterogeneous parts or finite. But to finite space we should give another space as boundary, and beneath heterogeneous parts of space we should imagine an homogeneous space as its foundation: in both cases it is to homogeneous and indefinite space that we should necessarily return. We cannot, then, hinder ourselves either from holding every place to be relative or from believing some motion to be absolute.

It may be urged that real movement is distinguished from relative movement in that it has a real cause, that it emanates from a force. But we must understand what we mean by this last word. In natural science force is only a function of mass and velocity: it is measured by acceleration: it is known and estimated only by the movements which it is supposed to produce in space. One with these movements, it shares their relativity. Hence the physicists, who seek the principle of absolute motion in force defined in this way, are led by the logic of their system back to the hypothesis of an absolute space which they had at first desired to avoid.[9] So it will become necessary to take refuge in the metaphysical sense of the word and attribute the motion which we perceive in space to profound causes, analogous to those which our consciousness believes it discovers within the feeling of effort. But is the feeling of effort really the sense of a profound cause? Have not decisive analyses shown that there is nothing in this feeling other than the consciousness of movements already effected or begun at the periphery of the body? It is in vain, then, that we seek to found the reality of motion on a cause which is distinct from it: analysis always brings us back to motion itself.

But why seek elsewhere? So long as we apply a movement to the line along which it passes, the same point will appear to us, by turns, according to the points or the axes to which we refer it, either at rest or in movement. But it is otherwise if we draw out of the movement the mobility which is its essence. When my eyes give me the sensation of a movement, this sensation is a reality, and something is effectually going on, whether it is that an object is changing its place before my eyes or that my eyes are moving before the object. A fortiori I am assured of the reality of the movement when I produce it, after having willed to produce it, and my muscular sense brings me the consciousness of it. That is to say, I grasp the reality of movement when it appears to me, within me, as a change of *state* or of *quality*. But then how should it be otherwise when I perceive changes of quality in things? Sound differs absolutely from silence, and also one sound from another sound. Between light and darkness, between colors, between shades, the difference is absolute. The passage from one to another is also an absolutely real phenomenon. I hold then the two ends of the chain, muscular sensations within me, the sensible qualities of matter without me, and neither in the one case nor in the other do I see movement, if there be movement, as a mere relation: it is an absolute. Now, between these two extremities lie the movements of external *bodies*, properly so-called. How are we to distinguish here between real and apparent movement? Of what object, externally perceived, can it be said that it moves, of what other, that it remains motionless? To put such a question is to admit that the discontinuity established by common sense between objects independent of each other, having each its individuality, comparable to kinds of persons, is a valid distinction. For, on the contrary hypothesis, the question would no longer be how, in given *parts* of matter are changes of position produced, but how, in the *whole*, is a change of aspect effected — a change of which we should then have to ascertain the nature. Let us then formulate at once our third proposition:

III. *All division of matter into independent bodies with absolutely determined outlines is an artificial division.*

A body, that is, an independent material object, presents itself at first to us as a system of qualities in which resistance and color — the data of sight and touch — occupy the center, all the rest being, as it were, suspended from them. Yet the data of sight and touch are those which most obviously have extension in space, and the essential character of space is continuity. There are intervals of silence between sounds, for the sense of hearing is not always occupied, between odors, between tastes, there are gaps, as though the senses of smell and taste only functioned accidentally: as soon as we open our eyes, on the contrary, the whole field of vision takes on color; and, since solids are necessarily in contact with each other, our touch must follow the surface or the edges of objects without ever encountering a true interruption. How do we parcel out the continuity of material extensity, given in primary perception, into bodies of which each is supposed to have its substance and individuality? No doubt the aspect of this continuity changes from moment to moment; why then do we not purely and simply realize that the whole has changed, as with the turning of a kaleidoscope? Why, in short, do we seek, in the mobility of the whole, tracks that are supposed to be followed by bodies supposed to be in motion? A *moving continuity* is given to us, in which everything changes and yet remains: why then do we dissociate the two terms, permanence and change, and then represent permanence by *bodies* and change by *homogeneous movements* in space? This is no teaching of immediate intuition; but neither is it a demand of science, for the object of science is, on the contrary, to rediscover the natural articulations of a universe we have carved artificially. Moreover, science, as we shall see, by an evermore complete demonstration of the reciprocal action of all material points upon each other, returns, in spite of appearances, to the idea of universal continuity. Science and consciousness are agreed at bottom, provided that we regard consciousness in its most immediate data and science in its remotest aspirations. Why then the irresistible tendency to set up a material universe that is discontinuous, composed of bodies which have clearly defined outlines and change their place, that is, their relation with each other?

Besides consciousness and science, there is life. Beneath the principles of speculation, so carefully analyzed by philosophers, there are tendencies of which the study has been neglected, and which are to be explained simply by the necessity of living, that is, of acting. Already the power conferred on the individual consciousness of manifesting itself in acts requires the formation of distinct material zones, which correspond respectively to living bodies: in this sense, my own body and, by analogy with it, all other living bodies are those which I have the most right to distinguish in the continuity of the universe. But this body itself, as soon as it is constituted and distinguished, is led by its various needs to distinguish and constitute other bodies. In the humblest living being nutrition demands research, then contact, in short, a series of efforts which converge toward a center: this center is just what is made into an object — the object which will serve as food. Whatever the nature of matter, it may be said that life will at once establish in it a primary discontinuity, expressing the duality of the need and of that which must serve to satisfy it. But the need of food is not the only need. Others group themselves round it, all having for object the conservation of the individual or of the species; and each of them leads us to distinguish, besides our own body, bodies independent of it which we must seek or avoid. Our needs are, then, so many searchlights which, directed upon the continuity of sensible qualities, single out in it distinct bodies. They cannot satisfy themselves except upon the condition that they carve out, within this continuity, a body which is to be their own and then delimit other bodies with which the first can enter into relation, as if with persons. To establish these special relations among portions thus carved out from sensible reality is just what we call *living*.

But if this first subdivision of the real answers much less to immediate intuition than to the fundamental needs of life, are we likely to gain a better knowledge of things by pushing the division yet further? In this way we do indeed prolong the vital movement, but we turn our back upon true knowledge. That is why the rough-and-ready operation, which consists in decomposing the body into parts of the same nature as itself, leads us down a blind alley, where we soon feel ourselves incapable of conceiving either why this division should cease or how it could go on ad infinitum. It is nothing, in fact, but the ordinary condition of *useful action*, unsuitably transported into the domain of *pure knowledge*. We shall never explain by means of particles, whatever these may be, the simple properties of matter: at most we can thus follow into corpuscles as artificial as the *corpus* — the body itself — the actions and reactions of this body with regard to all the others. This is precisely the object of chemistry. It studies *bodies* rather than *matter*; and so we understand why it stops at the atom, which is still endowed with the general properties of matter. But the materiality of the atom dissolves more and more under the eyes of the physicist. We have no reason, for instance, for representing the atom to ourselves as a solid, rather than as liquid or gaseous, nor for picturing the reciprocal action of atoms by shocks rather than in any other way. Why do we think of a solid atom, and why do we think of shocks? Because solids, being the bodies on which we clearly have the most hold, are those which interest us most in our relations with the external world, and because contact is the only means which appears to be at our disposal in order to make our body act upon other bodies. But very simple experiments show that there is never true contact between two neighboring bodies[10], and besides, solidity is far from being an absolutely defined state of matter.[11] Solidity and shock borrow, then, their apparent clearness from the habits and necessities of practical life — images of this kind throw no light on the inner nature of things.

Moreover, if there is a truth that science has placed beyond dispute, it is that of the reciprocal action of all parts of matter upon each other. Between the supposed molecules of bodies the forces of attraction and repulsion are at work. The influence of gravitation extends throughout interplanetary space. Something, then, exists between the atoms. It will be said that this something is no longer matter, but force. And we shall be asked to picture to ourselves, stretched between the atoms, threads which will be made more and more tenuous, until they are invisible and even, we are told, immaterial. But what purpose can this crude image serve? The preservation of life no doubt requires that we should distinguish, in our daily experience, between passive *things* and *actions* effected by these things in space. As it is useful to us to fix the seat of the *thing* at the precise point where we might touch it, its palpable outlines become for us its real limit, and we then see in its *action* a something, I know not what, which, being altogether different, can part company with it. But since a theory of matter is an attempt to find the reality hidden beneath these customary images which are entirely relative to our needs, from these images it must first of all set itself free. And, indeed, we see force and matter drawing nearer together the more deeply the physicist has penetrated into their effects. We see force more and more materialized, the atom more and more idealized, the two terms converging toward a common limit and the universe thus recovering its continuity. We may still speak of atoms; the atom may even retain its individuality for our mind which isolates it, but the solidity and the inertia of the atom dissolve either into movements or into lines of force whose reciprocal solidarity brings back to us universal continuity. To this conclusion were bound to come, though they started from very different positions, the two physicists of the last century who have most closely investigated the constitution of matter, Lord Kelvin and Faraday. For Faraday the atom is a center of force. He means by this that the individuality of the atom consists in the mathematical point at which cross, radiating throughout space, the indefinite lines of force which really constitute it: thus each atom occupies the whole space to which gravitation extends and all atoms are interpenetrating.[12] Lord Kelvin, moving in another order of ideas, supposes a perfect, continuous, homogeneous and incompressible fluid, filling space: what we term an atom he makes into a vortex ring, ever whirling in this continuity, and owing its properties to its circular form, its existence and, consequently, its individuality to its motion.[13] But on either hypothesis, the nearer we draw to the ultimate elements of matter the better we note the vanishing of that discontinuity which our senses perceived on the surface. Psychological analysis has already revealed to us that this discontinuity is relative to our needs: every philosophy of nature ends by finding it incompatible with the general properties of matter.

In truth, vortices and lines of force are never, to the mind of the physicist, more than convenient figures for illustrating his calculations. But philosophy is bound to ask why these symbols are more convenient than others and why they permit of further advance. Could we, working with them, get back to experience, if the notions to which they correspond did not at least point out the direction in which we may seek for a representation of the real? Now the direction which they indicate is obvious; they show us, pervading concrete extensity, *modifications, perturbations*, changes of *tension* or of *energy* and nothing else. It is by this, above all, that they tend to unite with the purely psychological analysis of motion which we considered to begin with, an analysis which presented it to us not as a mere change of relation between objects to which it was, as it were, an accidental addition, but as a true and, in some way, independent, reality. Neither science nor consciousness, then, is opposed to this last proposition:

IV. *Real movement is rather the transference of a state than of a thing.*

By formulating these propositions, we have, in reality, only been progressively narrowing the interval between the two terms which it is usual to oppose to each other — qualities, or sensations, and movements. At first sight, the distance appears impassable. Qualities are heterogeneous, movements homogeneous. Sensations, essentially indivisible, escape measurement; movements, always divisible, are distinguished by calculable differences of direction and velocity. We are inclined to put qualities, in the form of sensations, in consciousness, while movements are supposed to take place independently of us in space. These movements, compounded together, we confess, will never yield anything but movements; our consciousness, though incapable of coming into touch with them, yet by a mysterious process is said to translate them into sensations, which afterwards project themselves into space and come to overlie, we know not how, the movements they translate. Hence two different worlds, incapable of communicating otherwise than by a miracle — on the one hand, that of motion in space, on the other hand, that of consciousness with sensations. Now certainly the difference is irreducible (as we have shown in an earlier work[14]) between quality on the one hand and pure quantity on the other. But this is just the question: do real movements present merely differences of quantity, or are they not quality itself, vibrating, so to speak, internally, and beating time for its own existence through an often incalculable number of moments? Motion, as studied in mechanics, is but an abstraction or a symbol, a common measure, a common denominator, permitting the comparison of all real movements with each other; yet these movements, regarded in themselves, are indivisibles which occupy duration, involve a before and an after, and link together the successive moments of time by a thread of variable quality which cannot be without some likeness to the continuity of our own consciousness. May we not conceive, for instance, that the irreducibility of two perceived colors is due mainly to the narrow duration into which are contracted the billions of vibrations which they execute in one of our moments? If we could stretch out this duration, that is to say, live it at a slower rhythm, should we not, as the rhythm slowed down, see these colors pale and lengthen into successive impressions, still colored, no doubt, but nearer and nearer to coincidence with pure vibrations? In cases where the rhythm of the movement is slow enough to tally with the habits of our consciousness — as in the case of the deep notes of the musical scale, for instance — do we not feel that the quality perceived analyzes itself into repeated and successive vibrations, bound together by an inner continuity? That which usually hinders this mutual approach of motion and quality is the acquired habit of attaching movement to elements — atoms or what not — which interpose their solidity between the movement itself and the quality into which it contracts. As our daily experience shows us bodies in motion, it appears to us that there ought to be, in order to sustain the elementary movements to which qualities may be reduced, diminutive bodies or corpuscles. Motion becomes then for our imagination no more than an accident, a series of positions, a change of relations; and, as it is a law of our representation that the stable drives away the unstable, the important and central element for us becomes the atom, between the successive positions of which movement then becomes a mere link. But not only has this conception the inconvenience of merely carrying over to the atom all the problems raised by matter; not only does it wrongly set up as an absolute that division of matter which, in our view, is hardly anything but an outward projection of human needs; it also renders unintelligible the process by which we grasp, in perception, at one and the same time, a *state* of our consciousness and a *reality* independent of ourselves. This mixed character of our immediate perception, this appearance of a realized contradiction, is the principal theoretical reason that we have for believing in an external world which does not coincide absolutely with our perception. As it is overlooked in the doctrine that regards sensation as entirely heterogeneous with movements, of which sensation is then supposed to be only a translation into the language of consciousness, this doctrine ought, it would seem, to confine itself to sensations, which it had indeed begun to do by setting them up as the actual data, and not add to them movements which, having no possible contact with them, are no longer anything but their useless duplicate. Realism, so understood, is self-destructive. Indeed we have no choice: if our belief in a more or less homogeneous substratum of sensible qualities has any ground, this can only be found in an *act* which makes us seize or divine, *in quality itself*, something which goes beyond sensation, as if this sensation itself were pregnant with details suspected yet unperceived. Its objectivity — that is to say, what it contains over and above what it yields up — must then consist, as we have foreshadowed, precisely in the immense multiplicity of the movements which it executes, so to speak, within itself as a chrysalis. Motionless on the surface, in its very depth it lives and vibrates.

As a matter-of-fact, no one represents to himself the relation between quantity and quality in any other way. To believe in realities, distinct from that which is perceived, is above all to recognize that the order of our perceptions depends on them, and not on us. There must be, then, within the perceptions which fill a given moment, the reason of what will happen in the following moment. And mechanism only formulates this belief with more precision when it affirms that the states of matter can be deduced one from the other. It is true that this deduction is possible only if we discover, beneath the apparent heterogeneity of sensible quali-

ties, homogeneous elements which lend themselves to calculation. But if these elements are external to the qualities of which
they are meant to explain the regular order, they can no longer
render the service demanded of them, because then the qualities
must be supposed to come to overlie them by a kind of miracle,
and cannot correspond to them unless we bring in some pre-
established harmony. So, do what we will, we cannot avoid placing
those movements *within* these qualities, in the form of internal
vibrations, and then considering the vibrations as less homogeneous, and the qualities as less heterogeneous, than they appear,
and lastly attributing the difference of aspect in the two terms to
the necessity which lies upon what may be called an endless multiplicity of contracting into a duration too narrow to permit the
separation of its moments.

We must insist on this last point, to which we have already
alluded elsewhere, and which we regard as essential. The duration lived by our consciousness is a duration with its own determined rhythm, a duration very different from the time of the
physicist, which can store up, in a given interval, as great a number of phenomena as we please. In the space of a second, red light
— the light which has the longest wavelength, and of which, consequently, the vibrations are the least frequent — accomplishes
400 billion successive vibrations. If we would form some idea of
this number, we should have to separate the vibrations sufficiently
to allow our consciousness to count them or at least to record
explicitly their succession, and we should then have to enquire
how many days or months or years this succession would occupy.
Now the smallest interval of empty time which we can detect
equals, according to Exner, 0.002 seconds; and it is even doubt-
ful whether we can perceive in succession several intervals as short
as this. Let us admit, however, that we can go on doing so indefinitely. Let us imagine, in a word, a consciousness which should

watch the succession of 400 billion vibrations, each instantaneous, and each separated from the next only by the 0.002 of a second necessary to distinguish them. A very simple calculation shows that more than 25,000 years would elapse before the conclusion of the operation. Thus the sensation of red light, experienced by us in the course of a second, corresponds in itself to a succession of phenomena which, separately distinguished in our duration with the greatest possible economy of time, would occupy more than 250 centuries of our history. Is this conceivable? We must distinguish here between our own duration and time in general. In our duration – the duration which our consciousness perceives – a given interval can only contain a limited number of phenomena of which we are aware. Do we conceive that this content can increase; and when we speak of an infinitely divisible time, is it our own duration that we are thinking of?

As long as we are dealing with space, we may carry the division as far as we please; we change in no way, thereby, the nature of what is divided. This is because space, by definition, is outside us; it is because a part of space appears to us to subsist even when we cease to be concerned with it; so, even when we leave it undivided, we know that it can wait and that a new effort of our imagination may decompose it when we choose. As, moreover, it never ceases to be space, it always implies juxtaposition and, consequently, possible division. Abstract space is, indeed, at bottom, nothing but the mental diagram of infinite divisibility. But, with duration, it is quite otherwise. The parts of our duration are one with the successive moments of the act which divides it; if we distinguish in it so many instants, so many parts it indeed possesses; and if our consciousness can only distinguish in a given interval a definite number of elementary acts, if it terminates the division at a given point, there also terminates the divisibility. In vain does our imagination endeavor to go on, to carry division further still,

206

and to quicken, so to speak, the circulation of our inner phenomena: the very effort by which we are trying to effect this further division of our duration lengthens that duration by just so
much. And yet we know that millions of phenomena succeed each
other while we hardly succeed in counting a few. We know this
not from physics alone; the crude experience of the senses allows
us to divine it; we are dimly aware of successions in nature much
more rapid than those of our internal states. How are we to conceive them, and what is this duration of which the capacity goes
beyond all our imagination?

It is not ours, assuredly; but neither is it that homogeneous
and impersonal duration, the same for everything and for every
one, which flows onward, indifferent and void, external to all that
endures. This imaginary homogeneous time is, as we have endeavored to show elsewhere,[15] an idol of language, a fiction whose
origin is easy to discover. In reality there is no one rhythm of duration; it is possible to imagine many different rhythms which, slower
or faster, measure the degree of tension or relaxation of different
kinds of consciousness and thereby fix their respective places in
the scale of being. To conceive of durations of different tensions is
perhaps both difficult and strange to our mind, because we have
acquired the useful habit of substituting for the true duration, lived
by consciousness, an homogeneous and independent Time; however, in the first place, it is easy, as we have shown, to detect the
illusion which renders such a thought foreign to us, and, secondly,
this idea has in its favor, at bottom, the tacit agreement of our
consciousness. Do we not sometimes perceive in ourselves, in sleep,
two contemporaneous and distinct persons one of whom sleeps a
few minutes, while the other's dream fills days and weeks? And
would not the whole of history be contained in a very short time
for a consciousness at a higher degree of tension than our own,
which should watch the development of humanity while contract-

ing it, so to speak, into the great phases of its evolution? In short, then, to perceive consists in condensing enormous periods of an infinitely diluted existence into a few more differentiated moments of an intenser life, and in thus summing up a very long history. To perceive means to immobilize.

To say this is to say that we seize, in the act of perception, something which outruns perception itself, although the material universe is not essentially different or distinct from the representation which we have of it. In one sense, my perception is indeed truly within me, since it contracts into a single moment of my duration that which, taken in itself, spreads over an incalculable number of moments. But, if you abolish my consciousness, the material universe subsists exactly as it was; only, since you have removed that particular rhythm of duration which was the condition of my action upon things, these things draw back into themselves, mark as many moments in their own existence as science distinguishes in it; and sensible qualities, without vanishing, are spread and diluted in an incomparably more divided duration. Matter thus resolves itself into numberless vibrations, all linked together in uninterrupted continuity, all bound up with each other, and traveling in every direction like shivers through an immense body. In short, try first to connect together the discontinuous objects of daily experience; then, resolve the motionless continuity of their qualities into vibrations on the spot; finally, fix your attention on these movements, by abstracting from the divisible space which underlies them and considering only their mobility (that undivided act which our consciousness becomes aware of in our own movements): you will thus obtain a vision of matter, fatiguing perhaps for your imagination, but pure, and freed from all that the exigencies of life compel you to add to it in external perception. Now bring back consciousness, and with it the exigencies of life: at long, very long, intervals, and by as many leaps over enormous periods of the inner history of things, quasi-instantaneous views will be taken, views which this time are bound to be pictorial, and of which the more vivid colors will condense an infinity of elementary repetitions and changes. In just the same way the multitudinous successive positions of a runner are contracted into a single symbolic attitude, which our eyes perceive, which art reproduces, and which becomes for us all the image of a man running. The glance which falls at any moment on the things about us only takes in the effects of a multiplicity of inner repetitions and evolutions, effects which are, for that very reason, discontinuous, and into which we bring back continuity by the relative movements that we attribute to "objects" in space. The change is everywhere, but inward; we localize it here and there, but outwardly; thus we constitute bodies which are both stable as to their qualities and mobile as to their positions, a mere change of place summing up in itself, to our eyes, the universal transformation.

That there are, in a sense, multiple objects, that one man is distinct from another man, tree from tree, stone from stone, is an indisputable fact; for each of these beings, each of these things, has characteristic properties and obeys a determined law of evolution. But the separation between a thing and its environment cannot be absolutely definite and clear-cut; there is a passage by insensible gradations from the one to the other: the close solidarity which binds all the objects of the material universe, the perpetuality of their reciprocal actions and reactions, is sufficient to prove that they have not the precise limits which we attribute to them. Our perception outlines, so to speak, the form of their nucleus; it terminates them at the point where our possible action upon them ceases, where, consequently, they cease to interest our needs. Such is the primary and the most apparent operation of the perceiving mind: it marks out divisions in the continuity of the extended, simply following the suggestions of our requirement and the needs of practical life. But, in order to divide the real in this manner, we must first persuade ourselves that the real is divisible at will. Consequently we must throw beneath the continuity of sensible qualities, that is to say, beneath concrete extensity, a network, of which the meshes may be altered to any shape whatsoever and become as small as we please: this substratum which is merely conceived, this wholly ideal diagram of arbitrary and infinite divisibility, is homogeneous space. Now, at the same time that our actual and so to speak instantaneous perception effects this division of matter into independent objects, our memory solidifies into sensible qualities the continuous flow of things. It prolongs the past into the present, because our action will dispose of the future in the exact proportion in which our perception, enlarged by memory, has contracted the past. To reply, to an action received, by an immediate reaction which adopts the rhythm of the first and continues it in the same duration, to be in the present and in a present which is always beginning again — this is the fundamental law of matter: herein consists *necessity*. If there are actions that are really *free*, or at least partly indeterminate, they can only belong to beings able to fix, at long intervals, that becoming to which their own becoming clings, able to solidify it into distinct moments, and so to condense matter and, by assimilating it, to digest it into movements of reaction which will pass through the meshes of natural necessity. The greater or lesser tension of their duration, which expresses, at bottom, their greater or lesser intensity of life, thus determines both the degree of the concentrating power of their perception and the measure of their liberty. The independence of their action upon surrounding matter becomes more and more assured in the degree that they free themselves from the particular rhythm which governs the flow of this matter. So that sensible qualities, as they are found in our memory-shot perception, are, in fact, the successive moments obtained by a solidification of the real. But, in order to distinguish these moments, and also to bind them together by a thread which shall be common alike to our own existence and to that of things, we are bound to imagine a diagrammatic design of succession in general, an homogeneous and indifferent medium, which is to the flow of matter in the sense of length as space is to it in the sense of breadth: herein consists homogeneous time.

Homogeneous space and homogeneous time are then neither properties of things nor essential conditions of our faculty of knowing them: they express, in an abstract form, the double work of solidification and of division which we effect on the moving continuity of the real in order to obtain there a fulcrum for our action, in order to fix within it starting points for our operation, in short, to introduce into it real changes. They are the diagrammatic design of our eventual action upon matter. The first mistake, which consists in viewing this homogeneous time and space as properties of things, leads to the insurmountable difficulties of metaphysical dogmatism – whether mechanistic or dynamistic – dynamism erecting into so many absolutes the successive crosscuts which we make in the course of the universe as it flows along, and then endeavoring vainly to bind them together by a kind of qualitative deduction; mechanism attaching itself rather, in any one of these crosscuts, to the divisions made in its breadth, that is to say, to instantaneous differences in magnitude and position, and striving no less vainly to produce, by the variation of these differences, the succession of sensible qualities. Shall we then seek refuge in the other hypothesis, and maintain, with Kant, that space and time are forms of our sensibility? If we do, we shall have to look upon matter and spirit as equally unknowable. Now, if we compare these two hypotheses, we discover in them a common basis: by setting up homogeneous time and homogeneous space either as realities that are contemplated or as forms of contemplation, they both attribute to space and time an interest which is *speculative* rather than *vital*. Hence there is room, between metaphysical dogmatism, on the one hand, and critical philosophy, on the other hand, for a doctrine which regards homogeneous space and time as principles of division and of solidification introduced into the real, with a view to action and not with a view to knowledge, which attributes to things a real duration and a real extensity, and which, in the end, sees the source of all difficulty no longer in that duration and in that extensity (which really belong to things and are directly manifest to the mind), but in the homogeneous space and time which we stretch out beneath them in order to divide the continuous, to fix the becoming, and provide our activity with points to which it can be applied.

But our erroneous conceptions about sensible quality and space are so deeply rooted in the mind that it is important to attack them from every side. We may say then, to reveal yet another aspect, that they imply this double postulate, accepted equally by realism and by idealism: first, that between different kinds of qualities there is nothing common, and second, that neither is there anything common between extensity and pure quality. We maintain, on the contrary, that there is something common between qualities of different orders, that they all share in extensity, though in different degrees, and that it is impossible to overlook these two truths without entangling in a thousand difficulties the metaphysic of matter, the psychology of perception and, more generally, the problem of the relation of consciousness with matter. Without insisting on these consequences, let us content ourselves for the moment with showing, in the various theories of matter, the two postulates which we dispute and the illusion from which they proceed.

The essence of English idealism is to regard extensity as a property of tactile perceptions. As it sees nothing in sensible qualities but sensations, and in sensations themselves nothing but mental states, it finds in the different qualities nothing on which to base the parallelism of their phenomena. It is therefore constrained to account for this parallelism by a habit which makes the actual perceptions of sight, for instance, suggest to us potential sensations of touch. If the impressions of two different senses resemble each other no more than the words of two languages, we shall seek in vain to deduce the data of the one from the data of the other. They have no common element; consequently, there is nothing common between extensity, which is always tactile, and the data of the senses other than that of touch, which must then be supposed to be in no way extended.

But neither can atomistic realism, which locates movements in space and sensations in consciousness, discover anything in common between the modifications or phenomena of extensity and the sensations which correspond to them. Sensations are supposed to issue from the modification as a kind of phosphorescence, or, again, to translate into the language of the soul the manifestations of matter; but in neither case do they reflect, we are told, the image of their causes. No doubt they may all be traced to a common origin, which is movement in space; but, just because they develop outside of space, they must forego, qua sensations, the kinship which binds their causes together. In breaking with space they break also their connection with each other; they have nothing in common between them, nor with extensity.

Idealism and realism, then, only differ in that the first relegates extensity to tactile perception, of which it becomes the exclusive property, while the second thrusts extensity yet further back, outside of all perception. But the two doctrines are agreed in maintaining the discontinuity of the different orders of sensible qualities, and also the abrupt transition from that which is purely extended to that which is not extended at all. Now the principal

213

difficulties which they both encounter in the theory of perception arise from this common postulate.

For suppose, to begin with, as Berkeley did, that all perception of extensity is to be referred to the sense of touch. We may, indeed, if you will have it so, deny extension to the data of hearing, smell and taste; however, we must at least explain the genesis of a visual space that corresponds to tactile space. It is alleged, indeed, that sight ends by becoming symbolic of touch and that there is nothing more in the visual perception of the order of things in space than a suggestion of tactile perception. But we fail to understand how the visual perception of relief, for instance, a perception which makes upon us an impress sui generis, and indeed indescribable, could ever be one with the mere remembrance of a sensation of touch. The association of a memory with a present perception may complicate this perception by enriching it with an element already known, but it cannot *create* a new kind of impress, a new quality of perception: now the visual perception of relief presents an absolutely original character. It may be urged that it is possible to give the illusion of relief with a plane surface. This only proves that a surface, where the play of light and shadow on an object in relief is more or less well imitated, is enough to *remind* us of relief; but how could we be reminded of relief if relief had not been, at first, actually perceived? We have already said, but cannot repeat too often, that our theories of perception are entirely vitiated by the idea that if a certain arrangement produces, at a given moment, the illusion of a certain perception, it must always have been able to produce the perception itself – as if the very function of memory were not to make the complexity of the effect survive the simplification of the cause! Again, it may be urged that the retina itself is a plane surface, and that if we perceive by sight something that is extended, it can only be the image on the retina. But is it not true, as we have shown at the beginning of this

214

book, that in the visual perception of an object the brain, nerves, retina *and the object itself* form a connected whole, a continuous process in which the image on the retina is only an episode? By what right, then, do we isolate this image to sum up in it the whole of perception? And then, as we have also shown,[16] how could a surface be perceived as a surface otherwise than in a space that has recovered its three dimensions? Berkeley, at least, carried out his theory to its conclusion; he denied to sight any perception of extensity. But the objections which we raised only acquire the more force from this, since it is impossible to understand the spontaneous creation, by a mere association of memories, of all that is original in our visual perceptions of line, surface and volume, perceptions so distinct that the mathematician does not go beyond them and works with a space that is purely visual. But we will not insist on these various points, nor on the disputable arguments drawn from the observation of those, born blind, whose sight has been surgically restored: the theory of the acquired perceptions of sight, classical since Berkeley's day, does not seem likely to resist the multiplied attacks of contemporary psychology.[17] Passing over the difficulties of a psychological order, we will content ourselves with drawing attention to another point, in our opinion, essential. Suppose for a moment that the eye does not, at the outset, give us any information as to any of the relations of space. Visual form, visual relief, visual distance, then become the symbols of tactile perceptions. But how is it, then, that this symbolism succeeds? Here are objects which change their shape and move. Vision takes note of definite changes which touch afterwards verifies. There is, then, in the two series, visual and tactile, or in their causes, something which makes them correspond one to another and ensures the constancy of their parallelism. What is the principle of this connection?

For English idealism, it can only be some deus ex machina,

and we are confronted with a mystery again. For ordinary realism, it is in a space distinct from the sensations themselves that the principle of the correspondence of sensations one with another lies. But this doctrine only throws the difficulty further back and even aggravates it, for we shall now want to know how a system of homogeneous movements in space evokes various sensations which have no resemblance whatever with them. Just now the genesis of visual perception of space by a mere association of images appeared to us to imply a real creation ex nihilo; here all the sensations are born of nothing or at least have no resemblance with the movement that occasions them. In the main, this second theory differs much less from the first than is commonly believed. Amorphous space, atoms jostling against each other, are only our tactile perceptions made objective, set apart from all our other perceptions on account of the special importance which we attribute to them, and made into independent realities — thus contrasting with the other sensations which are then supposed to be only the symbols of these. Indeed, in the course of this operation, we have emptied these tactile sensations of a part of their content; after having reduced all other senses to being mere appendages of the sense of touch, touch itself we mutilate, leaving out everything in it that is not a mere abstract or diagrammatic design of tactile perception: with this design we then go on to construct the external world. Can we wonder that between this abstraction, on the one hand, and sensations, on the other hand, no possible link is to be found? But the truth is that space is no more without us than within us, and that it does not belong to a privileged group of sensations. *All* sensations partake of extensity; all are more or less deeply rooted in it; and the difficulties of ordinary realism arise from the fact that, the kinship of the sensations one with another having been extracted and placed apart under the form of an indefinite and empty space, we no longer see either how these sensations can partake of extensity or how they can correspond with each other.

Contemporary psychology is more and more impressed with the idea that all our sensations are in some degree extensive. It is maintained, not without an appearance of reason, that there is no sensation without extensity[18] or without a feeling "of volume."[19] English idealism sought to reserve to tactile perception a monopoly of the extended, the other senses dealing with space only insofar as they remind us of the data of touch. A more attentive psychology reveals to us, on the contrary, and no doubt will hereafter reveal still more clearly, the need of regarding all sensations as primarily extensive, their extensity fading and disappearing before the high intensity and usefulness of tactile, and also, no doubt, of visual, extensity.

So understood, space is indeed the symbol of fixity and of infinite divisibility. Concrete extensity, that is to say, the diversity of sensible qualities, is not within space; rather is it space that we thrust into extensity. Space is not a ground on which real motion is posited; rather is it real motion that deposits space beneath itself. But our imagination, which is preoccupied above all by the convenience of expression and the exigencies of material life, prefers to invert the natural order of the terms. Accustomed to seek its fulcrum in a world of ready-made motionless images, of which the apparent fixity is hardly anything else but the outward reflection of the stability of our lower needs, it cannot help believing that rest is anterior to motion, cannot avoid taking rest as its point of reference and its abiding place. Therefore, it comes to see movement as only a variation of distance, space being thus supposed to precede motion. Then, in a space which is homogeneous and infinitely divisible, we draw, in imagination, a trajectory and fix positions: afterwards, applying the movement to the trajectory, we see it divisible like the line we have drawn, and equally denuded of quality. Can we wonder that our understanding, working thenceforward on this idea, which represents precisely the reverse of the truth, discovers in it nothing but contradictions? Having assimilated movements to space, we find these movements homogeneous like space; and since we no longer see in them anything but calculable differences of direction and velocity, all relation between movement and quality is for us destroyed. So that all we have to do is to shut up motion in space, qualities in consciousness, and to establish between these two parallel series, incapable, by hypothesis, of ever meeting, a mysterious correspondence. Thrown back into consciousness, sensible qualities become incapable of recovering extensity. Relegated to space, and, indeed, to abstract space, where there is never but a single instant and where everything is always being born anew — movement abandons that solidarity of the present with the past which is its very essence. And as these two aspects of perception, quality and movement, have been made equally obscure, the phenomenon of perception, in which a consciousness, assumed to be shut up in itself and foreign to space, is supposed to translate what occurs in space, becomes a mystery. But let us, on the contrary, banish all preconceived idea of interpreting or measuring, let us place ourselves face-to-face with immediate reality: at once we find that there is no impassable barrier, no essential difference, no real distinction even, between perception and the thing perceived, between quality and movement.

So we return, by a roundabout way, to the conclusions worked out in the first chapter of this book. Our perception, we said, is originally in things rather than in the mind, without us rather than within. The several kinds of perception correspond to so many directions actually marked out in reality. But, we added, this perception, which coincides with its object, exists rather in theory than in fact: it could only happen if we were shut up within the present moment. In concrete perception, memory intervenes, and the subjectivity of sensible qualities is due precisely to the fact that our consciousness, which begins by being only memory, prolongs a plurality of moments into each other, contracting them into a single intuition.

Consciousness and matter, body and soul, were thus seen to meet each other in perception. But, in one aspect, this idea remained for us obscure because our perception and consequently, also our consciousness seemed thus to share in the divisibility which is attributed to matter. If, on the dualistic hypothesis, we naturally shrink from accepting the partial coincidence of the perceived object and the perceiving subject, it is because we are conscious of the undivided unity of our perception, whereas the object appears to us to be, in essence, infinitely divisible. Hence the hypothesis of a consciousness with inextensive sensations, placed over against an extended multiplicity. But, if the divisibility of matter is entirely relative to our action thereon, that is to say, to our faculty of modifying its aspect, if it belongs not to matter itself but to the space which we throw beneath this matter in order to bring it within our grasp, then the difficulty disappears. Extended matter, regarded as a whole, is like a consciousness where everything balances and compensates and neutralizes everything else; it possesses in very truth the indivisibility of our perception; so, inversely, we may without scruple attribute to perception something of the extensity of matter. These two terms, perception and matter, approach each other in the measure that we divest ourselves of what may be called the prejudices of action: sensation recovers extensity, the concrete extended recovers its natural continuity and indivisibility. And homogeneous space, which stood between the two terms like an insurmountable barrier, is then seen to have no other reality than that of a diagram or a symbol. It interests the behavior of a being which acts upon matter, but not the work of a mind which speculates on its essence.

Thereby also some light may be thrown upon the problem toward which all our enquiries converge, that of the union of body and soul. The obscurity of this problem, on the dualistic hypothesis, comes from the double fact that matter is considered as essentially divisible and every state of the soul as rigorously inextensive, so that from the outset the communication between the two terms is severed. And when we go more deeply into this double postulate, we discover, in regard to matter, a confusion of concrete and indivisible extensity with the divisible space which underlies it and also, in regard to mind, the illusory idea that there are no degrees, no possible transition, between the extended and the unextended. But if these two postulates involve a common error, if there is a gradual passage from the idea to the image and from the image to the sensation; if, in the measure in which it evolves toward actuality, that is to say, toward action, the mental state draws nearer to extension; if, finally, this extension once attained remains undivided and therefore is not out of harmony with the unity of the soul; we can understand that spirit can rest upon matter and, consequently, unite with it in the act of pure perception, yet nevertheless be radically distinct from it. It is distinct from matter in that it is, even then, *memory*, that is to say, a synthesis of past and present with a view to the future, in that it contracts the moments of this matter in order to use them and to manifest itself by actions which are the final aim of its union with the body. We were right, then, when we said, at the beginning of this book, that the distinction between body and mind must be established in terms not of space but of time.

The mistake of ordinary dualism is that it starts from the spatial point of view: it puts, on the one hand, matter with its modifications, in space; on the other hand, it places unextended sensations in consciousness. Hence the impossibility of understanding how the spirit acts upon the body or the body upon spirit. Hence hypotheses which are and can be nothing but disguised statements of the fact — the idea of a parallelism or of a preestablished harmony. But hence also the impossibility of constituting either a psychology of memory or a metaphysic of matter. We have striven to show that this psychology and this metaphysic are bound up with each other and that the difficulties are less formidable in a dualism which, starting from *pure* perception, where subject and object coincide, follows the development of the two terms in their respective durations: matter, the further we push its analysis, tending more and more to be only a succession of infinitely rapid moments which may be deduced each from the other and thereby are *equivalent to each other*; and spirit, being in perception already memory, and declaring itself more and more as a prolonging of the past into the present, a *progress*, a true evolution.

But does the relation of body and mind become thereby clearer? We substitute a temporal for a spatial distinction: are the two terms any the more able to unite? It must be observed that the first distinction does not admit of degree: matter is supposed to be in space, spirit to be extraspatial; there is no possible transition between them. But if, in fact, the humblest function of spirit is to bind together the successive moments of the duration of things, if it is by this that it comes into contact with matter and by this also that it is first of all distinguished from matter, we can conceive an infinite number of degrees between matter and fully developed spirit — a spirit capable of action which is not only undetermined, but also reasonable and reflective. Each of these successive degrees, which measures a growing intensity of life, corresponds to a higher tension of duration and is made manifest externally by a greater development of the sensori-motor system. But let us consider this nervous system itself: we note that its increasing complexity appears to allow an ever greater latitude to the activity of the living being, the faculty of waiting before reacting, and of putting the excitation received into relation with an ever richer variety of motor mechanisms. Yet this is only the outward aspect; and the more complex organization of the nervous system, which seems to assure the greater independence of the living being in regard to matter, is only the material symbol of that independence itself. That is to say, it is only the symbol of the inner energy which allows the being to free itself from the rhythm of the flow of things and to retain in an ever higher degree the past in order to influence ever more deeply the future — the symbol, in the special sense which we give to the word, of its memory. Thus, between brute matter and the mind most capable of reflection there are all possible intensities of memory or, what comes to the same thing, all the degrees of freedom. On the first hypothesis, that which expresses the distinction between spirit and body in terms of space, body and spirit are like two railway lines which cut each other at a right angle; on the second hypothesis, the rails come together in a curve, so that we pass insensibly from the one to the other.

But have we here anything but a metaphor? Does not a marked distinction, an irreducible opposition, remain between matter properly so-called and the lowest degree of freedom or of memory? Yes, no doubt, the distinction subsists, but union becomes possible, since it would be given, under the radical form of a partial coincidence, in *pure* perception. The difficulties of ordinary dualism come, not from the distinction between the two terms, but from the impossibility of seeing how the one is grafted upon the other. Now, as we have shown, pure perception, which is the lowest degree of mind — mind without memory — is really part of matter, as we understand matter. We may go further: memory does not intervene as a function of which matter has no presentiment and which it does not imitate in its own way. If matter does not remember the past, it is because it repeats the past unceasingly, because, subject to necessity, it unfolds a series of moments of which each is the equivalent of the preceding moment and may be deduced from it: thus its past is truly given in its present. But a being which evolves more or less freely creates something new every moment: in vain, then, should we seek to read its past in its present unless its past were deposited within it in the form of memory. Thus, to use again a metaphor which has more than once appeared in this book, it is necessary, and for similar reasons, that the past should be *acted* by matter, *imagined* by mind.

Summary and Conclusion

I. The idea that we have disengaged from the facts and confirmed by reasoning is that our body is an instrument of action, and of action only. In no degree, in no sense, under no aspect, does it serve to prepare, far less to explain, a representation. Consider external perception: there is only a difference of degree, not of kind, between the so-called perceptive faculties of the brain and the reflex functions of the spinal cord. While the spinal cord transforms the excitations received into movements which are more or less necessarily executed, the brain puts them into relation with motor mechanisms which are more or less freely chosen; but that which the brain explains in our perception is action begun, prepared or suggested, it is not perception itself. Consider memory. The body retains motor habits capable of acting the past over again; it can resume attitudes in which the past will insert itself; or, again, by the repetition of certain cerebral phenomena, which have prolonged former perceptions, it can furnish to remembrance a point of attachment with the actual, a means of recovering its lost influence upon present reality: but in no case can the brain store up recollections or images. Thus, neither in perception, nor in memory, nor a fortiori in the higher attainments of mind, does the body contribute directly to representation. By developing this hypothesis under its manifold aspects and thus pushing dualism to an extreme, we appeared to divide body and soul by an impassable abyss. In truth, we were indicating the only possible means of bringing them together.

II. All the difficulties raised by this problem, either in ordinary dualism, or in materialism and idealism, come from considering, in the phenomena of perception and memory, the physical and the mental as duplicates of one another. Suppose I place myself at the materialist point of view of the epiphenomenal consciousness: I am quite unable to understand why certain cerebral phenomena are accompanied by consciousness, that is to say, of what use could the conscious repetition of the material universe I have begun by positing be, or how could it ever arise. Suppose I prefer idealism: I then allow myself only perceptions, and my body is one of them. But whereas observation shows me that the images I perceive are entirely changed by very slight alterations of the image I call my body (since I have only to shut my eyes and my visual universe disappears), science assures me that all phenomena must succeed and condition one another according to a determined order, in which effects are strictly proportioned to causes. I am obliged, therefore, to seek, in the image which I call my body, and which follows me everywhere, for changes which shall be the equivalents — but the well-regulated equivalents, now deducible from each other — of the images which succeed one another around my body: the cerebral movements, to which I am led back in this way again are the duplicates of my perceptions. It is true that these movements are still perceptions, "possible" perceptions — so that this second hypothesis is more intelligible than the first; but, on the other hand, it must suppose, in its turn, an inexplicable correspondence between my real perception of things and my

226

possible perception of certain cerebral movements which do not in any way resemble these things. When we look at it closely, we shall see that this is the reef upon which all idealism is wrecked: there is no possible transition from the order which is perceived by our senses to the order which we are to conceive for the sake of our science, — or, if we are dealing more particularly with the Kantian idealism, no possible transition from sense to understanding. So my only refuge seems to be ordinary dualism. I place matter on this side, mind on that, and I suppose that cerebral movements are the cause or the occasion of my representation of objects. But if they are its cause, if they are enough to produce it, I must fall back, step-by-step, upon the materialistic hypothesis of an epiphenomenal consciousness. If they are only its occasion, I thereby suppose that they do not resemble it in any way, and so, depriving matter of all the qualities which I conferred upon it in my representation, I come back to idealism. Idealism and materialism are then the two poles between which this kind of dualism will always oscillate; and when, in order to maintain the duality of substances, it decides to make them both of equal rank, it will be led to regard them as two translations of one and the same original, two parallel and predetermined developments of a single principle, and thus to deny their reciprocal influence, and, by an inevitable consequence, to sacrifice freedom.

Now, if we look beneath these three hypotheses, we find that they have a common basis: all three regard the elementary operations of the mind, perception and memory, as operations of pure knowledge. What they place at the origin of consciousness is either the useless duplicate of an external reality or the inert material of an intellectual construction entirely disinterested: but they always neglect the relation of perception with action and of memory with conduct. Now, it is no doubt possible to conceive, as an ideal limit, a memory and a perception that are disinterested; but, in fact, it is toward action that memory and perception are turned; it is action that the body prepares. Do we consider perception? The growing complexity of the nervous system shunts the excitation received onto an ever larger variety of motor mechanisms and so sketches simultaneously an ever larger number of possible actions. Do we turn to memory? We note that its primary function is to evoke all those past perceptions which are analogous to the present perception, to recall to us what preceded and followed them, and so to suggest to us that decision which is the most useful. But this is not all. By allowing us to grasp in a single intuition multiple moments of duration, it frees us from the movement of the flow of things, that is to say, from the rhythm of necessity. The more of these moments memory can contract into one, the firmer is the hold which it gives to us on matter: so the memory of a living being appears indeed to measure, above all, its powers of action upon things and to be only the intellectual reverberation of this power. Let us start, then, from this energy, as from the true principle: let us suppose that the body is a center of action, and only a center of action. We must see what consequences then result for perception, for memory, and for the relations between body and mind.

III. To take perception first. Here is my body with its "perceptive centers." These centers vibrate, and I have the representation of things. On the other hand, I have supposed that these vibrations can neither produce nor translate my perception. It is, then, outside them. Where is it? I cannot hesitate as to the answer: positing my body, I posit a certain image, but with it also the aggregate of the other images, since there is no material image which does not owe its qualities, its determinations, in short, its existence, to the place which it occupies in the totality of the universe. My perception can, then, only be some part of these objects themselves; it is in them rather than they in it. But what is it exactly within them? I see that my perception appears to follow all the vibratory detail of the so-called sensitive nerves; yet I know that the role of their vibrations is solely to prepare the reaction of my body on neighboring bodies, to sketch out my virtual actions. Perception, therefore, consists in detaching, from the totality of objects, the possible action of my body upon them. Perception appears, then, as only a choice. It creates nothing; its office, on the contrary, is to eliminate from the totality of images all those on which I can have no hold, and then, from each of those which I retain, all that does not concern the needs of the image which I call my body. Such, at least, much simplified, is the way we explain or describe schematically what we have called pure perception. Let us mark out at once the intermediate place which we thus take up between realism and idealism.

That every reality has a kinship, an analogy — in short, a relation with consciousness — this is what we concede to idealism by the very fact that we term things "images." No philosophical doctrine, moreover, provided that it is consistent with itself, can escape from this conclusion. But, if we could assemble all the states of consciousness, past, present and possible, of all conscious beings, we should still only have gathered a very small part of material reality because images outrun perception on every side. It is just these images that science and metaphysic seek to reconstitute, thus restoring the whole of a chain of which our perception grasps only a few links. But, in order thus to discover between perception and reality the relation of the part to the whole, it is necessary to leave to perception its true office, which is to prepare actions. This is what idealism fails to do. Why is it unable, as we said just now, to pass from the order manifested in perception to the order which is successful in science, that is to say, from the contingency with which our sensations appear to follow each other to the determinism which binds together the phenomena of nature? Precisely because it attributes to consciousness, in perception, a speculative role, so that it is impossible to see what interest this consciousness has in allowing to escape, between two sensations, for instance, the intermediate links through which the second might be deduced from the first. These intermediaries and their strict order thus remain obscure, whether, with Mill, we make the intermediaries into "possible sensations," or, with Kant, hold the substructure of the order to be the work of an impersonal understanding. But suppose that my conscious perception has an entirely practical destination, simply indicating, in the aggregate of things, that which interests my possible action upon them: I can then understand that all the rest escapes me, and that, nevertheless, all the rest is of the same nature as what I perceive. My consciousness of matter is then no longer either subjective, as it is for English idealism, or relative, as it is for the Kantian idealism. It is not subjective, for it is in things rather than in me. It is not relative, because the relation between the "phenomenon" and the "thing" is not that of appearance to reality, but merely that of the part to the whole.

Here we seem to return to realism. But realism, unless corrected on an essential point, is as unacceptable as idealism and for the same reason. Idealism, we said, cannot pass from the order manifested in perception to the order which is successful in science, that is to say, to reality. Inversely, realism fails to draw from reality the immediate consciousness which we have of it. Taking the point of view of ordinary realism, we have, on the one hand, a composite matter made up of more or less independent parts, diffused throughout space, and, on the other hand, a mind which can have no point of contact with matter, unless it be, as materialists maintain, the unintelligible epiphenomenon. If we prefer the standpoint of the Kantian realism, we find between the "thing-in-itself," that is to say, the real, and the "sensuous manifold" from which we construct our knowledge, no conceivable relation, no common measure. Now, if we get to the bottom of these two extreme forms of realism, we see that they converge toward the same point: both raise homogeneous space as a barrier between the intellect and things. The simpler realism makes of this space a *real* medium, in which things are in suspension; Kantian realism regards it as an *ideal* medium, in which the multiplicity of sensations is coordinated; but for both of them this medium is given *to begin with*, as the necessary condition of what comes to abide in it. And if we try to get to the bottom of this common hypothesis, in its turn, we find that it consists in attributing to homogeneous space a disinterested office: space is supposed either merely to uphold material reality or to have the function, still purely speculative, of furnishing sensations with means of coordinating themselves. So the obscurity of realism, like that of idealism, comes from the fact that, in both of them, our conscious perception and the conditions of our conscious perception are assumed to point to pure knowledge, not to action. But now suppose that this homogeneous space is not logically anterior, but posterior to material things and to the pure knowledge which we can have of them; suppose that extensity is prior to space; suppose that homogeneous space concerns our action and only our action, being like an infinitely fine network which we stretch beneath material continuity in order to render ourselves masters of it, to decompose it according to the plan of our activities and our needs. Then, not only has our hypothesis the advantage of bringing us into harmony with science, which shows us each thing exercising an influence on all the others and, consequently, occupying, in a certain sense, the whole of the extended (although we perceive of this thing only its center and mark its limits at the point where our body ceases to have any hold upon it). Not only has it the advantage, in metaphysic, of suppressing or lessening the contradictions raised by divisibility in space — contradictions which always arise, as we have shown, from our failure to dissociate the two points of view, that of action from that of knowledge. It has, above all, the advantage of overthrowing the insurmountable barriers raised by realism between the extended world and our perception of it. For whereas this doctrine assumes, on the one hand, an external reality which is multiple and divided, and, on the other hand, sensations alien from extensity and without possible contact with it, we find that concrete extensity is not really divided, any more than immediate perception is in truth unextended. Starting from realism, we come back to the point to which idealism had led us; we replace perception in things. And we see realism and idealism ready to come to an understanding when we set aside the postulate, uncritically accepted by both, which served them as a common frontier.

To sum up: if we suppose an extended *continuum*, and, in this *continuum*, the center of real action which is represented by our body, its activity will appear to illuminate all those parts of matter with which at each successive moment it can deal. The same needs, the same power of action, which have delimited our body in matter, will also carve out distinct bodies in the surrounding medium. Everything will happen as if we allowed to filter through us that action of external things which is real, in order to arrest and retain that which is virtual: this virtual action of things upon our body and of our body upon things is our perception itself. But since the excitations which our body receives from surrounding bodies determine unceasingly, within its substance, nascent reactions — since these internal movements of the cerebral substance thus sketch out at every moment our possible action on things, the state of the brain exactly corresponds to the perception. It is neither its cause, nor its effect, nor in any sense its duplicate: it merely continues it, the perception being our virtual action and the cerebral state our action already begun.

IV. But this theory of "pure perception" had to be both qualified and completed in regard to two points. For the so-called "pure" perception, which is like a fragment of reality, detached just as it is, would belong to a being unable to mingle with the perception of other bodies that of its own body, that is to say, its affections; nor would it be able to mingle with its intuition of the actual moment that of other moments, that is to say, its memory. In other words, we have, to begin with, and for the convenience of study, treated the living body as a mathematical point in space and conscious perception as a mathematical instant in time. We then had to restore to the body its extensity and to perception its duration. By this we restored to consciousness its two subjective elements, affectivity and memory.

What is an affection? Our perception, we said, indicates the possible action of our body on others. But our body, being extended, is capable of acting upon itself as well as upon other bodies. Into our perception, then, something of our body must enter. When we are dealing with external bodies, these are, by hypothesis, separated from ours by a space, greater or lesser, which measures the remoteness in time of their promise or of their menace: this is why our perception of these bodies indicates only possible actions. But the more the distance diminishes between these bodies and our own, the more the possible action tends to transform itself into a real action, the call for action becoming more urgent in the measure and proportion that the distance diminishes. And when this distance is *nil*, that is to say, when the body to be perceived is our own body, it is a real and no longer a virtual action that our perception sketches out. Such is, precisely, the nature of pain, an actual effort of the damaged part to set things to rights, an effort

233

that is local, isolated, and thereby condemned to failure, in an organism which can no longer act except as a whole. Pain is, therefore, in the place where it is felt, as the object is at the place where it is perceived. Between the affection felt and the image perceived there is this difference, that the affection is within our body, the image outside our body. And that is why the surface of our body, the common limit of this and of other bodies, is given to us in the form both of sensations and of an image.

In this interiority of affective sensation consists its subjectivity; in that exteriority of images in general, their objectivity. But here again we encounter the ever-recurring mistake with which we have been confronted throughout this work. It is supposed that perception and sensation exist for their own sake; the philosopher ascribes to them an entirely speculative function; and, as he has overlooked those real and virtual actions with which sensation and perception are bound up and by which, according as the action is virtual or real, perception and sensation are characterized and distinguished, he becomes unable to find any other difference between them than a difference of degree. Then, profiting by the fact that affective sensation is but vaguely localized (because the effort it involves is an indistinct effort) at once he declares it to be unextended, and these attenuated affections or unextended sensations he sets up as the material with which we are supposed to build up images in space. Thereby he condemns himself to an impossibility of explaining either whence arise the elements of consciousness, or sensations, which he sets up as so many absolutes, or how, unextended, they find their way to space and are coordinated there, or why, in it, they adopt a particular order rather than any other, or, finally, how they manage to make up an experience which is regular and common to all men. This experience, the necessary field of our activity, is, on the contrary, what we should start from. Pure perceptions, therefore, or images,

234

are what we should posit at the outset. And sensations, far from being the materials from which the image is wrought, will then appear as the impurity which is introduced into it, being that part of our own body which we project into all others.

V. But, as long as we confine ourselves to sensation and to pure perception, we can hardly be said to be dealing with the spirit. No doubt we demonstrate, in opposition to the theory of an epiphenomenal consciousness, that no cerebral state is the equivalent of a perception. No doubt the choice of perceptions from among images in general is the effect of a discernment which foreshadows spirit. No doubt also the material universe itself, defined as the totality of images, is a kind of consciousness, a consciousness in which everything compensates and neutralizes everything else, a consciousness of which all the potential parts, balancing each other by a reaction which is always equal to the action, reciprocally hinder each other from standing out. But to touch the reality of spirit we must place ourselves at the point where an individual consciousness, continuing and retaining the past in a present enriched by it, thus escapes the law of necessity, the law which ordains that the past shall ever follow itself in a present which merely repeats it in another form and that all things shall ever be flowing away. When we pass from pure perception to memory, we definitely abandon matter for spirit.

VI. The theory of memory, around which the whole of our work centers, must be both the theoretic consequence and the experimental verification of our theory of pure perception. That the cerebral states which accompany perception are neither its cause nor its duplicate, and that perception bears to its physiological counterpart the relation of a virtual action to an action begun — this we cannot substantiate by facts, since on our hypothesis everything is bound to happen as if perception were a consequence of the state of the brain. For, in pure perception, the perceived object is a present object, a body which modifies our own. Its image is then actually given, and therefore, the facts permit us to say indifferently (though we are far from knowing our own meaning equally well in the two cases) that the cerebral modifications sketch the nascent reactions of our body or that they create in consciousness the duplicate of the present image. But with memory it is otherwise, for a remembrance is the representation of an *absent* object. Here the two hypotheses must have opposite consequences. If, in the case of a present object, a state of our body is thought sufficient to create the representation of the object, still more must it be thought so in the case of an object that is represented though absent. It is necessary, therefore, in this theory, that the remembrance should arise from the attenuated repetition of the cerebral phenomenon which occasioned the primary perception and should consist simply in a perception weakened. Therefore this double thesis: *Memory is only a function of the brain, and there is only a difference of intensity between perception and recollection.* If on the contrary, the cerebral state in no way begets our perception of the present object but merely continues it, it may also prolong and convert into action the recollection of it which we summon up, but it cannot give birth to that recollection. And as, on the other hand, our perception of the present object is something of that object itself, our representation of the absent object must be a phenomenon of quite another order than perception, since between presence and absence there are no degrees, no intermediate stages. Thus this double thesis, which is the opposite of the former: *memory is something other than a function of the brain, and there is not merely a difference of degree, but of kind, between perception and recollection.* The conflict between the two theories now takes an acute form, and this time experience can judge between them.

We will not here recapitulate in detail the proof we have tried to elaborate, but merely recall its essential points. All the arguments from fact, which may be invoked in favor of a probable accumulation of memories in the cortical substance, are drawn from localized disorders of memory. But, if recollections were really deposited in the brain, characteristic lesions of the brain would correspond to definite gaps in memory. Now, in those forms of amnesia in which a whole period of our past existence, for example, is abruptly and entirely obliterated from memory, we do not observe any precise cerebral lesion; on the contrary, in those disorders of memory where cerebral localization is distinct and certain, that is to say, in the different types of aphasia and in the diseases of visual or auditory recognition, we do not find that certain definite recollections are as it were torn from their seat, but it is the whole faculty of remembering that is more or less diminished *in vitality*, as if the subject had more or less difficulty in bringing his recollections into contact with the present situation. The mechanism of this contact was, therefore, what we had to study in order to ascertain whether the office of the brain is not rather to ensure its working than to imprison the recollections in cells.

We were thus led to follow through its windings the progressive movement by which past and present come into contact with each other, that is to say, the process of recognition. And we found, in fact, that the recognition of a present object might be effected in two absolutely different ways, but that in neither case did the brain act as a reservoir of images. Sometimes, by an entirely passive recognition, acted rather than thought, the body responds to a perception that recurs by a movement or attitude that has become automatic: in this case, everything is explained by the motor apparatus which habit has set up in the body, and lesions of the memory may result from the destruction of these mechanisms. Sometimes, on the other hand, recognition is actively produced by memory-images which go out to meet the present perception; but then it is necessary that these recollections, at the moment that they over-lie the perception, should be able to set going in the brain the same machinery that perception ordinarily sets to work in order to produce actions; if not foredoomed to impotence, they will have no tendency to become actual. And this is why, in all cases where a lesion of the brain attacks a certain category of recollec-tions, the affected recollections do not resemble each other by all belonging to the same period, for instance, or by any logical rela-tionship to each other, but simply in that they are all auditive or all visual or all motor. That which is damaged appears to be the various sensorial or motor areas, or, more often still, those append-ages which permit of their being set going from within the cor-tex, rather than the recollections themselves. We even went further, and by an attentive study of the recognition of words and also of the phenomena of sensory aphasia, we endeavored to prove that recognition is in no way effected by a mechanical awakening of memories that are asleep in the brain. It implies, on the contrary, a more or less high degree of tension in consciousness, which goes to fetch pure recollections in pure memory in order to material-ize them progressively by contact with the present perception.

But what is this pure memory and what are pure recollections? By the answer to this inquiry we completed the demonstration of our thesis. We had just established its first point, that is to say, that memory is something other than a function of the brain. We had still to show, by the analysis of "pure recollection," that there is not between recollection and perception a mere difference of degree but a radical difference of kind.

VII. Let us point out to begin with the metaphysical, and no longer merely psychological, bearing of this last problem. No doubt we have a thesis of pure psychology in a proposition such as this: rec-

238

ollection is a weakened perception. But let there be no mistake: if recollection is only a weakened perception, inversely, perception must be something like an intenser memory. Now the germ of English idealism is to be found here. This idealism consists in finding only a difference of degree, and not of kind, between the reality of the object perceived and the ideality of the object conceived. And the belief that we construct matter from our interior states and that perception is only a true hallucination, also arises from this thesis. It is this belief that we have always combated whenever we have treated of matter. Either, then, our conception of matter is false, or memory is radically distinct from perception.

We have thus transposed a metaphysical problem so as to make it coincide with a psychological problem which direct observation is able to solve. How does psychology solve it? If the memory of a perception were but this perception weakened, it might make us, for instance, take the perception of a slight sound for the recollection of a loud noise. Now such a confusion never occurs. But we may go further, and say that the consciousness of a recollection never occurs as an actual weak state which we try to relegate to the past so soon as we become aware of its weakness. How, indeed, unless we already possessed the representation of a past previously lived, could we relegate to it the less intense psychical states, when it would be so simple to set them alongside of strong states as a present experience which is confused, beside a present experience, which is clear? The truth is that memory does not consist in a regression from the present to the past, but, on the contrary, in a progression from the past to the present. It is in the past that we place ourselves at a stroke. We start from a "virtual state" which we lead onwards, step-by-step, through a series of different *planes of consciousness*, up to the goal where it is materialized in an actual perception; that is to say, up to the point where it becomes a present, active state — up to that extreme plane of our

239

consciousness against which our body stands out. In this virtual state, pure memory consists.

How is it that the testimony of consciousness on this point is misunderstood? How is it that we make of recollection a weakened perception, of which it is impossible to say either why we relegate it to the past, how we rediscover its date, or by what right it reappears at one moment rather than at another? We do so simply because we forget the practical end of all our actual psychical states. Perception is made into a disinterested work of the mind, a pure contemplation. Then, as pure recollection can evidently be only something of this kind (since it does not correspond to a present and urgent reality), memory and perception become states of the same nature, and between them no other difference than a difference of intensity can be found. But the truth is that our present should not be defined as that which is more intense: it is that which acts on us and which makes us act; it is sensory and it is motor — our present is, above all, the state of our body. Our past, on the contrary, is that which acts no longer but which might act, and will act by inserting itself into a present sensation from which it borrows the vitality. It is true that, from the moment when the recollection actualizes itself in this manner, it ceases to be a recollection and becomes once more a perception.

We understand then why a remembrance cannot be the result of a state of the brain. The state of the brain continues the remembrance; it gives it a hold on the present by the materiality which it confers upon it: but pure memory is a spiritual manifestation. With memory we are, in truth, in the domain of spirit.

VIII. It was not our task to explore this domain. Placed at the confluence of mind and matter, desirous chiefly of seeing the one flow into the other, we had only to retain, of the spontaneity of intellect, its place of conjunction with bodily mechanism. In this way we were led to consider the phenomena of association and the birth of the simplest general ideas.

What is the cardinal error of associationism? It is to have set all recollections on the same plane, to have misunderstood the greater or lesser distance which separates them from the present bodily state, that is from action. Thus associationism is unable to explain either how the recollection clings to the perception which evokes it, or why association is effected by similarity or contiguity rather than in any other way, or, finally, by what caprice a particular recollection is chosen among the thousand others which similarity or contiguity might equally well attach to the present perception. This means that associationism has mixed and confounded all the different *planes of consciousness* and that it persists in regarding a less complete recollection as one that is less complex, whereas it is in reality a recollection less *dreamed*, more impersonal, nearer to action and, therefore, more capable of molding itself — like a ready-made garment — upon the new character of the present situation. The opponents of associationism have, moreover, followed it onto this ground. They combat the theory because it explains the higher operations of the mind by association, but not because it misunderstands the true nature of association itself. Yet this is the original vice of associationism.

Between the plane of action — the plane in which our body has condensed its past into motor habits — and the plane of pure memory, where our mind retains in all its details the picture of our past life, we believe that we can discover thousands of different planes of consciousness, a thousand integral and yet diverse repetitions of the whole of the experience through which we have lived. To complete a recollection by more personal details does not at all consist in mechanically juxtaposing other recollections to this, but in transporting ourselves to a wider plane of consciousness, in going away from action in the direction of dream. Neither does the localizing of a recollection consist in inserting it mechanically among other memories, but in describing, by an increasing expansion of the memory as a whole, a circle large enough to include this detail from the past. These planes, moreover, are not given as ready-made things superposed the one on the other. Rather they exist virtually, with that existence which is proper to things of the spirit. The intellect, forever moving in the interval which separates them, unceasingly finds them again or creates them anew: the life of intellect consists in this very movement. Then we understand why the laws of association are similarity and contiguity rather than any other laws, and why memory chooses among recollections which are similar or contiguous certain images rather than other images, and, finally, how by the combined work of body and mind the earliest general ideas are formed. The interest of a living being lies in discovering in the present situation that which resembles a former situation, and then in placing alongside of that present situation what preceded and followed the previous one, in order to profit by past experience. Of all the associations which can be imagined, those of resemblance and contiguity are therefore at first the only associations that have a vital utility. But, in order to understand the mechanism of these associations and above all the apparently capricious selection which they make of memories, we must place ourselves alternately on the two extreme planes of consciousness which we have called the plane of action and the plane of dream. In the first are displayed only motor habits; these may be called associations which are acted or lived, rather than represented. Here resemblance and contiguity are fused together, for analogous external situations, as they recur, and have ended by connecting together certain bodily movements; thenceforth, the same automatic reaction, in which we unfold these contiguous movements, will also draw from the situation which occasions them its resemblance to former situations. But, as we pass from

242

movements to images and from poorer to richer images, resemblance and contiguity part company: they end by contrasting sharply with each other on that other extreme plane where no action is any longer affixed to the images. The choice of one resemblance among many, of one contiguity among others, is, therefore, not made at random: it depends on the ever-varying degree of the *tension* of memory, which, according to its tendency to insert itself in the present act or to withdraw from it, transposes itself as a whole from one key into another. And this double movement of memory between its two extreme limits also sketches out, as we have shown, the first general ideas — motor habits ascending to seek similar images, in order to extract resemblances from them, and similar images coming down toward motor habits, to fuse themselves, for instance, in the automatic utterance of the word which makes them one. The nascent generality of the idea consists, then, in a certain activity of the mind, in a *movement* between action and representation. And this is why, as we have said, it will always be easy for a certain philosophy to localize the general idea at one of the two extremities, to make it crystallize into words or evaporate into memories, whereas it really consists in the transit of the mind as it passes from one term to the other.

IX. By representing elementary mental activity in this manner to ourselves, and by thus making of our body and all that surrounds it the pointed end ever moving, ever driven into the future by the weight of our past, we were able to confirm and illustrate what we had said of the function of the body, and at the same time to prepare the way for an approximation of body and mind.

For after having successively studied pure perception and pure memory, we still had to bring them together. If pure recollection is already spirit, and if pure perception is still in a sense matter, we ought to be able, by placing ourselves at their meeting place,

243

to throw some light on the reciprocal action of spirit and matter. "Pure," that is to say, instantaneous, perception is, in fact, only an ideal, an extreme. Every perception fills a certain depth of duration, prolongs the past into the present, and thereby partakes of memory. So that if we take perception, in its concrete form, as a synthesis of pure memory and pure perception, that is to say, of mind and matter, we compress within its narrowest limits the problem of the union of soul and body. This is the attempt we have made especially in the latter part of this essay.

The opposition of the two principles, in dualism in general, resolves itself into the threefold opposition of the inextended and the extended, quality and quantity, freedom and necessity. If our conception of the function of the body, if our analyses of pure perception and pure memory, are destined to throw light on any aspect of the correlation of body and mind, it can only be on condition of suppressing or toning down these three oppositions. We will, then, examine them in turn, presenting here in a more metaphysical form the conclusions which we have made a point of drawing from psychology alone.

First. If we imagine on the one hand the extended really divided into corpuscles, for example, and, on the other hand, a consciousness with sensations, in themselves inextensive, which come to project themselves into space, we shall evidently find nothing common in such matter and such a consciousness to body and mind. But this opposition between perception and matter is the artificial work of an understanding which decomposes and recomposes according to its habits or its laws: it is not given in immediate intuition. What is given are not inextensive sensations: how should they find their way back to space, choose a locality within it, and coordinate themselves there so as to build up an experience that is common to all men? And what is real is not extension, divided into independent parts: how, being deprived of all possible relationship to our consciousness, could it unfold a series of changes of which the relations and the order exactly correspond to the relations and the order of our representations? That which is given, that which is real, is something intermediate between divided extension and pure inextension. It is what we have termed the *extensive*. Extensity is the most salient quality of perception. It is in consolidating and in subdividing it by means of an abstract space, stretched by us beneath it for the needs of action, that we constitute the composite and infinitely divisible extension. But it is in subtilizing it, in making it, in turn, dissolve into affective sensations and evaporate into a counterfeit of pure ideas, that we obtain those inextensive sensations with which we afterwards vainly endeavor to reconstitute images. And the two opposite directions in which we pursue this double labor open quite naturally before us because it is a result of the very necessities of action that extension should divide itself up for us into absolutely independent objects (whence an encouragement to go on subdividing extension) and that we should pass by insensible degrees from affection to perception (whence a tendency to suppose perception more and more inextensive). But our understanding, of which the function is to set up logical distinctions, and, consequently, clean-cut oppositions, throws itself into each of these ways in turn and follows each to the end. It thus sets up, at one extremity, an infinitely divisible extension and at the other, sensations which are absolutely inextensive. And it creates thereby the opposition which it afterwards contemplates amazed.

Second. Far less artificial is the opposition between quality and quantity, that is to say, between consciousness and movement: but this opposition is radical only if we have already accepted the other. For if you suppose that the qualities of things are nothing but inextensive sensations affecting a consciousness, so that these qualities represent merely, as so many symbols, homogeneous and cal-

245

culable changes going on in space, you must imagine between these sensations and these changes an incomprehensible correspondence. On the contrary, as soon as you give up establishing between them a priori this factitious contrariety, you see the barriers which seemed to separate them fall one after another. First, it is not true that consciousness, turned round on itself, is confronted with a merely internal procession of inextensive perceptions. It is inside the very things perceived that you put back pure perception, and the first obstacle is thus removed. You are confronted with a second obstacle, it is true: the homogeneous and calculable changes on which science works seem to belong to multiple and independent elements, such as atoms, of which these changes appear as mere accidents, and this multiplicity comes in between the perception and its object. But if the division of the extended is purely relative to our possible action upon it, the idea of independent corpuscles is a fortiori schematic and provisional. Science itself, moreover, allows us to discard it, and so the second barrier falls. A last barrier remains to be jumped over: that which separates the heterogeneity of qualities from the apparent homogeneity of movements that are extended. But, just because we have set aside the elements, atoms or whatnot, to which these movements had been affixed, we are no longer dealing with that movement which is the accident of a moving body, with that abstract motion which the mechanician studies and which is nothing, at bottom, but the common measure of concrete movements. How could this abstract motion, which becomes immobility when we alter our point of reference, be the basis of real changes, that is, of changes that are felt? How, composed as it is of a series of instantaneous positions, could it fill a duration of which the parts go over and merge each into the others? Only one hypothesis, then, remains possible; namely, that concrete movement, capable, like consciousness, of prolonging its past into its present, capable, by repeating itself, of engender-

ing sensible qualities, already possesses something akin to consciousness, something akin to sensation. On this theory, it might
be this same sensation diluted, spread out over an infinitely larger
number of moments, this same sensation quivering, as we have
said, like a chrysalis within its envelope. Then a last point would
remain to be cleared up: how is the contraction effected — the
contraction no longer of homogeneous movements into distinct
qualities, but of changes that are less heterogeneous into changes
that are more heterogeneous? But this question is answered by
our analysis of concrete perception: this perception, the living
synthesis of pure perception and pure memory, necessarily sums
up in its apparent simplicity of moments. Between sensible qualities, as regarded in our representation of them, and these same
qualities treated as calculable changes, there is therefore only a
difference in rhythm of duration, a difference of internal tension.
Thus, by the idea of *tension* we have striven to overcome the opposition between quality and quantity, as, by the idea of *extension*,
that between the inextended and the extended. Extension and
tension admit of degrees, multiple but always determined. The
function of the understanding is to detach from these two genera,
extension and tension, their empty container, that is to say, homogeneous space and pure quantity, and thereby to substitute, for
supple realities which permit of degrees, rigid abstractions born
of the needs of action, which can only be taken or left — to create
thus, for reflective thought, dilemmas of which neither alterna-
tive is accepted by reality.

Third. But if we regard in this way the relations of the extended
to the inextended, of quality to quantity, we shall have less difficulty in comprehending the third and last opposition, that of freedom and necessity. Absolute necessity would be represented by a
perfect equivalence of the successive moments of duration, each-
to-each. Is it so with the duration of the material universe? Can

each moment be mathematically deduced from the preceding moment? We have throughout this work, and for the convenience of study, supposed that it was really so; and such is, in fact, the distance between the rhythm of our duration and that of the flow of things, that the contingency of the course of nature, so profoundly studied in recent philosophy, must, for us, be practically equivalent to necessity. So let us keep to our hypothesis, though it might have to be attenuated. Even so, freedom is not in nature an *imperium in imperio*. We have said that this nature might be regarded as a neutralized and consequently, a latent consciousness, a consciousness of which the eventual manifestations hold each other reciprocally in check, and annul each other precisely at the moment when they might appear. The first gleams which are thrown upon it by an individual consciousness do not therefore shine on it with an unheralded light: this consciousness does but remove an obstacle; it extracts from the whole that is real a part that is virtual, chooses and finally disengages that which interests it; and although, by that intelligent choice, it indeed manifests that it owes to spirit its form, it assuredly takes from nature its matter. Moreover, while we watch the birth of that consciousness we are confronted, at the same time, by the apparition of living bodies, capable, even in their simplest forms, of spontaneous and unforeseen movements. The progress of living matter consists in a differentiation of function which leads first to the production and then to the increasing complication of a nervous system capable of canalizing excitations and of organizing actions: the more the higher centers develop, the more numerous become the motor paths among which the same excitation allows the living being to choose, in order that it may act. An ever greater latitude left to movement in space – this indeed is what is seen. What is not seen is the growing and accompanying tension of consciousness in time. Not only, by its memory of former experience, does

248

this consciousness retain the past better and better, so as to organize it with the present in a newer and richer decision; but, living
with an intenser life, contracting, by its memory of the immediate experience, a growing number of external moments in its present duration, it becomes more capable of creating acts of which
the inner indetermination, spread over as large a multiplicity of
the moments of matter as you please, will pass the more easily
through the meshes of necessity. Thus, whether we consider it
in time or in space, freedom always seems to have its roots
deep in necessity and to be intimately organized with it. Spirit
borrows from matter the perceptions on which it feeds and restores
them to matter in the form of movements which it has stamped
with its own freedom.

Notes

INTRODUCTION

1. We have laid stress on this particular point in an essay on "Le paralogisme psycho-physiologique," *Revue de Métaphysique et de Morale* (Nov., 1904).

2. F. Moutier, *L'Aphasie de Broca*, Paris, 1908; especially Chapter VII. Cf. the work of Professor Pierre Marie.

3. P. Janet, *Les Obsessions et la psychasthénie*, Paris, 1903; in particular, pp. 474–502.

CHAPTER I

1. The word representation is used throughout this book in the French sense, as meaning a mental picture, which mental picture is very often perception. (Translators' note.)

2. Lotze, *Metaphysic*, Oxford, 1887, vol. ii, p. 206.

3. Schwarz, *Das Wahrnehmungsproblem*, Leipzig, 1892, pp. 313ff.

4. The word "spiritualism" is used throughout this work to signify any philosophy that claims for spirit an existence of its own. (Translators' note.)

CHAPTER II

1. Robertson, "Reflex Speech," *Journal of Mental Science* (April, 1888). Cf. the article by Ch. Féré, "Le langage réflexe," *Revue Philosophique* (Jan., 1896).

2. Oppenheim, "Ueber das Verhalten der musikalischen Ausdrucksbewegungen bei Aphatischen," *Charité Annalen*, xiii (1888) pp. 348ff.

3. Ibid., p. 365.

4. See, on the subject of this sense of error, the article by Müller and Schumann, "Experimentelle Beiträge zur Untersuchung des Gedächthtnisses," *Zeitschr. f. Psych. u. Phys. der Sinnesorgane* (Dec., 1893), p. 305.

5. W.G. Smith, "The Relation of Attention to Memory," *Mind* (Jan., 1895).

6. Ibid., p. 23.

7. Something of this nature appears to take place in that affection which German authors call *Dyslexie*. The patient reads the first words of a sentence correctly, and then stops abruptly, unable to go on, as though the movements of articulation had inhibited memory. See, on the subject of dyslexie: Berlin, *Eine besondere Art der Wortblindheit* (*Dyslexie*), Weisbaden, 1887, and Sommer, "Die Dyslexie als functionelle Störung," *Arch. f. Psychiatrie* (1893). We may also compare with these phenomena the remarkable cases of word deafness in which the patient understands the speech of others, but no longer understands his own. (See examples cited by Bateman, *On Aphasia*, p. 200; by Bernard, *De l'aphasie*, Paris, 1889, pp. 143 and 144; and by Broadbent, "Case of Peculiar Affection of Speech," *Brain* [1878–79], pp. 484ff.)

8. Mortimer Granville, "Ways of Remembering," *Lancet*, Sept. 27, 1899, p. 458.

9. Kay, *Memory and How to Improve It*, New York, 1888.

10. See the systematic treatment of this thesis, supported by experiments, in Lehmann's articles, "Ueber Wiedererkennen," *Philos. Studien Wundt,* vol. v, pp. 96ff, and vol. vii, pp. 169ff.

11. Pillon, "La formation des idées abstraites et générales," *Crit. Philos.* (1885), vol. i, pp. 208ff. Cf. Ward, "Assimilation and Association," *Mind* (July, 1893 and Oct., 1894).

12. Brochard, "La loi de similarité," *Revue Philosophique,* vol. ix (1880), p. 258. M. Rabier shows himself also of this opinion in his "Leçons de philosophie," *Psychologie,* vol. i, pp. 187–92.

13. Pillon, "La formation des idées abstraites et générales," p. 207. Cf. James Scully, *The Human Mind*, vol. i, London, 1892, p. 331.

14. Höffding, "Ueber Wiedererkennen, Association und psychische Activität," *Vierteljahresschrift f. wissenschaftliche Philosophie* (1889), p. 433.

15. Munk, *Ueber die Functionen der Grosshirnrinde*, Berlin, 1881, pp. 108ff.

16. *Die Seelenblindheit als Herderscheinung*, Wiesbaden, 1887, p. 56.

17. "Ein Beitrag zur Kenntniss der Seelenblindheit," *Arch. f. Psychiatrie*, vol. xxiv (1892).

18. "Ein Fall von Seelenblindheit," *Arch. f. Psychiatrie* (1889).

19. Reported by Bernard, "Un cas de suppression brusque et isolée de la vision mentale," *Progrès Médical*, July 21, 1883.

20. Kussmaul, *Die Störungen der Sprache*, Leipzig, 1877, p. 181. Allen Starr, "Apraxia and Aphasia," *Medical Record*, Oct. 27, 1888. Cf. Laquer, "Zur Localisation der Sensorischen Aphasie," *Neurolog. Centralblatt*, June 15, 1888; and Dodds, "On Some Central Affections of Visions," *Brain* (1885).

21. "Les mouvements et leur importance psychologique," *Revue Philosophique*, vol. viii (1879), pp. 271ff. Cf. *Psychologie de l'attention*, Paris, 1889, p. 75.

22. *Physiology of Mind*, pp. 206ff.

23. In one of the most ingenious chapters of his *Psychologie*, vol. i, p. 242, Paris, 1893, Fouillée says that the sense of familiarity is largely due to the diminution of the inward *shock* which constitutes surprise.

24. *Arch. f. Psychiatrie* (1889–90), p. 224. Cf. Wilbrand, p. 140; and Bernhardt, "Eigenthümlicher Fall von Hirnerkrankung," *Berliner klinische Wochenschrift* (1877), p. 581.

25. *Arch. f. Psychiatrie*, vol. xxiv, p. 898.

26. *Arch. f. Psychiatrie* (1889–90), p. 233.

27. Marillier, "Remarques sur le mecanisme de l'attention," *Revue Philosophique*, vol. xxvii (1889). Cf. Ward, art. "Psychology" in the *Encyclopaedia Britannica*; and Bradley, "Is There a Special Activity of Attention?" *Mind*, vol. xi (1886) p. 305.

28. Hamilton, *Lectures on Metaphysics*, vol. i, p. 247.

29. Wundt, "Grundzüge der physiologischen," *Psychologie*, vol. iii, pp. 331ff.

30. Maudsley, *Physiology of Mind*, p. 299. Cf. Bastian, "Les processus nerveux dans l'attention," *Revue Philosophique*, vol. xxxiii, pp. 360ff.

31. W. James, *Principles of Psychology*, vol. i, p. 441.

32. *Psychologie de l'attention*, Paris, 1889.

33. Marillier, op. cit. Cf. J. Sully, "The Psycho-physical Process in Attention," *Brain* (1890) p. 154.

34. N. Lange, "Beitr. zur Theorie der Sinnlichen Aufmerksamkeit," Philos. Studien Wundt, vol. vii, pp. 390–422.

35. *Beiträge zur Experimentellen Psychologie*, vol. iv, pp. 15ff.

36. *Grundriss der Psychologie*, Leipzig, 1893, p. 185.

37. "Zur Physiologie und Pathologie des Lesens," *Zeitschr. f. Klinische Medicin* (1893). Cf. McKeen Cattell, "Ueber die Zeit der Erkennung von Schriftzeichen" *Philos. Studien* (1885–86).

38. "Ueber Aphasie und ihre Beziehungen zur Wahrnehmungen," *Arch. f. Psychiatrie* vol. xvi (1880).

39. Lichtheim, "On Aphasia," *Brain* (Jan., 1885), p. 447.

40. Ibid., p. 454.

41. Bastian, "On Different Kinds of Aphasia," *British Medical Journal* (Oct. and Nov., 1887) p. 935.

42. Romberg, *Lehrbuch der Nervenkrankheiten*, vol. ii (1853).

43. Quoted by Bateman, *On Aphasia*, London, 1890, p. 79. Cf. Marcé, "Mémoire sur quelques observations de physiologie pathologique," *Mém. de la Soc. de Biologie*, 2nd series, vol. ii, p. 102.

44. Forbes Winslow, *On Obscure Diseases of the Brain*, London, 1861, p. 505.

45. Kussmaul, *Die Störungen der Sprache*, Leipzig, 1877, pp. 55ff.

46. Arnaud, "Contribution à l'étude clinique de la surdité verbale," *Arch. de Neurologie* (1886), p. 192. Spamer, "Ueber Asymbolie," *Arch. f. Psychiatrie*, vol. vi, pp. 507 and 524.

47. See, in particular: P. Sérieux, "Sur un cas de surdité verbale pure," *Revue de Médecine*, 1893; pp. 733ff. Lichtheim, loc. cit.; p. 461; and Arnaud, "Contrib. à l'étude de la surdité verbale (2e article), "Arch. de Neurologie (1886), p. 366.

48. Adler, "Beitrag zur Kenntniss der seltneren Formen von sensorischer Aphasie," *Neurol. Centralblatt*, (1891). pp. 296ff.

49. Bernard, *De l'Aphasie*, Paris, 1889, p. 143.

50. Ballet, *Le Langage intérieur*, Paris, 1888, p. 85.

51. See the three cases cited by Arnaud in the *Archives de Neurologie* (1886),

pp. 366ff. ("Contrib. clinique à l'étude de la surdité verbale," 2nd article). Cf. Schmidt's case, "Gehors- und Sprachstörung in Folge von Apoplexie," *Allg. Zeitschriften f. Psychiatrie* vol. xxvii (1871), p. 304.

52. Stricker, *Studien über die Sprachvorstellung*, Vienna, 1880.

53. Bernard, pp. 172 and 179. Cf. Babilée, *Les Troubles de la mémoire dans l'alcoolisme*, Paris, 1886 (medical thesis), p.44.

54. Rieger, *Beschreibung der Intelligenzstörungen in Folge einer Hirnverletzung*, Wurzburg, 1889, p. 35.

55. Wernicke, *Der aphasische Symptomencomplex*. Breslau, 1874, p. 39. Cf. Valentin, "Sur un cas d'aphasie d'origine traumatique," *Revue Médicale de l'Est*, (1880), p. 171.

56. Ribot, *Les Maladies de la mémoire*, Paris 1881, pp. 131ff.

57. Forbes Winslow, *On Obscure Diseases of the Brain*, London, 1861.

58. Ibid., p. 372.

59. Pierre Janet, *Etat mental des hystériques*, vol. ii, Paris, 1894, pp. 263ff. Cf. *L'Automatisme psychologique*, Paris 1889, by the same author.

60. See Grashey's case, studied afresh by Sommer, and by him declared to be inexplicable according to the existing theories of aphasia. In this instance, the movements executed by the patient seem to me to have been *signals* addressed by him to an independent memory. (Sommer, "Zur Psychologie der Sprache," *Zeitschr. f. Psychol. u. Physiol. der Sinnesorgane*, vol. ii, (1891), pp. 143ff. Cf. Sommer's paper at the Congress of German Alienists, *Arch. de Neurologie*, vol. xxiv, (1892).

61. Wundt, *Grundzüge der physiologische Psychologie*, vol. i, Leipzig, 1903, pp. 314–15.

62. Bernard, *De l'Aphasie*, Paris, 1889, pp. 171 and 174.

63. Graves cites the case of a patient who had forgotten all names but remembered their initial, and by that means was able to recover them (quoted by Bernard, *De l'Aphasie*, p. 179).

64. Bernard, *De l'Aphasie*, p. 37.

65. Broadbent, "A Case of Peculiar Affection of Speech," *Brain* (1879), p. 494.

66. Kussmaul, *Die Störungen der Sprache*, p. 182.

67. Lichtheim, "On Aphasia," *Brain* (1885). Yet we must note the fact that Wernicke, the first to study sensory aphasia methodically, was able to do without a center for concepts (*Der aphasische Symptomencomplex*, Breslau, 1874).

68. Bastian, "On Different Kinds of Aphasia," *Brit. Med. Journal* (1887). Cf. the explanation (indicated as merely possible) of *optical aphasia* by Bernheim: "De la cécité psychique des choses," *Revue de Médecine* (1885).

69. Wysman, "Aphasie und verwandte Zustände," *Deutsches Archiv. für Klinische Medecin* (1880). Magnan had already opened the way, as Skwortzoff's diagram indicates, "De la cécité des mots," *Th. de Med.* (1881), p. i.

70. Moeli, "Ueber Aphasie bei Wahrnehmung der Gegenstände durch das Gesicht," *Berliner Klinische Wochenschrift*, Apr. 28, 1890.

71. Freud, *Zur Auffassung der Aphasien*, Leipzig, 1891.

72. Sommer, "Addressing a Congress of Alienists," *Arch. de Neurologie*, vol. xxiv (1892).

73. *The Senses and the Intellect*, p. 329. Cf. Spencer, *Principles of Psychology*, vol. i., p. 456.

74. Ribot, *Les Maladies de la mémoire*, Paris, 1881, p. 10.

75. See an enumeration of the most typical cases in Shaw's article, "The Sensory Side of Aphasia," *Brain* (1893), p. 501. Several authors, however, limit to the first convolution the lesion corresponding to the loss of verbal auditory images. See, in particular, Ballet, *Le Langage intérieur*, p. 153.

76. Luciani, quoted by J. Soury, *Les Fonctions du cerveau*, Paris, 1892, p. 211.

77. The theory which is here sketched out resembles, in one respect, that of Wundt. We will give the common element and the essential difference between them. With Wundt, we believe that distinct perception implies a centrifugal action; thereby we are led to suppose with him (although in a slightly different sense) that the so-called image centers are rather centers for the grouping of sense-impressions. But whereas, according to Wundt, the centrifugal action lies in an "apperceptive stimulation," the nature of which can only be defined in a general manner, and which appears to correspond to what is commonly called the fixing of the attention, we maintain that this centrifugal action bears in each case a distinct form, the very form of that "virtual object" which tends to actualize itself by successive stages. Hence an important difference in our understanding of the office of the centers. Wundt is led to assume: First, a general organ of apperception, occupying the frontal lobe; Second, particular centers which, though

most likely incapable of storing images, retain nevertheless a tendency or a disposition to reproduce them. Our contention, on the contrary, is that no trace of an image can remain in the substance of the brain, and that no such center of apperception can exist. Instead, there are merely, in that substance, organs of *virtual* perception, influenced by the intention of the memory, as there are at the periphery organs of *real* perception, influenced by the action of the object. (See *Grundzüge der physiologische Psychologie*, vol. i, pp. 320–27).

CHAPTER III

1. Kay, *Memory and How to Improve It*, p. 18.

2. Mathias Duval, "Théorie histologique du sommeil," *C. R. de la Soc. de Biologie* (1895), p. 74. Cf. Lépine, ibid., p. 85; and *Revue de Médecine* (Aug., 1894); and, especially, Pupin, *Le Neurone et les hypothèses histologiques*, Paris, 1896.

3. Forbes Winslow, *Obscure Diseases of the Brain*, pp. 25ff.; Ribot, *Maladies de la mémoire*, pp. 139ff.; Mauro, *Le Sommeil et les rêves*, Paris, 1878, p. 439; Egger, "Le Moi des mourants," *Revue philosophique* (Jan. and Oct., 1896). CF. Ball's dictum: "Memory is a faculty which loses nothing and records everything." (Quoted by Rouillard, *Les Amnésies* [medical thesis], Paris, 1885, p. 25.)

4. This idea has recently been developed by various authors. A systematic account of it will be found in the work of Cowles, "The Mechanism of Insanity," American Journal of Insanity (1890-91).

5. See, especially, Moreau de Tours, *Du Haschisch*, Paris, 1845.

6. Ball, *Leçons sur les maladies mentales*, Paris, 1890, pp. 608ff. Cf. a curious analysis: "Visions, a Personal Narrative," *Journal of Mental Science* (1896), p. 284.

7. See "Visions," p. 176.

8. Pierre Janet, *Les Accidents mentaux*, Paris, 1894, pp. 292ff.

9. Pierre Janet, *L'Automatisme psychologique*, Paris, 1898, pp. 95ff.

10. Ravaisson, *La Philosophie en France au xix siècle*, 3rd ed., p. 176.

CHAPTER IV

1. H. Bergson, *Time and Free Will*, Sonnenschein 1910. Translation of *Les Données immédiates de la conscience*.

257

2. We may here briefly recall this argument. Let there be a moving body which is displaced with a certain velocity, and which passes simultaneously before two bodies, one at rest and the other moving toward it with the same velocity as its own. During the same time that it passes a certain length of the first body, it naturally passes double that length of the other. Whence Zeno concludes that "a duration is the double of itself." A childish argument, it is said, because Zeno takes no account of the fact that the velocity is in the one case double that which it is in the other. Certainly, but how, I ask, could he be aware of this? That, in the same time, a moving body passes different lengths of two bodies, of which one is at rest and the other in motion, is clear for him who makes of duration a kind of absolute and places it either in consciousness or in something which partakes of consciousness. For while a *determined* portion of this absolute or conscious duration elapses, the same moving body will traverse, as it passes the two bodies, two spaces of which the one is the double of the other, without our being able to conclude from this that a duration is double itself, since duration remains independent of both spaces. But Zeno's error, in all his reasoning, is due to just this fact, that he leaves real duration on one side and considers only its objective track in space. How, then, should the two lines traced by the same moving body not merit an equal consideration, qua measures of duration? And how should they not represent the same duration, even though the one is twice the other? In concluding from this that "a duration is the double of itself," Zeno was true to the logic of his hypothesis, and his fourth argument is worth exactly as much as the three others.

3. Descartes, *Principes*, ii, 29.

4. *Principes*, part ii, § 37.

5. Leibniz, "Specimen dynamicum" *Mathem. Schriften*, Gerhardt, 2nd section, vol. ii. p. 246.

6. H. Morus, *Scripta Philosophica*, 1679, vol. ii, p. 248.

7. Newton, *Principia*, Thomson, ed, 1871, pp. 6ff.

8. Euler, *Theoria motus corporum solidorum*, 1765, pp. 30–33.

9. Newton, in particular.

10. See, on this subject, Clerk-Maxwell, "Action at a Distance," in *Scientific Papers*,

Cambridge, 1890, vol. ii, pp. 313–14.

11. Clerk-Maxwell, "Molecular Constitution of Bodies," in *Scientific Papers*, vol. ii. p. 618. Van der Waals has shown, on the other hand, the continuity of liquid and gaseous states.

12. Faraday, "A Speculation Concerning Electric Conduction," *Philos. Magazine*, 3rd series. vol. xxiv.

13. Thomson, "On Vortex Atoms," *Proc. of the Roy. Soc. of Edin.* (1867). An hypothesis of the same nature had been put forward by Graham, "On the Molecular Mobility of Gases," *Proc. of the Roy. Soc.* (1863), pp. 621ff.

14. Bergson, *Time and Free Will*.

15. Bergson, *Time and Free Will*.

16. Bergson, *Time and Free Will*.

17. See on this subject: Paul Janet, "La perception visuelle de la distance," *Revue philosophique*, vol. vii (1879), pp. 1ff.; William James, *Principles of Psychology*, vol. ii, chap. xxii. Cf. on the subject of the visual perception of extensity: Dunan, "L'espace visuel et l'espace tactile," *Revue Philosophique* (Feb. and Apr., 1888, Jan., 1889).

18. Ward, Art. "Psychology" in the *Encycl. Britannica*.

19. W. James, *Principles of Psychology*, vol. ii, pp. 134ff. We may note in passing that we might, in strictness, attribute this opinion to Kant, since *The Transcendental Æsthetic* allows no difference between the data of the different senses as far as their extension in space is concerned. But it must not be forgotten that the point of view of the *Critique* is other than that of psychology, and that it is enough for its purpose that all our sensations should *end* by being localized in space when perception has reached its final form.

Bibliography

Compiled by Bruno Paradis

The purpose of this bibliography is threefold: (1) to recall the dates of the original French publication of Bergson's works and to list the available English language translations; (2) to provide a selection of general commentaries as well as critical studies (all texts which specifically address *Matter and Memory* are marked by an asterisk); and (3) to allow for the possibility of dialogue, with a special focus on the question of time, between Bergson and great thinkers in the philosophical tradition, and between Bergson and important trends in contemporary science.

TEXTS BY BERGSON

Essai sur les données immédiates de la conscience. Paris: Presses Universitaires de France, 1889.

"Quid Aristoteles de loco senserit" (1889). French translation by R.-M. Mossé-Bastide in *Les Etudes Bergsoniennes*, 2 (1949):27–104.

Matière et mémoire. Paris: Presses Universitaires de France, 1896.

Le rire. Paris: Presses Universitaires de France, 1900.

L'évolution créatrice. Paris: Presses Universitaires de France, 1907.

L'énergie spirituelle. Paris: Presses Universitaires de France, 1919.

Durée et simultanéité. Paris: Presses Universitaires de France, 1922.

Les deux sources de la morale et de la religion. Paris: Presses Universitaires de France, 1932.

La pensée et le mouvant. Paris: Presses Universitaires de France, 1934.

Bergson, Ecrits et paroles. Edited by R.-M. Mossé-Bastide. 3 vols. (texts of 1878-1904, 1905-15, 1915-39). Paris: Presses Universitaires de France, 1957, 1958, 1959.

The above texts are also available in:

Bergson, Oeuvres (DI, MM, R, EC, ES, MR, PM), édition du centenaire. Paris: Presses Universitaires de France, 1963.

Bergson, Mélanges (QA, DS, Correspondance, Pièces diverses, Documents). Paris: Presses Universitaires de France, 1972.

ENGLISH TRANSLATIONS

Time and Free Will. Translated by F. L. Pogson. New York: Macmillan, 1919.

Matter and Memory. Translated by Nancy Margaret Paul and W. Scott Palmer. New York: Zone, 1991.

Creative Evolution. Translated by Arthur Mitchell. New York: Henry Holt, 1911.

Mind Energy. Translated by H. Wildon Carr. New York: Henry Holt, 1920.

Duration and Simultaneity. Translated by Leon Jacobson. Indianapolis: Bobbs-Merrill, 1965.

The Two Sources of Morality and Religion. Translated by R. Ashley Audra and Cloudesley Brereton with the assistance of W. Horsfall Carter. New York: Henry Holt, 1935.

The Creative Mind. Translated by Mabelle Andison. Westport, CT: Greenwood Press, 1946.

TEXTS ON BERGSON

Adam, M. *Die intellektuelle Anschauung bei Schelling in ihrem Verhältnis zur Methode der Intuition bei Bergson*. Paschkau, 1926.

Adolphe, Lydie. "Bergson et la science d'aujourd'hui." *Etudes Philosophiques*, 14, no. 4 (1959): 479-88.

Aichelle, Ronald B. "Russell on 'The Theory of Continuity.'" *Dianöia*, 5 (Spring, 1969): 1-11.

Alexander, J. W. *Bergson, Philosopher of Reflection*. London, 1957.

*Amidou, Philippe R. *Memory and Duration in Bergson: A Study of Terminology in Matter and Memory and an "Introduction to Metaphysics."* Ph. D. dissertation, St. Louis, 1968.

Armstrong, A. C. "Bergson, Berkeley, and Philosophical Intuition." *Philosophical Review*, 23, no. 4 (1914): 430-38.

Barthelemy-Madaule, Madeleine. *Bergson et Teilhard de Chardin*. Paris: Seuil, 1963.

_____. *Bergson, adversaire de Kant: étude critique de la conception bergsonienne du kantisme*. Paris: Presses Universitaires de France, 1966.

Barreau, Hervé. "Bergson et Zénon d'Elée." *Revue Philosophique de Louvain*, 67, no. 94 (May, 1969): 267-84; no. 95 (August, 1969): 389-430.

Berger, Gaston. "Le progrès de la réflexion chez Bergson et chez Husserl." In *Henri Bergson*, Béguin and Thévenax (Eds.), 257-63.

Bergson et nous. Actes du Xe Congrés. *Bulletin de la Société Française de Philosophie* (in 2 vols.). Paris: 1959.

Boudot, M. "L'espace selon Bergson." *Revue de Métaphysique et de Morale*, 85, no. 3 (1980): 332-56.

Bréhier, Emile. "Images plotiniennes, images bergsoniennes." *Les Etudes Bergsoniennes*, 2 (1949): 105-28.

Campanale, D. "Scienza e metafisica nei pensiero di Henri Bergson." *Rassegna di scienza filosofiche*, 7, no. 2 (1964): 137-67; no. 3 (1964): 306-33.

Canguilhem, Georges. "Commentaire du troisième chapitre de *L'evolution créatrice*." *Bulletin de la Faculté des Lettres de Strasbourg*, 21, nos. 5-6 (1943): 126-43; no. 7 (1943): 199-214.

Capek, Milic. "Stream of Consciousness and 'durée réelle.'" *Philosophy and Phenomenological Research*, 20, no. 3 (March, 1950): 331-53.

_____. "La genèse idéale de la matière chez Bergson: la structure de la durée." *Revue de Métaphysique et de Morale*, 57, no. 3 (1952): 325-48.

_____. "La théorie bergsonienne de la matière et la physique moderne." *Revue Philosophique de la France et de l'Etranger*, 43, nos. 1-3 (January–March, 1953).

_____. "La théorie biologique de connaissance chez Bergson et sa signification actuelle." *Revue de Métaphysique et de Morale*, 64, no. 2 (1959): 194–211.

_____. *The Philosophical Impact of Contemporary Physics*. New York: Van Nostrand, 1961.

_____. "La signification actuelle de la philosophie de James." *Revue de Métaphysique et de Morale*, 67, no. 3 (1962): 291–321.

* _____. *Bergson and Modern Physics: A Reinterpretation and Reevaluation*. Dordrecht: D. Reidel, 1971.

_____. "Bergson, Nominalism and Relativity." *The Southwestern Journal of Philosophy*, 9, no. 3 (1978): 127–33.

_____. "Ce qui est vivant et ce qui est mort dans la critique bergsonienne de la relativité." *Revue de Synthèse Française*, 101, no. 99 (1980): 313–44.

Cariou, Marie. *L'atomisme: trois essais: Gassendi, Leibniz, Bergson et Lucrèce*. Paris: Aubier-Montaigne, 1978.

Casey, E.S. "Habitual Body and Memory in Merleau-Ponty." *Man and World*, 17, no. 3-4 (1984): 279–97.

Chahine, O. *La durée créatrice dans la métaphysique de Bergson*. Paris, 1954.

* Couchoud, Paul Louis. "La métaphysique nouvelle: *Matière et mémoire* de M. Bergson." *Revue de Métaphysique et de Morale*, 10 (1902): 225–43.

Dayan, M. "L'inconscient chez Bergson." *Revue de Métaphysique et de Morale*, 70, no. 3 (1965): 287–324.

Delattre, Floris. "William James bergsonien." *Revue Anglo-Américaine*, 1, no. 2 (1923–24): 135–44.

*Delbos, Victor. "Matière et mémoire, étude critique." *Revue de Métaphysique et de Morale*, 5 (1897): 353–89.

Deleuze, Gilles. "La conception de la différence chez Bergson." *Les Etudes Bergsoniennes*, 4 (1956): 77–112.

_____. *Bergsonism*. New York: Zone Books, 1991.

Delhomme, Jeanne. "Durée et vie chez Bergson." *Les Etudes Bergsoniennes*, 2 (1949): 129–91.

_____. "L'exercice de la pensée et ses conditions dans la philosophie d'Henri Bergson." *Les Etudes Bergsoniennes*, 3 (1952): 151–58.

————. *Vie et conscience de la vie: essai sur Bergson.* Paris: Presses Universitaires de France, 1954.

————. "Le problème de l'intériorité: Bergson et Sartre." *Revue Internationale de Philosophie*, 48, no. 2 (1959): 201–19.

————. "Nietzsche et Bergson: la représentation de la vérité." *Les Etudes Bergsoniennes*, 5 (1960): 37–62.

Devaux, Philippe. "Le bergsonisme de Whitehead." *Revue Internationale de Philosophie*, 15, no. 56-57 (1961): 217–36.

*Dewey, John. "Perception and organic action." *The Journal of Philosophy*, 9, no. 24 (November, 1912): 645–68.

————. "Spencer and Bergson." *Revue de Métaphysique et de Morale*, 70, no. 3 (1965): 325–33.

Dumoncel, J.-C. "Popper et Bergson." *Revue d'Enseignement Philosophique*, 32, no. 3 (1982): 37–48.

Fabre-Luce de Gruson, Françoise. "Bergson, lecteur de Kant." *Les Etudes Bergsoniennes*, 5 (1960): 169–90.

————. "Sens commun et bon sens chez Bergson." *Revue Internationale de Philosophie*, 13, no. 2 (1959): 187–200.

*Fawcett, Edward Douglas. "Matter and Memory." *Mind*, 21, no. 82 (April, 1912): 201–32.

Felt, J. W. "Philosophy, Understanding and the Continuity of Becoming." *International Philosophical Quarterly*, 18, no. 4 (1978): 375–93.

Fressin, Augustin. *La perception chez Bergson et chez Merleau-Ponty.* Paris: Société d'éditions d'Enseignement supérieur, 1967.

Frieden-Markevitch, Nathalie. *La philosophie de Bergson, aperçu sur un stoïcisme inconscient.* Fribourg: Editions Universitaires, 1982.

George, André. "Bergson et Einstein." *Documents de la Vie Intellectuelle*, 1, no. 4 (January, 1930): 52–60.

Germino, Dante. *Political Philosophy and the Open Society.* Baton Rouge: Louisiana State University Press, 1982.

Gilson, Bernard. *L'individualité dans la philosophie de Bergson.* Paris: J. Vrin, 1978.

Gilson, Etienne. "Souvenir de Bergson." *Revue de Métaphysique et de Morale*, 64, no. 2 (April, 1959): 129–40.

Giroux, Laurent. *Durée pure et temporalité: Bergson et Heidegger.* Tournai (Belgium): Bellarmin, 1971.

————. "Bergson et la conception de temps chez Platon et chez Aristote." *Dialogue*, 10, no. 3 (1971): 479–503.

Gouhier, Henri. "Maine de Biran et Bergson." *Les Etudes Bergsoniennes*, 1 (1948): 129–73.

————. "Bergson et l'histoire des idées." *Revue Internationale de Philosophie*, 3, no. 10 (1949): 434–44.

————. *Bergson et le Christ des évangiles.* Paris: Fayard, 1961.

Gregoire, Franz. "La collaboration de l'intuition et de l'intelligence." *Revue Internationale de Philosophie*, 3, no. 3 (1949): 392–406.

*Grimaldi, Nicholas. "Matière et tradition." *Revue de Métaphysique et de Morale*, 76, no. 2 (April–June, 1971): 167–95.

Gross, David. "Bergson, Proust and the Revaluation of Memory." *International Philosophical Quarterly*, 25, no. 4 (1985): 369–80.

Gueroult, Martial. "Perception, idée, objet, chose chez G. Berkeley: la formule bergsonienne." *Revue Philosophique de la France et de l'Etranger*, 143, no. 2 (April, 1953): 181–200.

————. "Bergson en face des philosophes." *Les Etudes Bergsoniennes*, 5 (1960): 9–35.

*Gunter, Pete Addison Y. *Bergson and the Evolution of Physics.* Knoxville, TN: University of Tennessee Press, 1969.

*————. "Bergson's Theory of Matter and Modern Cosmology." *Journal of the History of Ideas*, 32, no. 4 (October–December, 1971): 525–42.

————. *Henri Bergson: A Bibliography.* Bowling Green, OH: Philosophy Documentation Center, Bowling Green University, 1974.

————. "Bergson, Conceptualism and Indeterminacy: A Rejoinder to Capek." *The Southwestern Journal of Philosophy*, 9, no. 3 (1978): 135–37.

Gurvitch, George. "Deux aspects de la philosophie de Bergson: temps et liberté." *Revue de Métaphysique et de Morale*, 65, no. 3 (1960): 307–11.

*Harward, J. "What Does Bergson Mean by Pure Perception?" *Mind*, 27, no. 106 (1918): 203–07; vol. 28, no. 112 (1919): 463–70.

Heidsieck, François. *Henri Bergson et la notion d'espace*. Paris, 1961.

Heintz, Joseph Walter. *La notion de conscience chez William James et Henri Bergson*. Ph.D. dissertation, Paris, 1950.

Herman, Daniel J. *The Philosophy of Henri Bergson*. Washington: University Press of America, 1980.

Horkheimer, Max. "Zur Henri Bergson Metaphysik der Zeit." *Zeitschrift für Sozialforschung*, 3 (1934): 321–42.

Husson, Léon. *L'intellectualisme de Bergson: genèse et développement de la notion bergsonienne d'intuition*. Paris, 1947.

––––––. "Les aspects méconnus de la liberté bergsonienne." *Les Etudes Bergsoniennes*, 4 (1956): 157–201.

Hyppolite, Jean. "Henri Bergson et l'existentialisme." *Les Etudes Bergsoniennes*, 2 (1949): 208–12.

*––––––. "Aspects divers de la mémoire chez Bergson." *Revue Internationale de Philosophie*, 3, no. 10 (1949): 373–92.

Ingarden, R. "Intuition und Intellekt bei Henri Bergson." *Jahrbuch für Philosophie und phänomenologische Forschung*, 5 (1922): 285–461.

James, William. "The Philosophy of Bergson." *Hibbert Journal*, 7, no. 3 (April, 1909): 562–77. Reprinted as "Bergson and His Critique of Intellectualism" in *A Pluralistic Universe*. New York: Longman, Green, Co., 1919, pp. 223–72.

––––––. "Bradley or Bergson?" *Journal of Philosophy*, 7, no. 2 (January, 1910): 29–33.

––––––. "A Great French Philosopher at Harvard." *Nation*, 90, no. 2335 (March 31, 1910): 312–14.

Janicaud, Dominique. *Une généalogie du spiritualisme français. Aux sources du bergsonisme: Ravaisson et la métaphysique*. The Hague: Martinus Nijhoff, 1969.

Jankelevitch, Vladimir. *Henri Bergson*. Paris: Presses Universitaires de France, 1954.

*Lattre, Alain de. "Remarques sur l'intuition comme principe régulateur de la connaissance chez Bergson." *Les Etudes Bergsoniennes*, 8 (1966): 195–215.

Joussain, A. "Schopenhauer et Bergson." *Archives de Philosophie*, no. 1 (1963): 71–89.

*Lechalas, Georges. "*Matière et mémoire*: d'après un nouveau livre de M. Bergson." *Annales de Philosophie Chrétienne*, 26 (1897): 146–64.

Leroy, André Louis. "Influence de la philosophie berkleyenne sur la pensée continentale." *Hermathema*, 82, no. 2 (November, 1953): 27–48.

Levi, Albert William. "Substance, Process, Being: A Whiteheadian–Bergsonian View." *Journal of Philosophy*, 55, no. 18 (August 29, 1958): 749–61.

*Marietti, Angèle. *Les formes du mouvement chez Bergson*. Paris: Les Cahiers du Nouvel Humanisme, 1953.

Marneff, J. "Bergson's and Husserl's Concepts of Intuition." *Philosophical Quarterly*, 23, no. 3 (1960): 169–80.

Mathieu, Vittorio. "Bergson technicien." *Revue Internationale de Philosophie*, 13, no. 48 (1959): 173–86.

————. "Il tempo ritrovato: Bergson e Einstein." *Filosofia*, 4, no. 4 (1953): 625–56.

*May, William Eugene. "The Reality of Matter in the Metaphysics of Bergson." *International Philosophical Quarterly*, 10, no. 4 (1970): 611–42.

Merleau-Ponty, Maurice. *L'union de l'âme et du corps chez Malebranche, Biran et Bergson*. Paris: Vrin, 1978.

*Milet, Jean. *Bergson et le calcul infinitésimal: la raison et le temps*. Paris: Presses Universitaires de France, 1974.

Mosse-Bastide, Rose-Marie. *Bergson éducateur*. Paris: Presses Universitaires de France, 1955.

————. *Bergson et Plotin*. Paris: Presses Universitaires de France, 1959.

*Mourelos, G. *Bergson et les niveaux de réalité*. Paris: Presses Universitaires de France, 1964.

Muirhead, J. "Philosophy of Bergson." *Hibbert Journal*, 9, no. 4 (July, 1911): 895–907.

Murillo, Zamora. *La notion de causalité dans la philosophie de Bergson*. San José, Costa Rica: Ciudad Universitaria, 1968.

Pariente, Jean-Claude. "Bergson et Wittgenstein." *Revue Internationale de Philosophie*, 23, nos. 88–89 (1969): 183–204.

*Paulus, Jean. "Les deux directions de la psychologie bergsonienne: behaviorisme et introspection dans *Matière et mémoire*." *Tijdschrift voor Philosophie*, 6, nos. 3–4 (1944): 297–332.

Peguy, Charles. *Note sur M. Bergson et la philosophie bergsonienne. Note sur Descartes et la philosophie cartésienne*. Paris: Gallimard, 1935.

Pennartz, C. M. A. "The Relationship between Time and Consciousness: A Study

Referring to Husserl and Bergson." In *Nature, Time and History* (vol. 2). P. A. Kroes (Ed.). Nijmegen: Fakulteit der Wiskunde en Natuurwetenschappen, Katholicke Universiteit, 1985 (pp. 21–32).

Piaget, Jean. "Lettre." *Revue de Théologie et de Philosophie*, 9, no. 1 (1959).

Pilkington, Andrew E. *Bergson and His Influence: A Reassessment.* Cambridge: Cambridge University Press, 1976.

*Rideau, Emile. *Les rapports de la nature et de l'esprit dans le bergsonisme.* Paris: Félix Alcan, 1932.

*Robinet, André. "Le passage à la conception biologique: De la perception de l'image et du souvenir chez Bergson: Notes pour un commentaire du chapitre II de *Matière et mémoire*." *Études Philosophiques*, 15, no. 3 (1960): 375–88.

_____. *Bergson et les métamorphoses de la durée.* Paris: Seghers, 1965.

Russell, Bertrand. "The Philosophy of Bergson." *Monist*, 22, no. 3 (July, 1912): 321–47.

_____. "On the Notion of Cause." *Proceedings of the Aristotelian Society*, 13 (1912–13): 1–26.

Sarnoff, S. "A Bergsonian View of Agent Causation." *International Philosophical Quarterly*, 25, no. 98 (1985): 185–96.

Scharfstein, Ben Ami. "Bergson and Merleau-Ponty: A Preliminary Comparison." *Journal of Philosophy*, 52, no. 14 (1955): 380–86.

Seyppel, Joachim H. "A Criticism of Heidegger's Time Concept with Reference to Bergson's 'durée.'" *Revue Internationale de Philosophie*, 10, no. 4 (1956): 503–08.

Stallknecht, Newton P. *Studies in the Philosophy of Creation with Especial Reference to Bergson and Whitehead.* Princeton: Princeton University Press, 1934.

*Taylor, Alfred Edward. "Review of *Matter and Memory* by Henri Bergson." *International Journal of Ethics*, 22, no. 1 (October, 1911): 101–07.

Thibaudet, Albert. *Le bergsonisme.* Paris: N.R.F., 1922.

Trotignon, Pierre. *L'idée de vie chez Bergson et la critique de la métaphysique.* Paris: Presses Universitaires de France, 1968.

Van Peursen, C. A. "Henri Bergson, phénoménologue de la perception." *Revue de Métaphysique et de Morale*, no. 3 (1960): 317–26.

Vinson, A. "Le fini, l'infini et l'indéfini." *Revue d'Enseignement Philosophique*, no. 3

(1986): 1–14.

Wahl, Jean. *Bergson*. Paris: Centre de Documentation Universitaire, 1965.

Texts Concerning Bergson: Dialogue and Debate

Aristotle. *Physics* IV (10–14).

———. *De anima.*

Augustine. *Confessions* (Book XI).

Bachelard, Gaston. *L'intuition de l'instant.* Paris: Stock, 1932.

———. *La dialectique de la durée.* Paris: Boivin, 1936.

———. *Les intuitions atomistiques: essaï de classifcation.* Paris: Boivin, 1933.

———. *L'activité rationaliste de la physique contemporaine.* Paris: Presses Universitaires de France, 1951.

Broglie, Louis de. *Matière et lumière.* Paris: Albin Michel, 1932.

———. "Individualité et interaction dans le monde physique." *Revue de Métaphysique et de Morale*, 1937.

———. *Continu et discontinu en physique moderne.* Paris: Albin Michel, 1941.

———. "L'espace et le temps dans la physique quantique." In *Ordre, désordre, lumière.* Paris: Vrin, 1952 (pp. 104–15).

———. *La physique quantique restera-t-elle indéterministe?* Paris: Gauthier-Villars, 1953.

Canguilhem, Georges. *La connaissance de la vie.* Paris: Vrin, 1965.

Cassirer, Ernst. *The Philosophy of Forms.* Translated by R. Manheim. New Haven: Yale University Press, 1965.

Costa, F. "La théorie du temps chez Brentano." *Revue de Métaphysique et de Morale*, no. 4 (1962): 450–74.

Costa de Beauregard, Olivier. *La notion du temps: équivalence avec l'espace.* Paris: Herman, 1963.

Deleuze, Gilles. *Différence et répétition* (cf. ch. 2, "La répétition pour elle-même" and *passim*). Paris: 1968.

———. *Cinema 1: The Movement-Image.* Translated by H. Tomlinson and B. Habberjam. Minneapolis: University of Minnesota Press, 1986.

———. *Cinema 2: The Time-Image.* Translated by H. Tomlinson. Minneapolis:

University of Minnesota Press, 1990.

Einstein, Albert. "A propos de la déduction relativiste de Meyerson." *Revue Philosophique de la France et de l'Etranger*, 105, nos. 3-4 (March–April, 1928): 161-66.

Evellin, François. *Infini et quantité: étude sur le concept de l'infini en philosophie et dans les sciences.* Paris: Baillière, 1880.

Freud, Sigmund. *Wit and Its Relation to the Unconscious.* New York: Moffat, Yard, 1916. (References to Bergson's *Laughter: An Essay on the Meaning of the Comic* on pages 301-60.)

Heisenberg, Werner. *Physicist's Conception of Nature.* Translated by A. Pomeraus. Westport, CT: Greenwood, 1958.

———. *Physics and Philosophy: The Revolution in Modern Science.* London: George Allen and Unwin, 1959.

Flournoy, Théodore. *Philosophy of William James.* Ayer, 1917.

Heidegger, Martin. *Being and Time.* Translated by J. Macquarrie. New York: Harper & Row, 1962.

Husserl, Edmund. *Phenomenology of Internal Time-Consciousness.* Translated by J. Churchill. Midland, 1961.

———. "Ideen zu einer reinen Phänomenologie und phänomenologischen Philosophie (1): Allgemeine Einführung in die reine Phänomenologie" (1913). In *Husserliana* (vol. 3), Walter Beimel (Ed.). The Hague: Martinus Nijhoff, 1950.

———. *The Idea of Phenomenology.* Translated by W. Alston and G. Nakhnikian. The Hague: Martinus Nijhoff, 1964.

Hyppolite, Jean. *Sens et existence dans la philosophie de Merleau-Ponty.* Oxford: Oxford University Press, 1963.

James, William. *Pragmatism.* Cambridge: Harvard University Press, 1975.

———. *A Pluralistic Universe.* Longman, Green, 1919.

Lévi-Strauss, Claude. *Totemism.* (cf. ch. 5). Translated by Rodney Needham. Boston: Beacon Press, 1963.

*Levinas, Emmanuel. *Time and the Other.* Translated by R. Cohen. Pittsburgh, PA: Duquesne University Press, 1987.

Merleau-Ponty, Maurice. *The Structure of Behavior*. Translated by Alden Fisher. Pittsburgh, PA: Duquesne University Press, 1983.

_____. *Eloge de la philosophie*. Paris: Gallimard, 1953.

_____. *Phenomenology of Perception*. Translated by C. Smith. New York: Humanities Press, 1962.

_____. *Signs*. Translated by R. C. McCleary. Evanston, IL: Northwestern University Press, 1964.

_____. *The Visible and the Invisible*. Translated by A. Lingis. Evanston, IL: Northwestern University Press, 1969.

Pariente, Jean-Claude. *Le langage et l'individuel* (cf. ch. 1, *"Hésitations bergsoniennes"*). Paris: Armand Colin, 1973.

Poulet, Georges. *Studies in Human Time*. Translated by E. Coleman. Westport, CT: Greenwood, 1956.

Plato. *Parmenides*.

_____. *Timaeus*.

Plotinus. *Enneades*. P. Henry and H. R. Schwyzer (Eds.). New York: Oxford University Press, 1964.

Poincaré, H. *Dernières pensées*. Paris: Flammarion, 1913.

_____. *La valeur de la science*. Paris: Flammarion, 1918.

Prigogine, Ilya, and Isabelle Stengers. *Order Out of Chaos: Man's New Dialogue with Nature*. New York: Bantam, 1984.

Russell, B. *An Essay on the Foundations of Geometry*. Cambridge: Cambridge University Press, 1897.

_____. *Mysticism and Logic, and Other Essays*. London: George Allen & Unwin, 1950.

Sartre, Jean-Paul. *The Psychology of Imagination* (cf. ch. 2.2). Westport, CT: Greenwood, 1978.

_____. *Being and Nothingness*. Translated by H. Barnes. New York: Philosophical Library, 1956.

Serres, Michel. *Hermes IV: La distribution* (cf. *"Boltzmann et Bergson"*). Paris: Minuit, 1977.

_____. *Hermes: Literature, Science, Philosophy*. J. Harari and D. Bell (Eds.). Baltimore: Johns Hopkins University Press, 1983.

Whitehead, Alfred N. *Science and the Modern World*. Cambridge: Cambridge University Press, 1926.

———. *Process and Reality: An Essay in Cosmology*. Cambridge: Cambridge University Press, 1929.

———. *Essays in Science and Philosophy*. New York: Philosophical Library, 1948.

———. *The Concept of Nature*. Cambridge: Cambridge University Press, 1955.

Index

This edition designed by Bruce Mau
Type composed by Archetype
Printed by Quebecor Printing/Kingsport
on Sebago acid-free paper